TIMELINES OF
WORLD WAR II

TIMELINES OF WORLD WAR II

DK

Penguin
Random
House

Produced for DK by
cobalt id
www.cobaltid.co.uk

Senior Editors Kay Celtel, Marek Walisiewicz
Senior Art Editors Paul Reid, Darren Bland

Senior Editor Christine Stroyan
Senior Art Editor Gillian Andrews
Cartographers Suresh Kumar, Mohammad Hassan
Managing Editor Gareth Jones
Senior Managing Art Editor Lee Griffiths
Production Editor Robert Dunn
Production Controller Nancy-Jane Maun
Senior Jackets Coordinator Priyanka Sharma Saddi

Jackets Design Development
Manager Sophia MTT
Jacket Designer Tanya Mehrotra
DTP Designer Rakesh Kumar
Art Director Karen Self
Design Director Phil Ormerod
Associate Publishing Director Liz Wheeler
Publishing Director Jonathan Metcalf

First published in Great Britain in 2024 by
Dorling Kindersley Limited
DK, One Embassy Gardens, 8 Viaduct Gardens,
London, SW11 7BW

The authorized representative in the EEA is
Dorling Kindersley Verlag GmbH. Arnulfstr. 124,
80636 Munich, Germany
Copyright © 2024 Dorling Kindersley Limited
A Penguin Random House Company
10 9 8 7 6 5 4 3 2 1
001–336904 June/2024

A CIP catalogue record for this book
is available from the British Library.
ISBN: 978-0-2416-3476-9

Printed and bound in UAE

For the curious
www.dk.com

CONSULTANT & CONTRIBUTOR

Adrian Gilbert is a military historian with a special interest in World War II. Among his recent books are *POW: Allied Prisoners In Europe 1939–45*; *Germany's Lightning War 1939–42*; and *Waffen-SS: Hitler's Army at War*.

CONTRIBUTORS

Tony Allan studied history at Oxford University and later served as series editor of the 24-volume Time-Life History of the World. His own books include *Vikings: The Battle at the End of Time* and *Ancient Rome: Life, Myth and Art*.

Dr Kay Celtel is a writer and editor specializing in history. She has contributed to a number of historical books and atlases, including several on World War II.

Dr Michelle Chew is a freelance social anthropologist, editor, and writer who has contributed to a number of academic and educational publications for adults, young people, and children.

Dr Jacob F. Field specializes in history and economics, and has written a number of books, including titles on Winston Churchill, the D-Day landings, and military speeches.

Philip Parker is a historian specializing in world and military history, and is author of *History of War in Maps*, *DK American Civil War Visual Encyclopedia* and *DK Companion Guide to World History*.

Half-title page The M18 Hellcat, a highly mobile tank-killer and infantry support vehicle used by the US Army.

Title page A corporal from the British Women's Auxiliary Air Force communicates with aircraft from the watch office of a Bomber Command station.

Above Having liberated Paris, victorious American soldiers march down the Champs-Elysées on 26 August 1944.

CONTENTS

1939–1945

NOVEMBER 1918–AUGUST 1939

SEPTEMBER 1939–JUNE 1941

JUNE 1941–OCTOBER 1942

NOVEMBER 1942–SEPTEMBER 1943

SEPTEMBER 1943–DECEMBER 1944

JANUARY 1945–SEPTEMBER 1945

SEPTEMBER 1945–SEPTEMBER 1951

Europe and North Africa, December 1941

KEY EVENTS AND BATTLES, 1936–45

1. **Axis alliance established** October 1936 (see p.44)
2. **Munich Agreement** September 1938 (see p.50)
3. **Molotov-Ribbentrop Pact** August 1939 (see p.53)
4. **Invasion of Poland** September 1939 (see p.56)
5. **The Winter War** November 1939–February 1940 (see p.63)
6. **Invasion of Norway** April–June 1940 (see p.68)
7. **Invasion of France** May 1940 (see p.70)
8. **French surrender** June 1940 (see p.77)
9. **Invasion of the Balkans** April 1941 (see p.103)
10. **Invasion of Syria and Lebanon** June 1941 (see p.108)
11. **Operation Barbarossa** June 1941 (see p.112)
12. **Siege of Leningrad** September 1941–January 1944 (see pp.118–19)
13. **Moscow counteroffensive** December 1941 (see p.128)
14. **Battle of Stalingrad** September 1942–November 1942 (see p.158)
15. **Second Battle of El Alamein** October 1942 (see p.161)
16. **Torch landings** November 1942 (see p.165)
17. **Casablanca Conference** January 1943 (see p.169)
18. **Invasion of Sicily** July 1943 (see p.191)
19. **Battle of Anzio** January–May 1944 (see p.212)
20. **D-Day landings** June 1944 (see p.228)
21. **Operation Bagration** June–August 1944 (see p.232)
22. **Yalta Conference** February 1945 (see p.263)
23. **Crossing the Rhine** March–April 1945 (see p.267)
24. **Victory in Italy** April 1945 (see p.272)
25. **Battle of Berlin** April–May 1945 (see p.274)
26. **Potsdam Conference** July 1945 (see p.283)

The first years of the war in Europe were marked by the territorial gains and alliances of the Axis, which brought much of the continent and North Africa under its control.

Archangel

U S S R

③ Moscow
⑬

Orel

Volga

Stalingrad

⑭

Don

Rostov

②② alta

Black Sea

Caucasus

Ankara

T Ü R K I Y E

S Y R I A

LEBANON
⑩

PALESTINE

TRANSJORDAN

IRAQ

Cairo

INTRODUCTION

World War II was the most devastating conflict in history, surpassing even the horrors of World War I in its scale, brutality, and impact. The war began as two separate conflicts sparked by German and Japanese expansionism. It developed into an ideological contest involving more than 70 nations, split between the Allies (led by Britain, the USA, the USSR, and France) and the Axis powers (led by Germany, Italy, and Japan). Up to 80 million people died, including around 60 million civilians – victims of a war on land, at sea, and in the air that encompassed genocide, unprecedented levels of bombing, and a terrifying new weapon, the atomic bomb. The war reshaped geopolitics, promoting the USA and the USSR to superpower status and speeding the process of decolonization.

War erupts in Europe

The Treaty of Versailles – the settlement that followed World War I – left Europe politically unstable and economically fragile. It provided fertile ground for the growth of nationalism and the emergence of right-wing dictators, such as Adolf Hitler, promising to build new empires and restore national pride and prosperity.

Exploiting nationalist sentiments, Adolf Hitler set out to establish a new German Reich ("empire"), using the claims of German minorities in Czechoslovakia and Poland to make territorial demands. When these were rejected, he ordered his armies to invade Poland on 1 September 1939. Britain and France responded by declaring war on Germany. World War II had begun.

The speed and success of the German campaign were devastating. The Polish capital of Warsaw – pounded by air and artillery bombardment – fell to the Germans on 28 September. When the USSR – having agreed to split Poland between itself and Germany – invaded eastern Poland, the country was crushed.

After a brief pause in hostilities – often known as the "phoney war" – German forces attacked Denmark and Norway in April 1940. German successes there were followed by the invasion of the Netherlands, Belgium, and France. In a six-week blitzkrieg ("lightning war") campaign, Germany defeated numerically superior Allied forces to leave Hitler in control of most of Europe.

Italy and North Africa

Italian dictator Benito Mussolini strove to emulate the success of his German Axis partner by invading Egypt and Greece. Thus, the European theatre of war expanded to include North Africa, the Middle East, and the Balkans, drawing in areas controlled by France and Britain, such as Tunisia, Syria, and Palestine, as well as new Axis allies in Europe, such as Romania and Bulgaria.

Italy's campaigns went badly, and Hitler was forced to step in to rescue his principal ally. The Germans successfully occupied Greece and Yugoslavia, but the campaigns

Key

■ Axis-controlled territory ■ Axis conquests, 1939 ■ Axis conquests, 1941 ■ Under British influence, 1941
■ Axis allies, 1941 ■ Axis conquests , 1940 ■ Allied-controlled territory, 1941

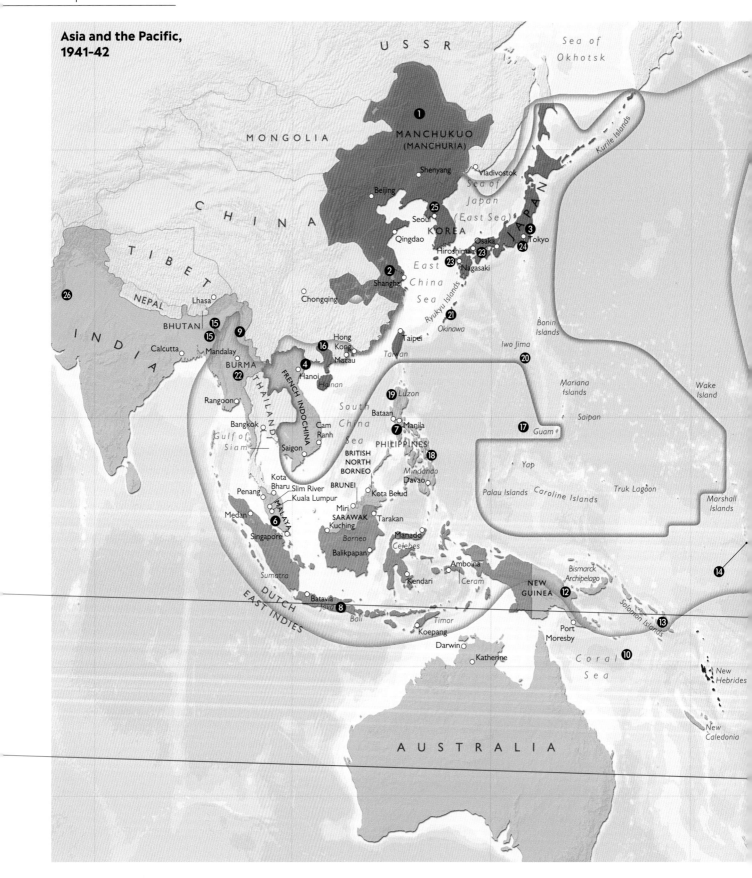

Asia and the Pacific, 1941–42

U S S R

MONGOLIA

Sea of Okhotsk

Kurile Islands

MANCHUKUO (MANCHURIA)

C H I N A

Shenyang

Vladivostok

Sea of Japan (East Sea)

J A P A N

25 Seoul

KOREA

Osaka 24 Tokyo 3

Beijing

Qingdao

Hiroshima 23 23 Nagasaki

T I B E T

NEPAL

Lhasa

Chongqing

2 Shanghai

East China Sea

Ryukyu Islands

21 Okinawa

Bonin Islands

26

BHUTAN

15

15

9

I N D I A

Calcutta

Mandalay

BURMA

22

16

Hong Kong

Macau

Taipei

Iwo Jima

20

Wake Island

Taiwan

4 Hanoi

FRENCH INDOCHINA

Hainan

South China Sea

19 Luzon

Mariana Islands

Saipan

Rangoon

THAILAND

Bangkok

Cam Ranh

Saigon

Bataan

7 Manila

PHILIPPINES

17 Guam

Gulf of Siam

Kota Bharu Slim River

Penang

Kuala Lumpur

MALAYA

Medan

6

Singapore

Sumatra

BRITISH NORTH BORNEO

BRUNEI

Kota Belud

Miri

SARAWAK

Kuching

Borneo

Tarakan

18

Mindanao

Davao

Yap

Palau Islands

Caroline Islands

Truk Lagoon

Marshall Islands

Manado

Celebes

Balikpapan

Kendari

Amboina

Ceram

Bismarck Archipelago

14

DUTCH EAST INDIES

Batavia

Java

8

Bali

Timor

Koepang

Darwin

Katherine

NEW GUINEA

12

Port Moresby

Solomon Islands

13

10

Coral Sea

New Hebrides

New Caledonia

A U S T R A L I A

The Empire of Japan became the dominant force in the Pacific until 1942, taking the Philippines, the East Indies, and Burma in a series of well-planned attacks.

P A C I F I C

O C E A N

⑪ *Midway Atoll*

⑤ *Hawaiian Islands*

Pearl Harbor ○-

KEY BATTLES AND ACTIONS, 1932–47
❶ **Manchukuo established** March 1932 (*see p.29*)
❷ **Nanjing Massacre** December 1937 (*see p.47*)
❸ **Greater East Asia Co-Prosperity Sphere established** July 1940 (*see p.79*)
❹ **Japanese invasion of French Indochina** August–September 1940 (*see p.80*)
❺ **Pearl Harbor** 7 December 1941 (*see p.126*)
❻ **Malayan Campaign** December 1941–January 1942 (*see p.126*)
❼ **Fall of the Philippines** December 1941–April 1942 (*see p.130*)
❽ **Invasion of the Dutch East Indies** January–March 1942 (*see p.131*)
❾ **Invasion of Burma** January 1942 (*see p.134*)
❿ **Battle of the Coral Sea** May 1942 (*see p.143*)
⓫ **Battle of Midway** June 1942 (*see p.149*)
⓬ **Invasion of New Guinea** July 1942 (*see p.153*)
⓭ **Battle of Guadalcanal** August 1942 (*see p.154*)
⓮ **Offensives in the Gilbert and Marshall Islands** November 1943–February 1944 (*see p.205*)
⓯ **Battles of Kohima and Imphal** March–April 1944 (*see pp.220–21*)
⓰ **Operation Ichi-Go** April–December 1944 (*see p.227*)
⓱ **Battle of the Philippine Sea** June 1944 (*see p.231*)
⓲ **Battle of Leyte Gulf** October 1944 (*see p.248*)
⓳ **Return to the Philippines** October–December 1944 (*see p.249*)
⓴ **Battle of Iwo Jima** February–March 1945 (*see p.264*)
㉑ **Battle of Okinawa** April–June 1945 (*see p.268*)
㉒ **Battles of Meiktila and Mandalay** December 1944–March 1945 (*see p.266*)
㉓ **Atomic bomb attacks** August 1945 (*see p.285*)
㉔ **Japanese surrender** August 1945 (*see p.285*)
㉕ **Division of Korea** September 1945 (*see p.292*)
㉖ **Partition of India** August 1947 (*see p.298*)

were a distraction from Hitler's great military preoccupation – the invasion and destruction of the USSR.

War with the USSR
On 22 June 1941, more than 3 million Axis troops smashed through the Soviet border. The Red Army was caught by surprise and fell back in disarray, and it seemed that the Germans might achieve their aims. However, Hitler had underestimated the material strength and resilience of the Red Army. By the end of 1941, the Soviets had launched a series of counterattacks that brought the German advance to a halt.

The Germans returned to the offensive in southern Russia during the summer of 1942 with some success, but Hitler was disastrously fixated on capturing Stalingrad. In November 1942, the powerful German 6th Army was trapped inside the city and was wiped out in a brutal struggle that finally ended in February 1943. From then on the German armed forces were on the defensive and slowly but inexorably driven out of the Soviet Union.

Allied successes mount
The tide began to turn against the Axis powers in Western Europe and North Africa in 1942–43. The Allies pushed the Germans out of North Africa following their victory at El Alamein in Egypt and the Allied Torch landings in Tunisia in November 1942. They then invaded Italy in September 1943, beginning the campaign to finally defeat the Axis powers in Europe.

Italy was, however, a sideshow, as the British and Americans (who joined the war in 1941) were in fact preparing to invade northern France. On D-Day, 6 June 1944, thousands of Western Allied troops landed

in Normandy and drove the Germans back through France towards their homeland. By the start of 1945, Germany's position was hopeless, its cities pounded by Allied bombers and its troops fighting a losing battle against forces closing in on Berlin from both east and west.

Asia and the Pacific
Japan began a campaign to extend its empire in 1931 by seizing territory in Manchuria, northern China. This brought it into conflict with Western powers that had interests in Asia. Faced with sanctions, Japan's increasingly militarist government decided to go to war through the creation by conquest of a "Greater East Asia Co-Prosperity Sphere" – a unified political and economic bloc to be centred around the resource-rich lands of Malaya, the Philippines, and the Dutch East Indies. It also joined the Axis alliance with Germany and Italy. Japan began its campaign in December 1941, hoping that the Allied nations – primarily concerned with events in Europe – would accept its victories and swiftly negotiate a peace. It was not to be.

Japan's campaign was breathtakingly effective at first. On 7 December 1941, its torpedo-bombers spearheaded an attack on the US Pacific Fleet at its base in Pearl Harbor, Hawaii. Elsewhere, Japanese forces struck at Wake Island and Hong Kong, attacked Malaya and Burma, made amphibious landings in Borneo, and instigated the conquest of the Philippines. Within six months, Japan had carved out a new empire stretching from the Kurile Islands to the Solomon Islands.

Japan's success was short-lived, however. A renewed offensive towards New Guinea and the Solomon Islands in 1942 foundered

Key
COLONIAL POSSESSIONS IN 1941
 USA
 The Netherlands
Britain and Commonwealth
 France
Portugal
Under British and French administration
Under Japanese control, Dec 1941
Under Japanese control, June 1942

in the face of determined US and Australian resistance. More serious still was Japan's defeat at the great naval encounter of Midway in June 1942. This was the pivotal battle of the war in the Pacific, after which Japan was forced onto the defensive.

In 1943, the Allies launched their great counteroffensive in the Asia-Pacific theatre. It consisted of two thrusts into Japanese-held territory. The first was a US Navy-led advance under Admiral Chester Nimitz through the Central Pacific. The second, commanded by General Douglas MacArthur, centred on an offensive in the southwest Pacific towards the Philippine Islands. Superior firepower and mobility allowed the Allies to secure the far-flung islands of Japan's Pacific empire and take control by the end of 1944.

Allied resurgence

The Allies now also began to make gains in mainland Asia. With its resources tied up in lengthy campaigns in China and Burma, and geographically isolated from its Axis allies, Japan found its forces thinly spread and unable to hold back Allied advances from late 1944. By mid-1945, Japan's naval and air forces were on the verge of collapse, and the Americans were bombing the Japanese homeland with minimal opposition. The Japanese government began to prepare for surrender, a once-unthinkable event that was hastened by the dropping of atomic bombs on Hiroshima and Nagasaki in August 1945, which brought the war to a shocking end.

The effects of war

Almost every major country in the world was sucked into World War II. The European nations with large overseas empires in Africa and Asia, notably Britain and France, drew manpower and materials from their colonies, while the USA encouraged Latin American nations to provide support against the Axis. Genuinely neutral countries were few and far between.

As the scope of the war increased, so too did the size of the armies deployed, the battles fought, and the casualties suffered. While the number of deaths may have reached 80 million, hundreds of millions were wounded, and millions displaced from their homes. About half of the casualties were civilians. Indeed, the killing of civilians was a central feature of the war, seen in the extermination policies that drove the Holocaust, the Allied strategic bombing of Germany and Japan, and the reprisals taken against resistance movements in Europe and Asia. In many places, starvation and disease were prevalent; as always, women, children, and the old and vulnerable were disproportionately affected.

A new order

The war helped reshape the world in radical ways. Britain and France's empires broke down as it became increasingly difficult to resist their colonies' demands for independence after many of them had provided soldiers to defend the freedom of other nations. Participation in the war also added weight to African-American demands for equality. The USA and the USSR emerged as superpowers. Their ideological opposition to each other drew the world into a "cold war", which played out in several conflicts in the 20th century but which was contained in part by the threat of nuclear war. The postwar period also ushered in a new era of transnational economic, political, and humanitarian cooperation, reflected, for example, in the creation of the United Nations.

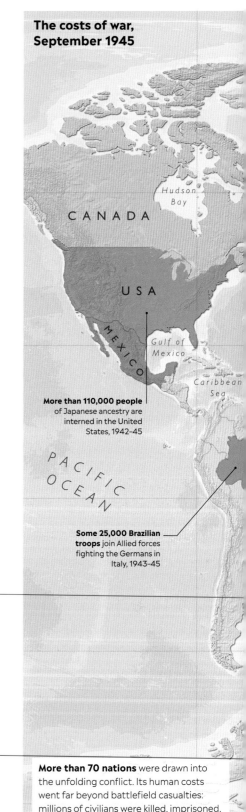

The costs of war, September 1945

Hudson Bay

CANADA

USA

MEXICO

Gulf of Mexico

Caribbean Sea

More than 110,000 people of Japanese ancestry are interned in the United States, 1942–45

PACIFIC OCEAN

Some 25,000 Brazilian troops join Allied forces fighting the Germans in Italy, 1943–45

More than 70 nations were drawn into the unfolding conflict. Its human costs went far beyond battlefield casualties: millions of civilians were killed, imprisoned, or displaced, and economies were ravaged.

Key

MILITARY DEAD

▩ Less than 1,000	▩ 10,000–50,000	▩ 100,000–500,000	▩ 1–3 million	👥 Civilian dead
▩ 1,000–10,000	▩ 50,000–100,000	▩ 500,000–1 million	▩ 3–14 million	

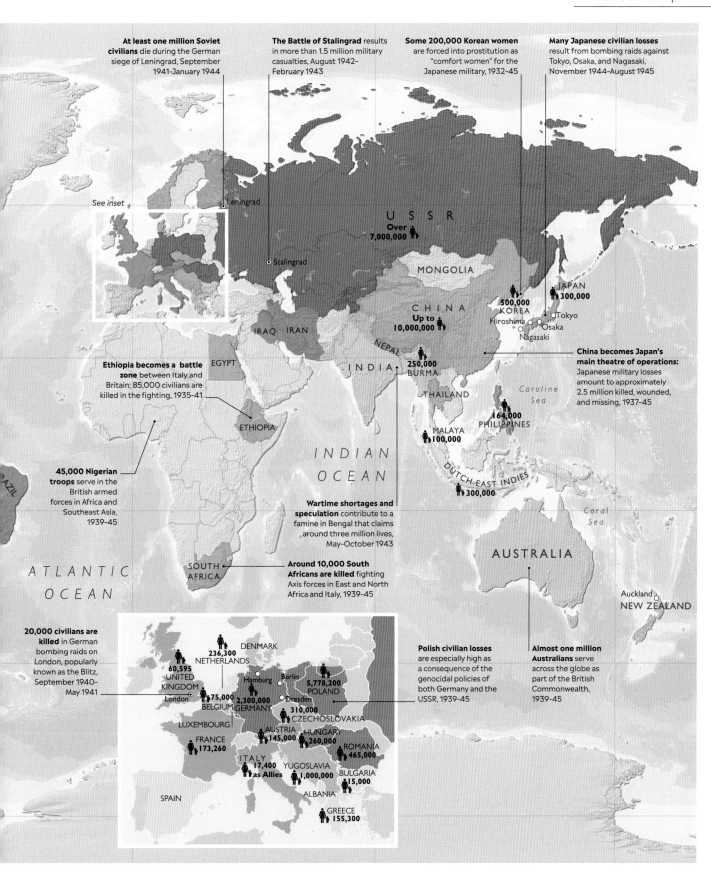

At least one million Soviet civilians die during the German siege of Leningrad, September 1941–January 1944

The Battle of Stalingrad results in more than 1.5 million military casualties, August 1942–February 1943

Some 200,000 Korean women are forced into prostitution as "comfort women" for the Japanese military, 1932–45

Many Japanese civilian losses result from bombing raids against Tokyo, Osaka, and Nagasaki, November 1944–August 1945

See inset

Leningrad

U S S R
Over 7,000,000

Stalingrad

MONGOLIA

JAPAN
300,000

KOREA
500,000

Hiroshima
Tokyo
Osaka
Nagasaki

CHINA
Up to 10,000,000

China becomes Japan's main theatre of operations: Japanese military losses amount to approximately 2.5 million killed, wounded, and missing, 1937–45

IRAQ   IRAN

EGYPT

NEPAL

INDIA

250,000
BURMA

THAILAND

Caroline Sea

Ethiopia becomes a battle zone between Italy and Britain; 85,000 civilians are killed in the fighting, 1935–41

ETHIOPIA

PHILIPPINES
164,000

MALAYA
100,000

INDIAN OCEAN

45,000 Nigerian troops serve in the British armed forces in Africa and Southeast Asia, 1939–45

Wartime shortages and speculation contribute to a famine in Bengal that claims around three million lives, May–October 1943

DUTCH EAST INDIES
300,000

Coral Sea

BRAZIL

SOUTH AFRICA

Around 10,000 South Africans are killed fighting Axis forces in East and North Africa and Italy, 1939–45

AUSTRALIA

ATLANTIC OCEAN

Auckland
NEW ZEALAND

20,000 civilians are killed in German bombing raids on London, popularly known as the Blitz, September 1940–May 1941

DENMARK

236,300
NETHERLANDS

60,595
UNITED KINGDOM

London

Hamburg   Berlin

75,000
BELGIUM

2,300,000
GERMANY

Dresden

5,778,200
POLAND

Polish civilian losses are especially high as a consequence of the genocidal policies of both Germany and the USSR, 1939–45

Almost one million Australians serve across the globe as part of the British Commonwealth, 1939–45

LUXEMBOURG

310,000
CZECHOSLOVAKIA

FRANCE
173,260

AUSTRIA
145,000

HUNGARY
260,000

ROMANIA
465,000

ITALY
17,400 as Allies

YUGOSLAVIA
1,000,000

BULGARIA
15,000

SPAIN

ALBANIA

GREECE
155,300

THE INTERWAR YEARS

World War II had its origins in the terms of the Treaty of Versailles, signed in Paris in June 1919 to bring a formal end to World War I. This, and other more minor treaties signed in Paris, represented an attempt by the victors of the Great War – Britain, France, Italy, and the USA – to create a more stable Europe and to prevent a repetition of the conflict. However, Versailles created more problems than it solved, and in combination with the profound economic crises that wracked postwar Europe, it sowed the seeds for a new world war, one even more deadly than its predecessor.

The structure of Central Europe was completely reshaped by the peace treaties. Germany was weakened economically, politically, and militarily. The Austro-Hungarian Empire was dismembered: Austria became a small, weak state, and Hungary was forced to cede large amounts of territory to Romania. New nation states – namely Poland, Czechoslovakia, and Yugoslavia – came into being.

National antagonisms

Although the concept of national self-determination had been one of the mainstays of Versailles, it failed to solve the competing nationalisms of Central Europe. Latent antagonisms between all the nations of this region harboured the potential for conflict. This was especially true of the substantial German-speaking minorities within Czechoslovakia and Poland.

The League of Nations, formed in 1920, seemed to offer a ray of hope. Its goal was to provide a forum for international negotiation and collective action that could prevent conflict. However, the League lacked the military backing necessary to enforce sanctions and soon proved to be a paper tiger.

The rise of fascism

The economic problems of the 1920s and 1930s encouraged the growth of right-wing political parties around the world. In Japan, Italy, and Germany these movements gained national power and determined to use military action to further their expansionist foreign policy aims. An autocratic, militarist Japan occupied the Chinese province of Manchuria in 1931 before launching a full-scale war against China in 1937, capturing Shanghai and advancing on Nanjing. And in 1935, Italy invaded Ethiopia to expand its colonial possessions in Africa.

The success of Adolf Hitler's Nazi Party in gaining power in Germany in 1933 was the single most important factor in pushing Europe towards war. Although Hitler became the German chancellor through legitimate means, once in control he immediately set about destroying Germany's democratic institutions. Amid new laws to suppress trade unions, opposition parties, and Jews and other "non-Aryans", a totalitarian dictatorship emerged.

Hitler was also active in the international sphere. Although an attempt to seize power in Austria in 1934 was thwarted, his long-term intentions were revealed when he overturned the conditions of the Versailles Treaty and began to rearm Germany.

The road to war

The way was now clear for Hitler to take more assertive action. This began in March 1936, when German troops unilaterally reoccupied the Rhineland. Germany's aggression went unopposed by Britain and France's leaders, who believed they could control Hitler. Thus emboldened, Hitler offered open support to General Franco's Nationalists in the Spanish Civil War (1936–39). Britain and France did nothing to prevent a Nazi takeover of Austria in March 1938 and even went so far as to sanction the dismemberment of Czechoslovakia six months later at the Munich Conference, in response to Hitler's demand for the incorporation of the German-speaking Sudetenland into Germany.

It took Germany's seizure of the remains of Czechoslovakia in March 1939 to demonstrate the inevitability of war. When Hitler made his next territorial demand, for the Polish (or Danzig) corridor, appeasement was replaced by firmer action. After Germany invaded Poland on 1 September 1939, Britain and France declared war on the Nazi state.

Germany lost c. 6.5 million people, one-tenth of its population, through the Treaty of Versailles

16 February 1919

THE AUSTRO-HUNGARIAN EMPIRE ENDS

The Austro-Hungarian Empire broke apart at the end of World War I into Austria and Hungary, two fragile new republics. Both were unable to take a strong role in negotiating their peace treaties with the Allies, as Austria's chancellor was excluded from the discussions, while Hungary was unsettled by a communist coup in March. Thus, neither was able to make a claim for more land as the empire was dismantled.

LE SORT TRAGIQUE DE LA HONGRIE

△ "The tragic fate of Hungary", poster, 1919

28 November The Estonian War of Independence begins when Russia lays claim to Estonian territory; Estonia prevails in 1920

1918

11 NOVEMBER

11 November The Armistice finally ends World War I after more than four years of fighting

19 January 1919 Germany holds its first free democratic elections since the abdication of Kaiser Wilhelm II (9 Nov 1918)

23 March In Italy, Benito Mussolini (*p.74*) forms the paramilitary Fasci Italiani di Combattimento

5–12 January 1919

THE SPARTACIST UPRISING

In Germany, communist revolutionaries the Spartacists attempted to overthrow the government, based in the town of Weimar. The uprising was brutally suppressed, and its leaders, Rosa Luxemburg and Karl Liebknecht, were murdered.

△ Rosa Luxemburg

19 May 1919

THE TURKISH WAR OF INDEPENDENCE

After the Allies partitioned and occupied the Ottoman Empire following World War I, army general Mustafa Kemal Atatürk fought to create a strong new country. By 1923, he had overthrown the ineffectual Ottoman caliph, establishing the Republic of Türkiye.

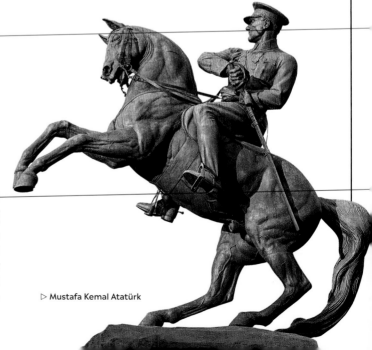

▷ Mustafa Kemal Atatürk

28 June 1919

THE TREATY OF VERSAILLES

At the Palace of Versailles in Paris, the Allied Powers and Germany agreed the terms for peace. Germany lost 13 per cent of its territory in Europe and had its colonies confiscated. Its armaments were strictly limited, and it was to pay reparations worth US$33 billion to the Allies.

◁ The signing of the Treaty of Versailles

1919

31 DECEMBER

3 June The Emirate of Afghanistan seeks a ceasefire with Britain in the Third Anglo-Afghan War, ongoing since Afghans invaded British India on 6 May

12 September Italian nationalists under proto-fascist Gabriele D'Annunzio occupy the city of Fiume, awarded to Yugoslavia after the war

1919-23

EUROPE RESHAPED

In the peace treaties that followed World War I, the map of Europe was redrawn. The Austro-Hungarian, German, Ottoman, and Russian empires were crudely carved up to make way for new states: Türkiye, Poland, Czechoslovakia, Hungary, Austria, Finland, Estonia, Latvia, Lithuania, and the Kingdom of the Serbs, Croats, and Slovenes (Yugoslavia). The new borders often split ethnic groups, leaving large numbers of German speakers in Poland, for example, and ethnic Hungarians in Romania. In that confusion, and in the harsh conditions imposed on the defeated powers, lay the seeds of World War II.

New states, new problems

The treaties served to destabilize Europe, leaving a myriad of new states in Central Europe caught between a crippled, angry Germany and a Russia keen to spread communism and regain its former territories.

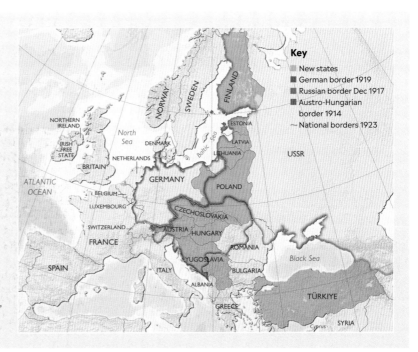

△ **Palais des Nations**, Geneva, home to the League

10 January 1920

THE LEAGUE OF NATIONS

Founded under the terms of the Treaty of Versailles to maintain peace through a commitment to disarmament and collective security, the League initially had 42 members. However, the USA never joined, the USSR was only briefly a member, and Germany and Italy left in the 1930s. With states acting in their own interests, the League could not stop the slide towards war.

1920

1 JANUARY

13 March The Kapp Putsch sees the Freikorps, German right-wing paramilitary forces, try to seize power; the German government flees to Dresden

11 February 1921 The Soviet Russian Red Army invades Georgia and establishes the Georgian Soviet Socialist Republic

4 June The Treaty of Trianon formally ends the war between the Allies and Hungary

10 August The harsh terms of the Treaty of Sèvres fuel support for Atatürk in the Ottoman Empire

△ **NSDAP badge with swastika**

24 February 1920

THE NAZI PARTY

In 1920, the German Workers' Party was renamed the National Socialist German Workers' Party (NSDAP), or Nazi Party. It was an extreme nationalist organization, dedicated to eliminating communism and promoting the theory of an "Aryan master race", which was used to justify the Nazis' vicious antisemitism and Germany's later invasions of other countries.

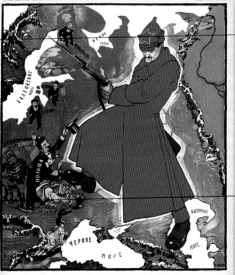

△ **Soviet propaganda poster** from the Polish–Soviet war

18 March 1921

THE POLISH–SOVIET WAR ENDS

Begun in 1919, the Polish-Soviet War was driven by Soviet Russia's attempt to claim more territory for communism. Poland crushed the Red Army at the Battle of Warsaw in August 1920, and a ceasefire followed. The Peace of Riga then firmly established the Russian–Polish border.

29 July 1921

HITLER BECOMES LEADER OF THE NAZI PARTY

Adolf Hitler joined the Nazi Party in late 1919. He soon became a dominant figure as the Nazis' most talented orator and recruiter. In July, angry at the party's direction, he resigned and refused to return unless made chairman. On 29 July, he was elected chairman, replacing the party's founder, Anton Drexler.

▷ **Adolf Hitler** in 1921 (hand-coloured image)

12 November 1921–6 February 1922

NAVAL DISARMAMENT

In 1921, the USA invited nine nations, including the UK and Japan, to Washington, DC, to discuss naval disarmament and tensions in East Asia. In the resulting treaties, the Imperial Japanese Navy was limited to two-fifths the size of the British and US navies and the signatories' possessions in the Far East were to be respected.

△ Washington naval conference attendees

"Our programme is simple: we wish to govern Italy."

BENITO MUSSOLINI, SPEECH AT UDINE, 20 SEPTEMBER 1922

1922

26 JANUARY

23 May The Leipzig trials begin the prosecution of alleged German war criminals

26 January 1922 Italian troops occupy Misrata in Libya as part of Italy's colonization of the country

9 November 1921

MUSSOLINI FOUNDS THE FASCIST PARTY

Benito Mussolini transformed his fascist organization, the Fasci Italiani di Combattimento ("Italian fighting bands"), into the Partito Nazionale Fascista ("National Fascist Party"). Its policies were vague and its methods openly violent, but the party gained support with its strident opposition to communism and promises of an end to weak government and the creation of a modern Italian empire.

▷ **Benito Mussolini** in the 1930s

1919-39
THE RISE OF FASCISM

The philosophy of fascism, which arose in the late 19th century, supported the idea of autocratic leadership over a regimented and monolithic nation. Democracy was seen as a weakness, and the "nation" was often forged through the demonization of groups considered to be a threat or outsiders. The word "fascism" comes from *fasces*, a bundle of rods around an axe that was a symbol of authority in ancient Rome.

The first fascist political party was created by Benito Mussolini. Inspired by D'Annunzio's bold actions in Fiume (*see below*), Mussolini seized power in 1922 by ordering his militia, the *squadristi* (known as Blackshirts), to march on Rome, forcing the king to name him prime minister. He then transformed Italy into a one-party police state, with himself as dictator, Il Duce.

The Great Depression of the 1930s and the threat of communism provided fertile ground for the movement to grow. Fascist parties emerged around the world but remained fringe groups in most places. The movement was most successful in Europe, particularly in Germany, where Adolf Hitler rose to power in 1933, and the following year made himself Führer (Leader), with sweeping powers. Other countries followed, with dictatorial fascist regimes established in Austria, Spain, Romania, Croatia, Norway, and Hungary over the subsequent decade.

GABRIELE D'ANNUNZIO

KEY MOMENTS

1919 Seizing the moment
Gabriele D'Annunzio was a right-wing poet and pilot who, in 1919, temporarily seized the port city of Fiume (now Rijeka in Croatia), which had a large Italian population. He declared it the independent "Regency of Carnaro", with himself as its *duce* ("leader").

1930 Romania's Iron Guard
In 1930, fascist Romanian politician Corneliu Zelea Codreanu founded the Iron Guard as the paramilitary wing of his party, the Legion of the Archangel Michael. Despite Codreanu's arrest and execution in 1938, his party became increasingly influential and dominated Romanian politics in 1940–41.

1932 Blackshirts in Britain
Oswald Mosley founded the British Union of Fascists (*see symbol, left*) in 1932. Known as Blackshirts, like the Italian Fascists, Britain's Fascists frequently clashed with opponents, most notoriously in the Battle of Cable Street in London, in 1936.

Hitler and Mussolini, here pictured together in 1937 reviewing SS soldiers, first met in Venice in 1934. Despite becoming allies and sharing political beliefs, the two leaders were often critical of one another in private.

▷ Postcard marking the March on Rome

27–31 October 1922
MUSSOLINI'S MARCH ON ROME

Mussolini mobilized thousands of supporters of the Fascist Party to march to Rome and seize power. Fearing civil war, Italy's king, Victor Emmanuel III, persuaded the prime minister to resign and offered Mussolini the premiership as the crowds approached the city.

▷ French soldier guarding coal in the Ruhr (hand-coloured image)

11 January 1923
FRENCH TROOPS OCCUPY THE RUHR

When Germany defaulted on its reparation payments to the Allies, French troops occupied the Ruhr, an important industrial area in Germany, and seized goods in compensation. The German workers refused to co-operate, paralysing the area's mines and factories.

31 Aug Italy invades Corfu after a border dispute with Greece. Italy ignores demands by the League of Nations that it leave Corfu

1922

27 JANUARY

16 April The Treaty of Rapallo creates an alliance between Russia and Germany that enables Germany to rearm

20 April 1923 Virulently antisemitic newspaper and tool of Nazi propaganda *Der Stürmer* is first published

30 December 1922
THE USSR IS CREATED

The Russian civil war, ongoing since the anti-monarchy revolutions of 1917, finally ended in October 1922. By then, the Communist Party, led by Vladimir Lenin, was firmly in control of Russia, which had become a Soviet republic, along with Belarus, Ukraine, and Transcaucasia (comprising Georgia, Azerbaijan, and Armenia). In December, these republics joined together in the Union of Soviet Socialist Republics (USSR) – a vast one-party Communist state controlled from Moscow in Russia.

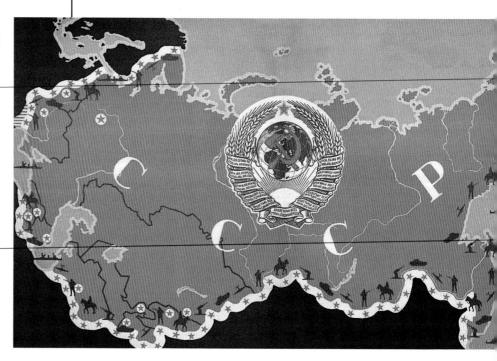

▷ Map of the Soviet Union from the 1930s

November 1923

GERMAN HYPERINFLATION

The German economy was already faltering under the burden of reparations payments when the French occupation of the Ruhr ushered in a period of hyperinflation. The country's currency collapsed, and millions of people lost their savings and found their wages worthless. Nazi promises of a strong government and economy became even more appealing.

◁ **Children playing** with worthless banknotes, 1923

1878-1953

JOSEPH STALIN

Born into poverty in Georgia, Joseph Dzhugashvili adopted the name Stalin ("steel" in Russian). A key figure in the 1917 Russian Revolution, he went on to lead the Soviet Union until his death from a stroke in 1953.

10 June 1924 Italian socialist leader
Giacomo Matteotti is kidnapped and murdered by Fascist thugs after denouncing the violence seen at Italy's recent elections

1924

24 DECEMBER

8-9 November In the Beer Hall Putsch, Hitler plans to overthrow the government; he is arrested and imprisoned for five years

16 August The USA's Dawes Plan reduces Germany's reparations payments and introduces the Reichsmark in an attempt to boost the German economy

24 December A communist coup aiming to create a Soviet republic in Estonia fails

By November 1923, 1 US dollar was worth 4,200,000 million German marks

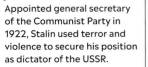

1924-38

STALIN'S PATH TO POWER

Appointed general secretary of the Communist Party in 1922, Stalin used terror and violence to secure his position as dictator of the USSR.

1924 Lenin dies and Stalin positions himself as Lenin's political heir. His plan to strengthen the Soviet Union proves popular.

1927 Stalin removes ideological rivals and opponents such as Leon Trotsky, who is exiled then expelled from the USSR.

1929 Stalinist propaganda creates a cult of the leader that encourages personal devotion to Stalin and makes opposition difficult.

1936-38 The Great Purge, a violent campaign of political repression, further stifles dissent and brings terror to the population.

4 July 1926
THE HITLER YOUTH

The Hitlerjugend ("Hitler Youth") was an organization for German boys, and later girls, aged between 10 and 18. Modelled on the Sturmabteilung or SA ("assault division"), the Nazi Party's paramilitary wing, it became a tool for indoctrination. Boys were given military training while girls were trained to be wives, mothers, and guardians of Nazi ideology. Other youth groups were banned in 1936; 90 per cent of Germany's youth were members of the Hitler Youth by 1939.

▷ **Hitler Youth on parade,** c. 1933 (hand-coloured image)

1924

25 DECEMBER

3 January 1925 Mussolini becomes dictator in Italy, styling himself "Il Duce" ("The Leader")

5–16 October The Locarno Pact confirms Germany's western border with France and Belgium

7 April 1926 Irish woman Violet Gibson shoots at Mussolini in one of several attempts to assassinate him

9 November 1925
HITLER'S BODYGUARDS

The Schutzstaffel or SS ("defence squadron") was created as Hitler's personal bodyguard. However, under the leadership of Heinrich Himmler from 1929, its numbers grew from just 280 to 52,000 in 1933. The SS came to be responsible for security, intelligence gathering, and enforcing the Nazis' racial policies, and its black-uniformed members were feared across Nazi-occupied territories.

◁ **SS cap** with death's-head badge

4–12 May 1926
GENERAL STRIKE IN BRITAIN

An argument over the handling of the coal industry by the British government and mine owners developed into one of the largest industrial disputes in British history. Millions walked out from the road transport, rail, electricity, gas, printing, iron, and steel industries in a huge demonstration of working-class solidarity and anger at poor working conditions and decreasing pay. On 12 May, the strike was called off, having achieved nothing. The government introduced legislation that made another general strike impossible.

▷ **English workers** demonstrating during the General Strike

△ **A Japanese destroyer** being launched

3–11 May 1928
THE JINAN INCIDENT
KMT forces advancing to Beijing clashed with Japanese forces protecting Japanese commercial interests at Jinan, in Shandong province. Thousands of KMT soldiers died, and the incident highlighted the increasing tensions between China and Japan.

△ **Cigarette card** showing KMT forces in combat with the Japanese

20 June–4 August 1927
THE NAVAL ARMS RACE
At the Geneva Naval Conference, the USA, Japan, and Great Britain discussed extending the limitations on naval capacity set at Washington in 1922 (*see p.19*). Talks ended in stalemate, and, with the USA planning new ships, the pace of the arms race accelerated.

15 March 1928 The Japanese government arrests over 1,600 people in a crackdown on communism

1928

11 MAY

24 March 1927 In China, US and British naval vessels bombard Nanjing to protect foreign residents from looting by the Kuomintang's army as it captures the city

1 August 1927
CIVIL WAR IN CHINA
In 1926, China's Nationalist Party (the Kuomintang or KMT) and Communist Party (the CCP) embarked on the Northern Expedition to defeat China's regional warlords and unite the country. However, in 1927 the KMT turned on the CCP. On 1 August 1927, the Communists launched an uprising against the KMT government in Wuhan province, beginning an intermittent civil war that lasted until 1949.

▷ **Chiang Kai-shek,** KMT leader

27 August 1928
WAR OUTLAWED

In Paris, 15 nations, including France, the USA, the UK, Germany, Italy, and Japan, signed the Kellogg-Briand Pact, which outlawed wars of agression and called for disagreements to be settled peacefully. Another 47 nations, including the Soviet Union, subsequently joined the pact. Nations could act in self-defence, but it was unclear what might constitute self-defence. Moreover, there was no way to enforce the pact or sanction belligerents.

▷ **The Kellogg-Briand Pact** with the first 15 signatures

1928

12 MAY

20 May The Nazi Party wins just 12 seats out of 491 in the Reichstag elections; the party begins to focus on becoming attractive to Germany's electorate

9 February 1929 In the Litvinov Protocol, the USSR, Poland, Estonia, Romania, and Latvia agree not to use force to settle disputes

4 June Japan's Kwantung Army assassinates Manchurian warlord Zhang Zuolin, whom Japan has previously supported, after his defeat by KMT forces

"… a frank renunciation of war as an instrument of national policy should be made…"

PREAMBLE TO THE KELLOGG-BRIAND PACT, 1928

7 June 1929
VATICAN CITY FOUNDED

Since 1870, when it lost control of Rome, the Holy See had been in conflict with the Italian state. Aware of the power of the Roman Catholic Church in Italy, Mussolini set out to win over the Holy See. With the Lateran Treaty, he healed the rift, recognizing Vatican City as a sovereign state, compensating the Holy See for its losses, and making Catholicism Italy's official state religion.

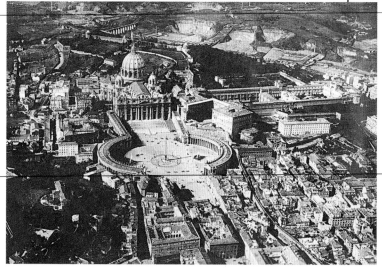

△ **Vatican City** from the air in the 1920s

19 December 1929

INDIA DEMANDS INDEPENDENCE

After several hundred Indians were killed by British troops in Amritsar in 1919, anti-British sentiment and demands for a return to self-rule grew in the British colony. In 1929, the Indian National Congress, a political party led by Mahatma Gandhi and Jawaharlal Nehru, passed the "Purna Swaraj" declaration, calling for nothing less than India's total independence.

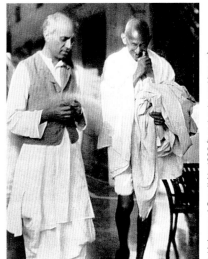

△ Nehru and Gandhi in 1929 (hand-coloured image)

31 August 1929

THE YOUNG PLAN

The Young Plan aimed to relieve the economic pressure on Germany by further reducing its reparations to around US$29 billion, to be paid over 58 years. The last occupying troops were also to leave German soil. However, the Wall Street Crash derailed the plan.

◁ **Cartoon satirizing** American attempts to secure German reparations

27 July The Geneva Convention requires that prisoners of war be treated humanely

16 October The Nazi Party organizes mass rallies in support of the proposed Liberty Law, which rejects reparations and German "war guilt"

1929

31 DECEMBER

July–December War breaks out in Manchuria between Russia and China; the bloody conflict reveals the limitations of the Kellogg-Briand Pact

December In Italy, the Fascist Party puts plans in place requiring teachers to take oaths of loyalty and to teach children loyalty to Fascism

24–29 October 1929

THE WALL STREET CRASH

In September, the buying of shares on the New York Stock Exchange on Wall Street began to slow. Panicking, investors began to sell their stocks, causing prices to tumble. Investors, banks, and businesses were ruined as billions of dollars were wiped off share values on three consecutive days of trading from 24 October (Black Thursday). Millions of people were left unemployed as the Great Depression took hold worldwide. In Germany, disenchantment with the government grew as the US loans the country relied on dried up.

▷ **Ruined by the Crash,** a man sells his car for cash (hand-coloured image)

$100 WILL BUY THIS CAR MUST HAVE CASH. LOST ALL ON THE STOCK MARKET

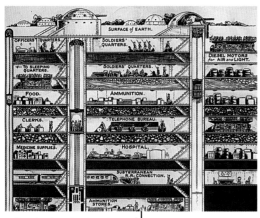

△ Sketch of the Maginot Line

January 1930
FRANCE READIES ITS DEFENCES

French minister of war, André Maginot, convinced the government to construct a defensive line along the border between France and Germany. The fortifications, completed in 1938, were enormous. Below the surface, they ran deep underground to stores, hangars, soldiers' quarters, offices, and a railway that linked various strongpoints.

14 September 1930
NAZI ELECTION GAINS

In the federal election, the Nazi Party took 107 seats in the Reichstag to become Germany's second largest party, behind the Social Democratic Party (SDP). The Nazi Party, among many other parties, refused to cooperate with the minority government appointed by President Hindenburg, leaving it unable to deal with Germany's problems.

△ SDP election poster

30 June France withdraws from the Rhineland, a buffer zone occupied in 1923, after the Young Plan guarantees that Germany will pay its reparations

1930

1 JANUARY

22 April The London Naval Treaty is another flawed attempt to extend the terms of 1922's Washington Treaty (*see p.19*) and control the naval arms race

19 May 1931
GERMANY LAUNCHES ITS FIRST BATTLE CRUISER

Needing to replace its antiquated prewar dreadnoughts, yet having to adhere to the limits imposed on its navy by the Treaty of Versailles, Germany developed the Deutschland-class cruiser. These were heavily armoured ships, which the British called "pocket battleships". The first, the *Deutschland*, was launched in May 1931; the *Admiral Scheer* and the *Admiral Graf Spee* followed.

▽ *Deutschland*, a "pocket battleship"

△ **Japanese soldiers** in occupied Manchuria (hand-coloured image)

"... Japan... used me as a puppet to help them rule the Northeast."

PUYI, IN HIS AUTOBIOGRAPHY, FROM EMPEROR TO CITIZEN, 1964

18–19 September 1931

THE MUKDEN INCIDENT

On the night of 18 September, a section of track on the Japanese-owned railway near Mukden in Manchuria, northeast China, was destroyed by an explosion. The Japanese Kwantung Army, based in Manchuria, blamed Chinese Nationalists and used the incident as a pretext to seize Mukden and invade Manchuria.

28 January 1932 Japanese officers foment conflict in Shanghai, China, increasing international concerns about Japanese aggression

1932

12 MARCH

17 October 1931 In Japan, members of the ultranationalist Cherry Blossom Society (Sakurakai) are arrested after planning a coup

◁ **Puyi,** the emperor of Manchukuo

February 1932–November 1934

THE GENEVA CONFERENCE FOR WORLD DISARMAMENT

Sixty countries met in Geneva, Switzerland, to discuss disarmament. The conference ended in deadlock over Germany's demands to be allowed arms equal to those of other nations and France's need for security guarantees.

△ **Postcard marking** the Geneva Conference

1 March 1932

JAPAN TAKES CONTROL IN MANCHURIA

By February 1932, the Kwantung Army was in control of Manchuria. The following month, it helped install the last emperor of China, the 26-year-old Puyi, as ruler of the newly created State of Manchuria, known as Manchukuo. Puyi was then made emperor in 1934. Although the League of Nations refused to recognize the legitimacy of Manchukuo, it did nothing to penalize Japan for its aggression in the region.

15 May 1932
MILITARISM RISES IN JAPAN

The Japanese prime minister, Inukai Tsuyoshi, was assassinated by a group of militarist, nationalist naval officers, army cadets, and civilians in an attempted coup. The light sentences given to the assassins at their trial strengthened the militarists' position and weakened the rule of law in Japan.

△ **Trial of Tsuyoshi's** assassins in Tokyo

▷ Hermann Göring at the Reichstag

31 July 1932
THE NAZI PARTY DOMINATES THE REICHSTAG

In the federal elections, the Nazi Party won 230 of the Reichstag's 609 seats, becoming the German parliament's biggest party. Hitler made Hermann Göring president of the Reichstag, but refused to form a coalition government with other parties. The Reichstag was unable to function, and another election was held in November.

13 March Hitler gains 30 per cent of the vote in the German presidential election, but 85-year-old President Hindenburg wins

16 June–9 July At the Lausanne Conference, the UK and France agree to suspend Germany's reparations payments

1932

13 MARCH

4 May Estonia and the Soviet Union sign a non-aggression pact; it remains in force until 31 December 1945

6 November The Nazi Party loses 35 seats in the last free elections before Hitler seizes power; it again fails to form a coalition

30 January 1933
HITLER BECOMES GERMAN CHANCELLOR

Desperate to get the government working to stabilize Germany's economy and reduce unemployment, and believing he could control Hitler, President Hindenburg gave in to Hitler's demands to be made chancellor. A new coalition was formed, but with Nazis in only 3 out of 11 cabinet positions, Hitler called for a new election on 5 March.

▷ *The 30th January 1933,* painting by Arthur Kampf, 1938

27 February 1933
THE REICHSTAG FIRE

When an arsonist set fire to the Reichstag building, Hitler persuaded President Hindenburg that communists were to blame and were planning an uprising that could be prevented only by emergency legislation. The Reichstag Fire Decree suspended many civil rights, giving the Nazis free rein to suppress opposition before the 5 March election, which it dominated.

◁ **The Reichstag building on fire**

22 March 1933 Dachau concentration camp opens; it is Germany's first. The earliest inmates are mainly communists and other opponents of the Nazi Party

27 March Japan leaves the League of Nations after rejecting its approach to events in Manchuria

1933

31 MARCH

23 March SS and SA troops surround the Reichstag to prevent opponents from voting while the Nazis force through the Enabling Act, granting Hitler dictatorial powers

4 March 1933
ROOSEVELT BECOMES PRESIDENT OF THE USA

Franklin D. Roosevelt began the first of four terms as US president after being elected in November 1932. The country faced huge economic problems, with 13 million people unemployed and many banks closed. In his "First 100 Days", Roosevelt outlined a recovery and reform programme that would help businesses, agriculture, and the unemployed and begin to rebuild America's economy.

◁ **Inaugural programme** of Franklin D. Roosevelt and Vice President John Garner

"We want the bill, or fire and murder."

NAZI CHANT DEMANDING THE PASSING OF THE ENABLING ACT, 1933

△ **The Gestapo headquarters** on Briennerstrasse, Munich, 1933

26 April 1933
ESTABLISHMENT OF GERMANY'S SECRET POLICE

The Geheime Staatspolizei, shortened to Gestapo, was Nazi Germany's secret state police. Created after the Reichstag Fire Decree (*see p.31*) suspended citizens' legal rights, including the right to privacy, the Gestapo became feared for its use of surveillance, violence, and torture in its mission to root out subversion and opposition.

△ **German drag queen** Hansi Sturm, c.1927

6 May 1933
THE NAZIS TARGET GAY MEN

Before the rise of the Nazis, Germany was a liberal country in which queer culture flourished, and homosexuality was close to being legalized in 1929. In May 1933, the Nazis closed the pioneering Institute for Sexual Sciences and burned its library of books on gender and same-sex love. This began a campaign of persecution in which thousands of gay men were arrested, harassed, sent to concentration camps, and even castrated.

1933

1 APRIL

29 April Japanese-backed warlord Liu Guitang advances into Inner Mongolia's Dolonor region, which Japan's Kwantung Army then seizes

2 May Trade Unions in Germany are banned as the Nazis continue to crack down on dissent

"No to decadence and moral corruption! Yes to decency and morality in family and state!"

JOSEPH GOEBBELS, SPEECH AT THE BOOK BURNINGS IN BERLIN, 10 MAY 1933

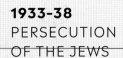

1933–38
PERSECUTION OF THE JEWS

From 1933, the Nazi Party began to use intimidation and legislation to restrict the rights and freedom of Germany's Jewish population.

1 April 1933 The Nazis organize a nationwide, one-day boycott of Jewish-owned shops; many ignore the boycott.

10 May 1933 More than 25,000 books written by Jews and others the Nazis deemed "un-German" are publicly burned in Berlin's Opernplatz.

25 July 1938 Jewish doctors have their medical licences revoked. Only 700 remain as "patient handlers" to treat patients in Jewish hospitals.

15 November 1938 Jewish children are expelled from Germany's public schools, in which their numbers have been restricted since 1933.

15 May 1933
GERMANY REVIVES ITS AIR FORCE

Work began in the newly created Air Ministry on secretly rebuilding Germany's Luftwaffe, disbanded in 1920 under the terms of the Treaty of Versailles. When Hitler publicly announced the air force's existence in February 1935, it had more than 1,800 aircraft and 20,000 personnel, and an operational doctrine focused on tactical bombing in support of ground operations.

◁ **Observer's Badge,** awarded to members of the Luftwaffe

The Nazi Party's rally grounds in Nuremberg could hold up to 1 million people and covered 11 sq km (7 sq miles)

14 July Germany legalizes the forcible sterilization of Roma, Afro-Germans, and people with physical and mental disabilities or mental illness

2 September Italy and the USSR sign a non-aggression pact; it lasts until 22 June 1941, when Italy declares war on the USSR

1933
2 SEPTEMBER

12 June At the London Economic Conference, 66 countries meet to discuss a way out of the worldwide economic depression

30 August German-Jewish philosopher and critic of the Nazis Theodor Lessing is murdered by Nazi supporters in Czechoslovakia

30 August–3 September 1933
THE NUREMBERG RALLIES

The rallies the Nazis had held since the 1920s became annual events after the "Rally of Victory" in 1933, which marked Hitler's appointment as chancellor. Hundreds of thousands gathered at the purpose-built grounds in Nuremberg to listen to speeches and take part in choreographed displays of military strength and discipline. Some of the rallies were filmed by Leni Riefenstahl, whose film *Triumph of the Will* helped mythologize the Nazis.

▷ Scene from Leni Riefenstahl's *Triumph of the Will*

6 February 1934
RIGHT-WING RIOTS IN PARIS

Angry at the alleged corruption of France's centre-left government, thousands of far-right activists and nationalist veterans gathered at the Place de la Concorde in Paris. The government narrowly avoided a coup when protesters attempted to force their way into parliament buildings, prompting police to open fire, killing 26. More protests by both left- and right-wing movements followed, helping entrench political divisions in France.

▷ **Women from the nationalist Solidarité Française** marking the riot's first anniversary, 1935

1933
3 SEPTEMBER

12 September Hungarian physicist Leo Szilard conceives of the idea of the nuclear chain reaction, which underpins the development of the atomic bomb

26 January 1934 A 10-year pact of non-aggression is signed by Germany and Poland

19 October Germany leaves the League of Nations, removing one barrier to German rearmament

1882–1945
FRANKLIN D. ROOSEVELT

As an adult, Roosevelt was paralysed by poliomyelitis. With characteristic determination, he taught himself to walk again using iron leg and hip braces. He applied the same single-mindedness to America's problems on becoming president in 1933.

15 November 1933
DIPLOMATIC RELATIONS RESTORED

By 1933, the USSR and USA were keen to re-establish relations, which had been broken off in 1917. Roosevelt hoped to find an ally against Japan's expansionism in Asia, and the USSR craved the legitimacy of formal recognition from the USA. Talks between Roosevelt and Soviet diplomat Maxim Litvinov gave rise to a "gentleman's agreement" that allowed the USA to resume full diplomatic relations and appoint its first ambassador to the USSR.

◁ **William Christian Bullitt,** the first US ambassador to the USSR

△ Poster for the National Industrial **Recovery Act,** one of Roosevelt's new agencies

30 June 1934

THE NIGHT OF THE LONG KNIVES

As Hitler consolidated his power, he ordered a purge of potential rivals, primarily the SA and its leader, Ernst Röhm. Röhm wanted the SA to be incorporated into Germany's armed forces. This was unacceptable to Germany's generals, who viewed the Brownshirts and Röhm as thugs, and whose support Hitler needed. On the night of 30 June, the SS shot Röhm and many other leaders of the SA, along with other enemies of Hitler, such as former chancellor Kurt von Schleicher.

▽ SA honour dagger

28 June 1934

ROOSEVELT'S NEW DEAL

By June 1934, the first phase of Roosevelt's New Deal was ending. It had created and mobilized a host of federal agencies, whose abbreviated names were likened to "alphabet soup", to lift America out of economic depression. In his "fireside chat" on 28 June, the President asked the nation to judge his success and outlined the controversial idea at the heart of the next phase: social insurance.

9 February In the Balkans, Greece, Türkiye, Romania, and Yugoslavia sign a defensive pact to reduce tensions in the area; Bulgaria refuses to join

17 April Japan rejects the League of Nations' authority and claims sole responsibility for the maintenance of peace in Asia

1934

25 JULY

25 July 1934

THE JULY PUTSCH

In June 1933, Austria's right-wing chancellor, Engelbert Dollfuss, banned the Austrian Nazi Party after weeks of terrorist activity. Some Nazis remained in Austria while others fled to Germany, where they were given military training. On 25 July, Austria's Nazis attempted a coup on Hitler's orders, during which Dollfuss was shot dead. The coup failed, but it made clear that Germany represented a serious threat to Austria's independence.

◁ Engelbert Dollfuss

"We seek the security of the men, women, and children of the Nation."

FRANKLIN D. ROOSEVELT IN HIS "FIRESIDE CHAT", 28 JUNE 1934

Ein Volk, ein Reich, ein Führer!

2 August 1934

HITLER BECOMES FÜHRER

Since January 1933, Germany had undergone a process of *Gleichschaltung* ("synchronization"), which removed opponents of the Nazis from politics and the legal system, and Nazified social and cultural life. The process reached its apogee when President Hindenburg died on 2 August 1934 and Hitler subsumed the role of president, becoming Führer ("the Leader").

◁ **Nazi propaganda poster** (the slogan reads "One People, one State, one Leader")

5 December 1934

ITALY AND ETHIOPIA CLASH

Ethiopian troops arrived at the Walwal oasis, on the Ethiopian side of the buffer zone with Italian Somaliland, to ask the Dubats (Somali soldiers) stationed there to withdraw. Skirmishes followed, in which 150 died. The League of Nations' weak response to the incident emboldened Italy.

▷ **Dubat working for Italy's** Royal Corps of Colonial Troops

20 August The Hitler Oath requires all officers and soldiers in the German armed forces and civil servants to swear allegiance to Hitler

1934

26 JULY

9 October King Alexander I of Yugoslavia is assassinated in Marseille, France, by a Macedonian separatist

16 October 1934

THE LONG MARCH

From 1 August 1927, China's government, headed by the Kuomintang (KMT), was engaged in a civil war with the Chinese Communist Party (CCP). By 1934, the Communists were encircled at their base in southwest China. Faced with destruction, on 16 October, Mao Zedong secured a reputation for heroism by breaking out almost 100,000 Communists. He then led them on the Long March into northern China. In 368 days, the Communists covered more than 9,600 km (6,000 miles).

▷ **Mao Zedong** on horseback during the Long March

13 January 1935
THE SAAR RETURNS TO GERMANY

From 1920, the Saar, part of Germany since 1815, was under League of Nations control. When that mandate ended in 1935, a plebiscite was held on whether the Saar should return to Germany or join France. More than 90 per cent voted for its return to Germany.

△ "Back to the Fatherland", Nazi propaganda for the plebiscite

▽ The first public appearance of Germany's Wehrmacht (armed forces), 1935

16 March 1935
GERMANY BUILDS ITS ARMY

After revealing the existence of the Luftwaffe on 9 March, Hitler announced on 16 March that he was increasing the German Army to 36 divisions and introducing conscription for all men aged between 18 and 45. This rearmament directly contravened the terms of the Treaty of Versailles.

26 February 1935 The Japanese Army stamps out factionalism in its ranks and increases its influence over Japan's civilian government

1935

7 APRIL

29 December Japan warns that it will consider itself bound by naval treaty limitations only for two more years

7 April In the Free City of Danzig, Nazis dominate the elections as pressure to rejoin Germany grows among the German-speaking population

GERMANY'S CULTURE WAR

The Nazification of German culture was in the hands of Joseph Goebbels, Minister of Public Enlightenment and Propaganda, who set about purging the arts of "un-German" influences. This meant, for example, banning jazz music because of its Black cultural origins and promoting the works of German composers such as Richard Wagner. After Hitler made clear his disgust for modern art, thousands of works, including those of Picasso and Van Gogh, were sold or destroyed. Nazi art exhibitions reflected Nazi ideology, with themes such as "Blood and Soil", or mocked art considered "degenerate" by the Nazis.

Poster for the *Degenerate "Art"* exhibition held in Munich, 1937

1889–1945
ADOLF HITLER
Born in Austria, Hitler was a clever child with dreams of being an artist. He moved into politics after World War I and, as head of the Nazi Party, became one of history's most notorious and reviled figures.

15 September 1935
THE NUREMBERG LAWS

Germany enacted two race laws – the "Reich Citizenship Law" and the "Law for the Protection of German Blood and German Honour" – together known as the Nuremberg Laws. The definition of citizens as people "of German or related blood" excluded Jews, stripping them of German citizenship and their political rights. The laws also forbade Jewish people from marrying or having sexual relations with those of "German blood".

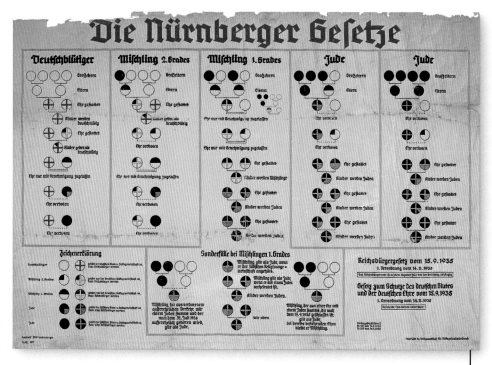

▷ **Nuremberg Laws poster** showing the categorization of people as Jewish, German, or "mixed race" according to their ancestry

1935

8 APRIL

14 April France, Britain, and Italy form the Stresa Front to oppose German rearmament and further attempts to defy the Treaty of Versailles

12 September Britain declares to the League of Nations Assembly that it stands "for steady and collective resistance to all acts of unprovoked aggression"

24 June Britain's foreign secretary, Anthony Eden, meets Mussolini in Rome to try to resolve tensions between Italy and Ethiopia; Mussolini rejects Eden's proposals

△ German naval flag 1935-45

18 June 1935
ANGLO-GERMAN NAVAL AGREEMENT

Britain and Germany agreed that the size of Germany's surface fleet would be limited to 35 per cent of that of the Commonwealth. An act of appeasement that reassured Britain there would be no arms race, this undermined the Stresa Front and angered France.

◁ Senator Gerald Nye

31 August 1935
US NEUTRALITY

After Senator Nye's investgation into US involvement in World War I, Congress passed a Neutrality Act, which embargoed the trade in arms and war materials with any parties in a war. The act was favoured by America's isolationists, but Roosevelt secured a "cash and carry" concession in 1937, allowing belligerents to buy goods (including arms, from 1939) with cash and transport them on their own ships.

By the outbreak of the war in 1939, Britain had 17 infantry divisions; Germany had 86

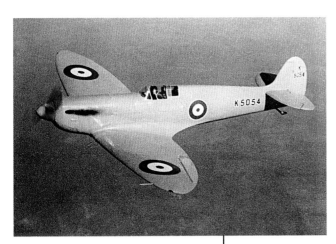

31 December 1935

BRITAIN REARMS

Britain began to rearm at the end of 1935. It prioritized the Royal Air Force (RAF), with a series of expansion plans that focused initially on bombers and increasingly on fighters, including the Supermarine Spitfire, of which the RAF ordered 310 in June 1936. The British Army, however, was held back by the doctrine of limited liability, aimed at minimizing potential losses in another European war. By September 1939, Britain's troop numbers were far below those of Germany.

◁ **A prototype** Vickers Supermarine Spitfire

7 October The League of Nations imposes weak economic sanctions on Italy that, crucially, do not include oil

1936

26 FEBRUARY

10–19 February 1936 Italy is victorious in the Battle of Amba Aradam in the Second Italo-Ethiopian War

26 February Extremists from the Imperial Way faction try to overthrow Japan's conservative government

3 October 1935

ITALY INVADES ETHIOPIA

Determined to carve out an Italian empire, Mussolini used Italy's footholds in Eritrea and Somaliland to launch an invasion of the independent empire of Ethiopia (then called Abyssinia). The Italian forces bombed villages, poisoned water supplies, and used gas against local troops. On 2 May 1936, Emperor Haile Selassie (*see p.103*) fled into exile in London. Five days later, Mussolini announced the annexation of Ethiopia.

◁ **Map of Ethiopia** after the invasion of Italian troops in 1935

Sailors scrutinize a navy radar scope on a US warship in 1944. The scope provided crew members with an invaluable visual plot of an enemy ship or aircraft, including location and direction of travel. Radar technology improved steadily over the course of World War II.

1935-45
RADIO VISION

The development of radar (an acronym of "radio detection and ranging") began in the USA, Europe, and the USSR in the early 20th century. The technology, which allows the detection of moving objects at long range, relies on antennas that emit radio signals and pick up their reflections from faraway targets. Radar is capable, for example, of revealing the height and bearing of enemy aircraft.

The first large-scale aircraft tracking system, known as "Chain Home", was developed in Britain shortly before the outbreak of WWII. With its tall antennas erected along the coast, Chain Home was instrumental in the defeat of German aerial attacks during the Battle of Britain.

Radar technology advanced very rapidly during the war with the development of the cavity magnetron. This was a powerful vacuum tube capable of producing high-intensity radio pulses transmitted using an aerial just a few centimetres long. This meant that radar could be fitted, for example, inside night fighters so that they could track enemy bombers in complete darkness.

Radar had many wartime applications. Allied patrol aircraft used radar to track surfaced U-boats at long range; during the day and at night, ships could see over the horizon; and gun-laying radars improved the accuracy of naval artillery fire.

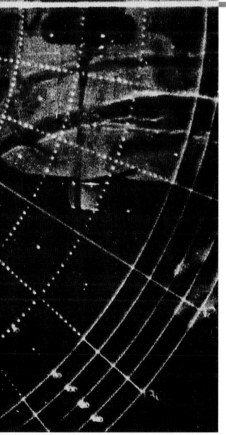

KEY MOMENTS

1935 Pioneer of radar
Scottish physicist Robert Watson-Watt (*right*) was asked by Britain's Air Ministry to develop a radio-based "death-ray" to destroy enemy aircraft. In proving that this was technically impossible, he showed that radio could be used to detect flying objects.

1940 The Battle of Britain
German pilots flying over southern England during the Battle of Britain were surprised to be regularly and accurately intercepted by British fighters. This was because a network of radar stations along the coast (*right*) guided the RAF pilots to their targets.

1942 The Bruneval raid
In 1942, the British realized that Germany's new Würzburg-Riese radar was proving very effective in detecting RAF bombers. To discover more, the British dropped paratroopers to dismantle an example of the technology near the French village of Bruneval (*right*) and gather parts for analysis.

7 March 1936
GERMANY REOCCUPIES THE RHINELAND

The Rhineland – a strip of German territory bordering France, Belgium, and the Netherlands – had been demilitarized under the Treaty of Versailles in 1919. On the pretext that a mutual assistance pact between France and the USSR (May 1935) threatened Germany's safety, Hitler ordered 35,000 German troops to march into and reoccupy the Rhineland. France was outraged, but there was little real opposition to Hitler's move.

◁ **Children greet** German soldiers in the Rhineland

1936

27 FEBRUARY

9 March The Japanese prime minister, Keisuke Okada, is replaced by radical militarist Koki Hirato

25 March The Second London Naval Treaty tries to limit the naval arms race; Japan and Germany are not signatories

2 May Emperor Haile Selassie flees Ethiopia for the UK, where he sets up a government-in-exile

5 May Italian troops enter Addis Ababa, ending the Second Italo-Ethiopian war; Italy then annexes Ethiopia

15 April 1936
ARAB REVOLT IN PALESTINE

From 1919, Palestine came to be administered by the British under the League of Nations' Mandate for Palestine. The ultimate aim of the mandate was to prepare the territory for self-rule. However, the independence process was complicated by tensions between Jewish and Arab inhabitants, exacerbated by the arrival of Jewish immigrants seeking to establish a Zionist state. In 1936, the Arab Higher Committee (a nationalist coalition) called for a general strike. Arab rebels began attacking Jewish settlements and British installations. British troops restored order by the end of the year, but unrest continued.

▷ **A British soldier** searches Arab men for arms

1892–1975
FRANCISCO FRANCO

Born into a military family, Franco became a general in the Spanish army. In 1936, he joined Spain's right-wing Nationalist rebels, leading them to victory in the civil war and establishing himself as dictator.

◁ **Jesse Owens** at the start of the 200 metres at the Berlin Olympic Games (hand-coloured image)

17 July 1936
THE SPANISH CIVIL WAR BEGINS

Spanish generals sympathetic to the fascist Falange party launched a military revolt against the country's left-wing Republican government, sparking a civil war. Under the leadership of General Francisco Franco, Spain's right-wing factions gathered together under a Nationalist banner; they gained control of Spain and finally defeated the Republicans after capturing Madrid in March 1939. Franco then set up a brutal fascist regime.

◁ **Nationalist propaganda poster** from the Spanish Civil War

1–16 August 1936
THE BERLIN OLYMPICS

Germany's Nazi regime used the Summer Olympics in Berlin as a propaganda exercise. However, its ambition to showcase to the world's media the supposed physical superiority of the Aryan "master race" was undone by the spectacular success of Black American athlete Jesse Owens, who won gold medals in the 100m, 200m, 4x400m relay, and long jump.

July Sachsenhausen concentration camp goes into operation in Oranienberg, Germany

1936

16 AUGUST

> "To all of you who feel holy love for Spain...
> the nation calls you to defend it."

FRANCISCO FRANCO, IN A RADIO BROADCAST, 18 JULY 1936

1936-39
FOREIGN FORCES IN SPAIN

Although agreeing not to intervene in Spain's civil war, Germany and Italy aided the Nationalists, and the USSR supported the Republicans.

27 July 1936 Germany's Condor Legion begins transporting 13,500 troops of Spain's Army of Africa to the mainland.

14 October 1936 The first volunteers from the Soviet-backed International Brigades arrive in Spain from across Europe and North America.

26 April 1937 The Condor Legion and Italy's Aviazione Legionaria bomb Guernica in northern Spain at the request of Franco's Nationalists.

23 March 1937 Republican forces prevail over Nationalist and Italian volunteer troops at the Battle of Guadalajara.

25 November 1936
THE ANTI-COMINTERN PACT

Germany and Japan united against the Communist International (Comintern) – a Soviet-led organization dedicated to the spread of communism. The two countries also secretly agreed that should either be at war with the USSR, the other would stay neutral. This emboldened Japan, whose plans for expansion in China would bring it into conflict with Communist Party forces.

△ **Japanese girls celebrating** the second anniversary of the Anti-Comintern Pact in 1938

25 October 1936
THE ROME—BERLIN AXIS

Attempts by Britain and France to maintain close relations with Italy ended when Mussolini made an alliance with Hitler. This created, as Mussolini put it, "an axis around which all European States animated by a desire for peace may collaborate on troubles".

▷ **Postcard marking** the Axis

ACHSE BERLIN – ROMA

1936

17 AUGUST

1 December Hitler makes membership of the Hitler Youth mandatory for boys aged 10–18

8–14 September At the 8th Nazi Party Congress, Hitler outlines his ambition to restore Germany's prewar colonies

14 November Japan backs an attempt by Mongol and Han Chinese forces to take control of China's Suiyuan province

An estimated 750,000 people died between 1936 and 1938 in Stalin's Great Purge

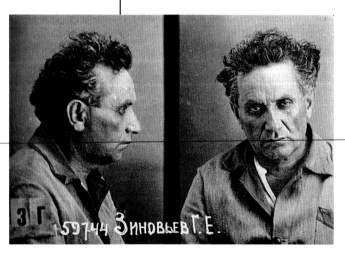

19 August 1936
STALIN'S GREAT PURGE

Paranoid about his hold on the Communist Party, Stalin ordered a purge of "Old Bolsheviks" – party members who had founded the Soviet Union. Confessions were gathered under torture by the secret police (NKVD) and used to condemn many – including prominent politician Grigory Zinoviev – to death. As the purge widened, hundreds of thousands of ordinary people were detained, executed, or sent to forced labour camps. Moreover, 81 out of 103 of the Soviet Union's highest-ranking military leaders were executed.

◁ **NKVD mugshot** of the Bolshevik Grigory Zinoviev

▷ A Nationalist Chinese anti-Japanese propaganda poster with offensive caricature of Japanese soldiers

我愈戰愈強
敵愈戰愈弱

國際侵略運動中國分會製

7 July 1937

THE SINO-JAPANESE WAR BEGINS

With tensions between China and Japan already high over the invasion of Manchuria, an exchange of fire between Chinese and Japanese forces near the Marco Polo Bridge, southwest of Beijing, lit the touchpaper on all-out war. Japan invaded north China from its puppet state of Manchukuo and advanced south. The Sino-Japanese War became enmeshed with World War II and is seen by some as the latter's true starting point.

> ## "Politics is war without bloodshed, while war is politics with bloodshed."

CHINESE COMMUNIST LEADER MAO ZEDONG, 1938

24 December The Chinese Communist Party and Kuomintang suspend the Chinese Civil War and join together to fight the Japanese

15 July 1937 Buchenwald concentration camp opens; it goes on to administer 88 sub-camps across Germany

8 August Japanese forces occupy Beijing after forcing the Chinese to retreat

1937

13 AUGUST

25 July Japanese and Chinese forces clash at Langfang, south of Beijing; Japan then bombs the city

13 August–26 November 1937

THE BATTLE OF SHANGHAI

On 13 August, Japanese soldiers attacked the Chinese at Shanghai while Japan's 3rd Fleet bombarded the city. It was the first major battle in the Sino-Japanese war and one of the bloodiest. The Chinese clung on for three months, losing an estimated 250,000 men, before being forced to retreat.

▷ Soldiers of the Imperial Japanese Army celebrating their victory at Shanghai

21 August 1937

THE SINO-SOVIET NON-AGRESSION PACT

By signing a friendship agreement with China, the USSR successfully closed down the possibility that China would join the Anti-Comintern pact. In return, the USSR sent aircraft and economic aid to support China in its war with Japan but would not be drawn into fighting.

▽ **Polikarpov I-16** Soviet Air Force fighter aircraft

> "Germany's future was therefore wholly conditional upon the solving of the need for space."

MINUTES FROM THE BERLIN MEETING ON LEBENSRAUM, 5 NOVEMBER 1937

1937

14 AUGUST

13 October Germany guarantees Belgium's sovereignty as long as it takes no part in military action against Germany

5 October Roosevelt calls for aggressors to be "quarantined" by the international community, angering non-interventionists in the USA

6 November Italy joins the Anti-Comintern pact with Japan and Germany, unifying what will become the primary Axis powers

26 November Japanese forces capture Shanghai after three months of fighting

5 November 1937

HITLER OUTLINES HIS PLANS FOR EXPANSION

In a secret meeting in Berlin, Hitler laid out his foreign policy plans for the coming years. He wanted to create a Greater Germany that expanded beyond Germany's 1914 borders and provided sufficient *Lebensraum* ("living space") and autarky (self-sufficiency) for the German people. Hitler planned to take this living space from Austria and Czechoslovakia in 1943–45, but events proceeded much more quickly.

▷ **German propaganda poster** justifying the need for *Lebensraum*

Der deutsche Wirtschaftsraum hat 2½ mal so viel Konsumenten wie Frankreich oder England.

(in Millionen Einwohnern)

42   47   108,6

Die Weltwirtschaft kann ohne den deutschen Markt nicht bestehen!

13 December 1937
ATROCITY AT NANJING

The Chinese city of Nanjing fell to the Japanese on 13 December. Over the following six weeks, it was the scene of great brutality and cruelty as the Japanese embarked on an orgy of killing and rape. Up to 400,000 Chinese died in organized massacres or random killings, and tens of thousands were raped. Japan's military leadership did nothing to hold back its soldiers, and even encouraged them. Worried about Japan's reputation abroad, Emperor Hirohito ordered the expansion of Japan's "comfort stations", aiming to prevent indiscriminate rape; instead, it led to a new abomination – the forced prostitution of thousands of women (*see p.131*).

◁ **Destroyed houses**
in Nanjing, 1937

11 December **Mussolini announces** to crowds in Rome that Italy has left the League of Nations

26 January 1938 **US consul John Allison** is struck by a Japanese officer and American property is looted in Nanjing; the incident further strains Japanese–US relations

1938

4 FEBRUARY

△ **The USS *Panay*,** which was sunk by Japanese bombs off Nanjing

12 December 1937
THE PANAY INCIDENT

Japanese naval aircraft opened fire on the USS *Panay* and three other American ships as they moved up China's river Yangzi, having rescued American refugees from Nanjing. Three died and 48 were injured in the attack. Later, the Japanese government apologized for attacking neutral vessels and compensated the USA, but the incident alerted the USA to the increasing dangers posed to its interests overseas.

4 February 1938
HITLER CREATES THE OBERKOMMANDO DER WEHRMACHT

Hitler dissolved the Reich War Ministry and created the Armed Forces High Command (Oberkommando der Wehrmacht or OKW). This brought the heads of Germany's armed forces under his direct control, allowing him to dictate military strategy for his commanders to execute, and to maintain control by playing the armed forces off against each other.

▽ **Close combat clasp,** awarded to infantry of the Wehrmacht

24 April–19 May 1938
SUDETEN CRISIS

After annexing Austria, Hitler turned his attention to dismantling Czechoslovakia, using Konrad Henlein, leader of the 3.5 million Sudeten Germans that lived in Czechoslovakia, as his puppet. Claiming that the Germans were being mistreated, Henlein demanded autonomy for the Sudetenland in a manifesto called the *Karlsbader Programm*. Clashes erupted between Czechs and Germans, and Hitler intimated that he would take military action if necessary. The Czech government mobilized its considerable army in response.

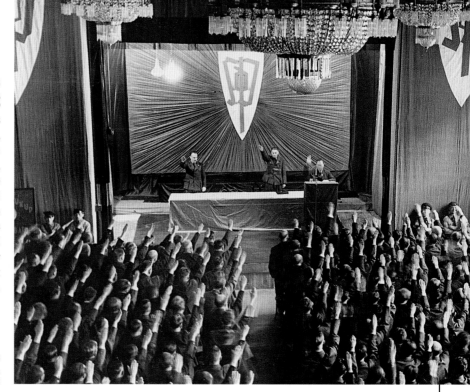

▷ **Konrad Henlein** reads out his eight-point programme in Karlsbad, Germany, 24 April 1938

1938

5 FEBRUARY

30 March Mussolini is made First Marshal of the Empire, giving him and Italy's king equal power over the military

10 April Eduoard Deladier becomes France's prime minister; he has a clear understanding of the threat posed by Hitler to European peace

16 April Britain recognizes Italian control of Ethiopia in return for Italy withdrawing its troops from Spain when the civil war ends

In a confirmatory referendum held on 10 April, 99.73 per cent of Germans were in favour of Austria's union with Germany

11–13 March 1938
GERMANY ANNEXES AUSTRIA

As Italy moved closer to Germany, Austria became isolated and increasingly under threat. On 9 March, Chancellor Kurt von Schuschnigg announced plans for a plebiscite to decide if Austria should remain independent of Germany. Fearing support for independence, Hitler threatened to invade if von Schuschnigg did not resign and cancel the vote. On 11 March, the Austrian chancellor gave in. Nonetheless, the next day, German troops entered Austria. On 13 March, Austria's "reunification" with Germany was announced.

◁ **Poster marking the Anschluss ("union")** of Austria and Germany, 1938

6–15 July 1938

THE EVIAN CONFERENCE

At Evian in France, delegates from 32 countries met to discuss the increasing number of Jewish refugees fleeing Germany and Austria. While most were sympathetic to the Jewish plight, they refused to increase their immigration quotas; some even tightened their criteria. The USA, for example, would accept only 27,000 Jews a year.

△ **Delegates** at the Evian Conference

▽ **Red Army** soldiers at Lake Khasan

29 July–11 August 1938

JAPAN AND THE SOVIET UNION CLASH

The Battle of Lake Khasan, also known as the Changkufeng Incident, saw fighting erupt at the border between the Soviet Union and Manchuria near the Korean border. Long believed to have been caused by a Japanese incursion into Soviet territory, it may in fact have been the result of a Soviet false-flag operation.

30 May Hitler issues a directive for Fall Grün, the invasion of Czechoslovakia, planned for 1 October 1938

5 August The Fascist magazine *La Difesa della Razza* publishes the *Manifesto of Race* – a prelude to the introduction of Italy's racial laws

1938

31 AUGUST

26 April Jewish people inside the German Reich are required to register any property worth more than 5,000 Reichsmarks

1 August SS officer Adolf Eichmann establishes the Office of Jewish Emigration to speed up the process of making Germany *judenrein* ("clean of Jews")

1933–39

JEWISH REFUGEES

Between 1933 and 1938, about 150,000 of Germany's 525,000 Jews left the country, but Austria's annexation brought another 185,000 under Nazi rule, sparking further emigration. Some went to neighbouring countries, such as Czechoslovakia, France, the Netherlands, and Belgium, only to be rounded up during later German occupations. Some made it further afield. For example, by September 1939, the UK had accepted around 60,000 Jews, including 10,000 unaccompanied children brought by the Kindertransport, but it had also refused entry to 500,000 more.

▷ **A train** carrying refugee children from Vienna to Switzerland

△ **Neville Chamberlain** waves a paper signed by Hitler and himself on his return from Munich

29 September 1938

THE MUNICH AGREEMENT

The British prime minister, Neville Chamberlain, negotiated for weeks to find a peaceful solution to the Sudeten crisis (*see p.48*). Finally, at Munich on 29 September, an agreement was reached between Britain, France, Italy, and Germany that allowed Germany to annex the whole Sudetenland in exchange for peace. Chamberlain declared this meant "Peace for our time".

21 October 1938

THE JAPANESE CAPTURE GUANGZHOU

For more than a year, the Japanese bombarded Guangzhou (then known as Canton), an important port on the Pearl River in southern China, in an attempt to blockade the coast and disrupt supplies to the Chinese. On 12 October, Japanese troops landed 75 km (47 miles) southwest of Guangzhou. Supported by air cover, they captured the city, which had been set on fire by retreating Chinese forces, by 21 October. Within days, Japanese warships entered the harbour.

△ **Japanese soldiers** above Guangzhou

1938

1 SEPTEMBER

24 September Hitler issues an ultimatum to Czechoslovakia over the Sudetenland; the Czech government rejects his demands

5 October Germany invalidates the passports of Jews and reissues passports marked with a "J"

21 October In a secret memorandum, Hitler prepares Wehrmacht leaders for the "liquidation" of Czechoslovakia

"All is over. Silent, mournful, abandoned, broken, Czechoslovakia recedes into the darkness."

WINSTON CHURCHILL, ON THE MUNICH AGREEMENT, 5 OCTOBER 1938

21 September 1938

CHURCHILL'S WARNINGS

From the early 1930s, Winston Churchill issued warnings in parliament and in the press about the threat posed by Nazi Germany, particularly after it began rearming. While Chamberlain negotiated with Hitler over Czechoslovakia, Churchill warned of the consequences of partitioning the country. He claimed that it was delusional to believe that "throwing a small state to the wolves" would bring security and peace; instead, such appeasement would weaken Britain and France and threaten democracy.

◁ **French cartoon showing** Churchill warning neutral nations of the dangers of Nazi Germany, 1935

1909-2015
SIR NICHOLAS WINTON
Knighted in 2003 for his work on the Kindertransport, Nicholas Winton was a 29-year-old London stockbroker when he began organizing the rescue of 669 Jewish children from Czechoslovakia in 1938.

1938
APPEASEMENT
In the 1930s, Britain – desperate to avoid another world war – followed a policy of appeasement with Germany and Italy. Its leaders believed that Europe's dictators could be controlled by showing that reasonable demands could be met by negotiation rather than force. Moreover, the perception in Britain was that the USSR was the greater threat, and that Nazi Germany provided a bulwark against communism.

△ **Postcard** celebrating the signing of the Munich Agreement, 29 September 1938

1,406 synagogues and prayer rooms were destroyed in Germany on *Kristallnacht*

28 October 17,000 Polish Jews living in Germany are deported to Poland, which refuses to admit them; thousands are stranded in the frontier village of Zbaszyn

15 December President Roosevelt announces the extension of US$25 million credit to the Chinese government for its fight against Japan

1938

31 DECEMBER

2 December 200 Jewish children from an orphanage in Berlin destroyed on Kristallnacht arrive in England with the first Kindertransport

9–10 November 1938
KRISTALLNACHT (THE NIGHT OF BROKEN GLASS)
Jewish businesses, synagogues, and homes across Germany, Sudetenland, and Austria were attacked. Around 7,500 shops were looted, their shattered glass windows giving the night its name. There were 91 official deaths, but probably hundreds more, and around 30,000 Jewish males were arrested and sent to concentration camps. The violence was blamed on spontaneous demonstrations, but was really carried out by Hitler Youth units and Nazi paramilitaries.

◁ **A synagogue in Hanover** on fire, 9 November 1938

14–15 March 1939
CZECHOSLOVAKIA DISMANTLED

After Germany took control of the Sudetenland, Hungary annexed land in southern Slovakia, and Poland took territory in Czech Silesia. Then, on 14 March, Slovakia seceded from Czechoslovakia, becoming the First Slovak Republic. Its government, led by Jozef Tiso, aligned itself with Germany. The next day, Germany invaded what remained of Czechoslovakia, turning it into a Reich protectorate. This clearly contravened the agreement made at Munich, but Britain raised little protest.

◁ Hitler marching past an honorary company in the castle district in the Czech capital, Prague, after Germany's invasion

1939

1 JANUARY

27 January Hitler orders Plan Z, aiming to expand the German fleet so that it will be able to defeat Britain's navy by 1944

20–23 March Germany demands the return of the Free City of Danzig and that Lithuania cede Klaipeda, on the Baltic coast

3 April Hitler orders planning to begin for the invasion of Poland, scheduled for 25 August 1939

1 April The Spanish Civil War ends in a Nationalist victory. Francisco Franco is made dictator

"We are rearming, but do not dream of attacking other nations."

ADOLF HITLER, SPEECH AT WILHELMSHAVEN, 1 APRIL 1939

1883–1946
JOACHIM VON RIBBENTROP
A top German diplomat, von Ribbentrop served as foreign secretary from 1938 to 1945. He negotiated Germany's non-aggression pact with the USSR, which made possible the invasion of Poland. In 1946, he was found guilty of war crimes.

7–12 April 1939
ITALY INVADES ALBANIA
Determined to show that he was equal to Hitler in his militarism and empire-building, Mussolini bombarded Albania's coast, after its king, Zog I, refused to let Italy annex the country. Italian troops landed on 7 April, and Zog fled to London. Albania's government resigned on 12 April, and the country became an Italian protectorate.

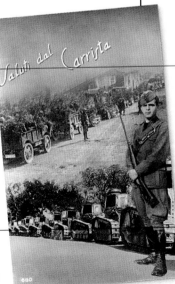

▷ Italian propaganda postcard marking the invasion of Albania

11 May–16 September 1939
THE BATTLE OF KHALKHIN GOL

Japanese and Soviet clashes at the Mongolia–Manchuria border escalated in July when Japanese forces occupied the region. The Soviets launched a blistering attack, defeating the Japanese 6th Army by 16 September. Stunned by the Soviet victory, Japan turned its attention from the USSR towards European- and American-held territories in the Pacific.

△ **Stalin (*right*) celebrates** the signing of the Nazi-Soviet Pact

△ **Soldiers** of the Soviet-backed Mongolian People's Army at Khalkhin Gol

23 August 1939
THE NAZI–SOVIET PACT

Although ideologically opposed, Germany and the USSR joined together in a pact, negotiated by their foreign ministers, Joachim von Ribbentrop and Vyacheslav Molotov, to advance their interests. Publicly, the two pledged to maintain neutrality if either country was at war. In secret clauses, however, they carved up Eastern Europe into spheres of influence and agreed to split Poland between them.

28 April Hitler renounces Germany's 1934 non-aggression pact with Poland

30 August Germany issues an ultimatum over the return of the Free City of Danzig

1939
31 AUGUST

10 July Neville Chamberlain reaffirms that Britain will intervene in Poland if hostilities break out

Britain's Land Army employed 80,000 women at its height in 1944

1 June 1939
THE LAND GIRLS

The Women's Land Army (WLA) was originally created in 1917 to help maintain food production during World War I. With war imminent, it was re-formed in 1939 and called, initially, for women to volunteer for farm work where needed across Britain. Between 1939 and 1950, more than 200,000 women worked in the Land Army. An additional 4,000 "Lumber Jills" worked for the Women's Timber Corps from 1942.

◁ **Propaganda image** of one of Britain's "land girls", Suffolk, 1940

THE EUROPEAN WAR

The speed and success of the German conquest of Poland in September 1939 caught the world by surprise. In a whirlwind campaign lasting less than a month, the Polish Army was destroyed and, in a secret, agreement, the entire country was divided between Germany and the Soviet Union.

Although the Soviet Union had gained dominion over eastern Poland and the Baltic states of Estonia, Latvia, and Lithuania, its leader, Joseph Stalin, demanded Finnish territory close to the city of Leningrad (now St Petersburg). The Winter War followed Finland's rejection of Stalin's claim. The Soviet Red Army made a poor start but eventually prevailed, and the Finnish government surrendered the territory.

War in Western Europe

In April 1940, German forces seized Denmark and then invaded Norway. The British and French sent troops to support the Norwegians, but in a series of confused engagements, they failed to prevent the German conquest. While the fighting in Norway was still ongoing, Hitler launched his offensive in the west.

On 10 May 1940, German troops swept into the Netherlands and Belgium, and then France, in a "blitzkrieg" (a "lightning war" designed to achieve a quick victory). Ten days after the opening of the offensive, German tanks had reached the English Channel, establishing a panzer corridor that cut the

Allied armies in two. Outflanked and facing disaster, the British fell back towards the port of Dunkirk to prepare for evacuation.

Germany triumphant

The Germans then turned south to deal with the remainder of the French Army, which was attempting to establish new lines to protect Paris and the French interior. On 5 June, the Germans sliced through the French defences: Paris fell on 14 June, and Marshal Philippe Pétain, the newly installed French president, signed an armistice with Germany on 22 June. Within the space of six weeks, Hitler had defeated France and forced the British Army to scuttle back across the Channel to England.

The Battle of Britain

Hitler assumed Britain would come to terms with Germany, but when his offers of peace were rebuffed, he told his generals to prepare to invade. Germany's opening move was to attempt to gain air supremacy over southern England. However, between July and September 1940, Britain's Royal Air Force held off Germany's Luftwaffe in a series of aerial engagements known as the Battle of Britain. The failure to knock Britain out of the war would come back to haunt Hitler, but at the time he could take comfort in a series of victories that made him master of continental Europe.

Hitler spent the opening months of 1941 preparing his forces for an invasion of the Soviet Union. In the diplomatic sphere, this entailed convincing the Balkan nations to accept the free passage of German troops through their territories. Most fell into line, although Yugoslavia and Greece refused to accept German overlordship. Hitler's preparations were interrupted by the antics of his junior partner in the Rome–Berlin Axis, Italy's leader, Benito Mussolini.

Italy intervenes

In September 1940, Italy had advanced into Egypt from Libya, prompting a British counter-response that threw the Italians back. Hitler felt obliged to send an expeditionary force, Erwin Rommel's Afrika Korps, to North Africa in early 1941 to stabilize the Italian retreat. Italy's invasion of Greece in October 1940 had proved another disaster, and Hitler was again forced to come to Mussolini's aid. By then, Britain and Greece were allies, and the RAF had established air bases in Greece that made the Romanian oil fields – vital to Germany's war effort – vulnerable to aerial attack.

In April 1941, German forces invaded Yugoslavia and Greece. There, the Germans achieved another remarkable blitzkrieg success, but the campaign drew them into a largely unwanted war that delayed and drained resources away from the main campaign against Soviet Russia.

△ **Adolf Hitler saluting**
Wehrmacht and SS troops
as they march into Poland

1 September 1939

GERMANY INVADES POLAND

After staging several incidents to justify its actions, Germany invaded Poland. Around 1.5 million soldiers and more than 2,000 aircraft and 2,500 tanks poured across Poland's borders from Germany, Slovakia, and the German enclave of East Prussia. The German armies made rapid progress and had surrounded Warsaw by 15 September.

3 September 1939

THE BATTLE OF THE ATLANTIC BEGINS

Germany's campaign against Allied shipping in the Atlantic (*see p.64*) began when German submarine *U-30* torpedoed and sank the SS *Athenia*, a British passenger liner, killing 128 civilian passengers and crew.

▷ The sinking of the SS *Athenia*

1939

1 SEPTEMBER

3 September Reaffirming US neutrality, President Roosevelt commits the government to keeping the country out of the war

3 September Prime Minister Neville Chamberlain announces that Britain and Germany are at war; France follows suit later in the day

> ## "You can imagine what a bitter blow it is to me that all my long struggle to win peace has failed."

NEVILLE CHAMBERLAIN, RADIO ADDRESS, 3 SEPTEMBER 1939

1 September 1939
BLITZKRIEG IN POLAND

Germany's invasion of Poland was a carefully coordinated assault. Air, sea, and ground forces combined to rapidly sweep away opposition.

c. 4:40am The Luftwaffe starts carpet bombing Wieluń; most of the town's buildings are destroyed in hours.

c. 4:45am The German battleship *Schleswig-Holstein* begins shelling the Polish garrison at Westerplatte, in Danzig harbour.

c. 8am German soldiers attack Polish forces near Mokra in one of the first battles of the invasion. The Polish secure a victory.

c. 7:45pm Postal workers at Danzig's Polish post office surrender after 15 hours of attacks by pro-German paramilitary groups.

△ Soviet troops at Brest-Litovsk

1904-42
REINHARD HEYDRICH

An arrogant former naval officer, Heydrich was drawn into the Nazis' leadership. He became Hitler's ruthlessly efficient head of security and intelligence, and masterminded the Holocaust.

17 September 1939
THE USSR INVADES POLAND FROM THE EAST

Alarmed by German advances into Polish territory that they had agreed should belong to the USSR, the Soviet Union invaded Poland. It attacked on two fronts – from western Belorussia and western Ukraine. The Polish government fled to Romania, where its members were interned.

14-16 September Polish forces break the German line of defence as they attempt to reach Lwów (now Lviv) in the Battle of Jaworow

19 September Soviet and German forces link up at Brest-Litovsk, in central Poland

1939

7 September The French begin the Saar offensive, attempting to invade Germany along its weak western border, but the offensive fails by 16 September

19 September Hitler enters Danzig; he denounces Poland and warns that Germany will never capitulate

21 SEPTEMBER

21 September 1939
THE POLISH GHETTOS

Germany's invasion of Poland brought more than 2 million Polish Jews under its control. To manage this population, Reinhard Heydrich ordered the establishment of more than 1,000 ghettos in cities and towns across Poland. Jews and some Roma, were relocated to the ghettos. These became hugely overcrowded, particularly after the arrival of Jews from Germany and Austria in 1941.

▷ **Jews photographed** in Poland's Lodz Ghetto

△ President Risto Ryti of Finland

28 September 1939
POLAND SURRENDERS

With its forces trapped between Soviet and German armies, Poland surrendered on 28 September. The country was then split into three. Germany annexed territories to the west and occupied a central zone known as the General Government. The USSR took the eastern half of Poland and incorporated it into Soviet Ukraine and Belorussia.

24 September–12 October 1939
SOVIET PRESSURE ON THE BALTIC STATES

According to the terms of the Nazi-Soviet Pact (*see p.53*), the Baltic states and Finland fell into the Soviet sphere of influence. While Lithuania, Estonia, and Latvia bowed to pressure and allowed Soviet troops to be stationed in their territory, Finland's president, Risto Ryti, refused to cede strategically important territory to the Soviet Union.

△ A German Heinkel bombing Warsaw

1939

22 SEPTEMBER

25 September Germany begins rationing food, but allowances are initially generous

27 September Soviet forces secure a victory in the Battle of Vladypol in central Poland

26 September 1939
GERMANY UNLEASHES ITS SURFACE RAIDERS

Hitler ordered the pocket battleships *Deutschland* and *Graf Spee* to attack Allied shipping in the North and South Atlantic. On 30 September, the *Graf Spee* claimed the SS *Clement* off Brazil. The ship was a constant threat to the trade routes off Africa and South America. The British Admiralty, under Sir Dudley Pound, swiftly organized task forces to hunt down the German ships; six vessels were assigned to finding the *Graf Spee*. The Allies finally cornered the ship off Argentina in December (*see p.62*).

▷ The *Graf Spee,* a German pocket battleship

14 October 1939

THE SINKING OF THE ROYAL OAK

At 12:58am on 14 October 1939, German torpedoes struck HMS *Royal Oak* at the British naval base at Scapa Flow, in the Orkney Islands, Scotland. The battleship sank quickly, and 833 lives were lost. The incident was a major blow to British morale and boosted Germany's confidence.

△ Illustration of the sinking of HMS *Royal Oak* from a Dutch magazine, 1939

> "The place where the German U-boat sank the British battleship *Royal Oak* was none other than the middle of Scapa Flow, Britain's greatest naval base! It sounds incredible."

JOURNALIST WILLIAM L. SHIRER, 18 OCTOBER 1939

2 October The USA and other neutral nations create the Pan-American Security Zone, a zone 480 km (300 miles) wide around the Americas, to be patrolled by the US Navy

12 October Britain rejects Hitler's offer of peace, made in a speech to the Reichstag, as too vague to be meaningful

1939

14 OCTOBER

6 October The Battle of Changsha ends with a Chinese victory over the Japanese

9 October Hitler issues Directive No. 6, outlining his plan for the conquest of the Low Countries and northern France

September 1939–March 1940

THE PHONEY WAR

A period of very little military action, which became known as the Phoney War, followed the Allies' declaration of war in 1939. This lull suited Germany, which was preoccupied with Poland, and gave the Allies time to put emergency powers and plans in place and build up their armed forces. The British Expeditionary Force, for example, was able to take up defensive positions in France, and the evacuation began of more than 1.5 million people (mostly children) from Britain's cities to the countryside, in anticipation of German air raids. The Phoney War ended abruptly on 1 April 1940, when Germany invaded Denmark and Norway.

▷ British propaganda poster, 1940

1877–1943

SIR DUDLEY POUND

Pound served as captain of the battleship HMS *Colossus* in World War I. He was promoted to admiral in 1933. As Admiral of the Fleet from July 1939, he led the Royal Navy in the Battle of the Atlantic.

1–5 November 1939

THE OSLO REPORT

In early November, German physicist Hans Mayer sent British intelligence a report on Nazi military technology. This included references to the German rocket programme and details of the Junkers Ju 88 production programme, German air-raid warning equipment, and torpedoes. The report was initially dismissed as a hoax, but a young scientist working in intelligence, Dr R. V. Jones, believed it to be real. It led to the development of radar-jamming countermeasures that later saved many Allied lives in the air campaign over Germany.

◁ **Junkers Ju 88** German World War II multi-role aircraft

1939

15 OCTOBER

18 October 21,000 Red Army soldiers enter Estonia under the terms of the Bases Treaty signed with the USSR

18 October French troops occupy the Maginot Line defences; the British fortify the area between the line and the Channel

4 November The US Neutrality Act is amended to allow belligerents to buy arms from the United States

3 November Norwegian authorities free the SS City of Flint from its German captors after they illegally drop anchor in Norwegian waters

1939–45

CIVILIANS AT SEA

In 1939, Britain was dependent on its Merchant Navy for its oil, most of its raw materials, and half its food. It had the largest merchant fleet in the world, with around 1,900 ocean-going vessels and 190,000 civilian seafarers, predominantly men aged between 14 and 70, drawn from Britain, the Commonwealth, Europe, Ireland, Scandinavia, China, Japan, and Africa. As soon as war broke out, a convoy system was put in place to keep the Merchant Navy safe as it worked around the clock keeping vital supply lines in the Atlantic open.

◁ **A convoy of merchant ships** crossing the Atlantic Ocean

9 November 1939

THE ALLIES PREPARE FOR AN INVASION

With an invasion of the Low Countries imminent, the Allied Supreme Council adopted General Maurice Gamelin's Plan D. Assuming that the Germans would advance through the Low Countries to France, the plan was to send the left wing of the Allied armies racing into Belgium and pushing eastward to the river Dyle. However, unbeknown to the Allies, the Germans had a different route mapped out (*see p.70*).

△ Maurice Gustave Gamelin (*centre*), 1939

26 November 1939

THE SHELLING OF MAINILA

With Finland continuing to resist Soviet demands (*see p.58*), the USSR orchestrated a "false flag" incident that would provide a pretext for war. The Soviets claimed that, at 3:45pm on 26 November, its troops at Mainila near the Russo-Finnish border had been subjected to Finnish artillery fire. The Finnish artillery, however, was out of range at the time, having been withdrawn to prevent such incidents.

13 November Britain loses its first destroyer when HMS *Blanche* is sunk by a German mine in the Thames Estuary

21 November German battle cruisers *Scharnhorst* and *Gneisenau* head into the North Atlantic

29 November The USSR breaks off diplomatic relations with Finland

1939

29 NOVEMBER

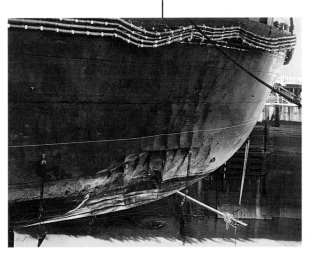

▷ **Degaussing cables** sitting just below the ship's deck edge

21 November 1939

GERMAN MAGNETIC MINES CLAIM FIRST VICTIM

By 1939, Germany had developed magnetic mines that would remain hidden under the sea until triggered by a ship's magnetic field. Britain lost its first ship to the mines on 21 November, when HMS *Belfast* was sunk off Scotland. The British quickly discovered that they could cancel a ship's magnetic field by passing an electric current through a cable around its hull (degaussing) and stop it triggering the mines.

23 November 1939

JEWISH PEOPLE MARKED OUT

In German-occupied Poland, all Jewish people over the age of 10 were ordered to wear a white armband emblazoned with a blue six-pointed star over their garments. In September 1941, Reinhard Heydrich ordered that all Jews aged six years and older were to wear a badge with a yellow Star of David and the word "Jew" in the local language. Many of Germany's allies subsequently introduced their own markers.

△ **Star of David badge** inscribed with the word *Jude* (German for "Jew")

▽ Finnish soldiers wearing white mantles to blend in with the wintry background

30 November 1939
THE USSR INVADES FINLAND

Aiming to aim reach Helsinki and install a compliant regime, the USSR invaded Finland. It launched a three-pronged assault – in the Arctic north, in the east, and in the Karelian Isthmus, where most of the Finnish forces were deployed along the fortifications known as the Mannerheim Line. The Finns were heavily outnumbered, but drove the Soviets to a stalemate by December, using *motti* ("encirclement") tactics, skiing through the dense forests to outflank the enemy formations. They also invented the Molotov cocktail, a simple but effective explosive, to destroy Soviet tanks.

14 December The USSR is expelled from the League of Nations for its aggression against Finland

8 January 1940 Britain begins rationing food, restricting purchases of sugar, meat, fats, and cheese; it has already begun encouraging people to "Dig for Victory" and grow their own food

1939
30 NOVEMBER

18 January Germany authorizes unrestricted submarine warfare, allowing U-boats to sink ships, including merchant vessels, without warning

13 December 1939
BATTLE OF THE RIVER PLATE

In the early hours of 13 December, the German pocket battleship *Admiral Graf Spee* engaged a British Navy squadron, sent to hunt it down, in the South Atlantic. The ship hit HMS *Exeter* and *Ajax* before withdrawing to Montevideo, Uruguay, to inspect its own damage. Tricked into believing that a large British force was approaching, *Graf Spee*'s captain, Hans Langdorff, moved the ship to the River Plate estuary, where he scuttled it on 17 December.

▷ The *Admiral Graf Spee* being scuttled by charges detonated on board (hand-coloured image)

16–17 February 1940

THE ALTMARK INCIDENT

The German supply vessel *Altmark* was heading home carrying some 300 prisoners of war from Allied merchant ships sunk in the Atlantic when it was chased into the neutral waters of Norway's Jøssingfjord by Britain's HMS *Cossack*. On 16 February, three officers and 30 men armed with rifles, bayonets, and a cutlass boarded the *Altmark* and freed the POWs, killing eight German guards in the process.

△ **British merchant seamen** on board the destroyer HMS *Cossack*

1874–1965
WINSTON CHURCHILL
An experienced British soldier and statesman, Churchill was First Lord of the Admiralty before leading Britain as prime minister in 1940–45 and 1951–55. A prolific author, he won the Nobel Prize in Literature in 1953.

12 March Finland's surrender ends Allied plans for an invasion of Scandinavia to secure iron ore and prevent the region from falling into German hands

1940
12 MARCH

1 March In Directive No. 10a, Hitler orders his generals to prepare for the invasion of Denmark and Norway, anticipating British action in Scandinavia

> "You should board *Altmark*, liberate the prisoners, and take possession of the ship… "

WINSTON CHURCHILL, INSTRUCTIONS TO HMS COSSACK, *FEBRUARY 1940*

1939–40
THE WINTER WAR

The war began well for Finland, whose troops held off the Soviets for two months before exhaustion brought an end to the fighting.

30 November 1939–7 January 1940 Finnish forces hold back the Soviets at Suomussalmi in the east and around Lake Ladoga in the southeast, isolating the Soviet forces in the north.

1 February 1940 Soviet forces renew their offensive. They breach the Mannerheim Line on 12 February and take Summa. The Finns withdraw as the Red Army pours into Finland.

2 March 1940 The Soviets launch a three-sided attack on Viipuri, Finland's second largest city. Fighting is so intense that by mid-March, both sides are exhausted and Finland sues for peace.

1939-43
THE U-BOAT WAR

As an island nation, Britain relied heavily on maritime trade for its survival and ability to wage war. In 1939, the German Navy launched a campaign using its U-boats (a shortening of *Unterseeboot* or "under-sea boat") to destroy merchant ships sailing in and out of British ports; this became known as the Battle of the Atlantic.

The campaign repeatedly see-sawed between the two sides. German advances opened up new ports from Norway to France, allowing their U-boats even better access to the North Atlantic; and the development of wolfpack tactics, in which several U-boats worked together to hunt Allied ships, initiated a period called the "happy time" by German submariners.

New British tactics turned the war in the Allies' favour after February 1941, but a second "happy time" occurred between January and June 1942, when inexperienced US merchant ships provided easy targets for U-boats operating in the Atlantic. By April 1943, superior Allied organization and technology had ended the U-boat threat.

Submarines were in operation in theatres other than the Atlantic. Axis and British submarines were engaged in a sustained campaign in the Mediterranean. In the Pacific, the US submarine fleet fought a highly effective war against Japanese merchant shipping, so that by the middle of 1945, lack of fuel had rendered most Japanese ships and aircraft inoperable.

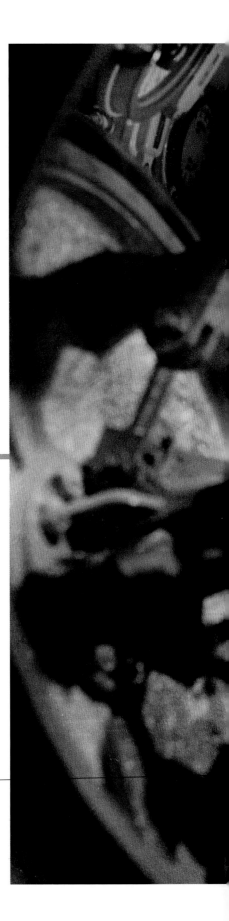

KEY MOMENTS

1939 The sinking of the *Royal Oak*
U-boat ace Günther Prien commanded *U-47* (*left*) in a daring attack that sank HMS *Royal Oak* within the battleship's supposedly impregnable Scottish harbour of Scapa Flow, in the Orkney Islands, on 14 October 1939.

1940-41 The U-boat "happy time"
The "happy time" saw the emergence of several U-boat aces. Otto Kretschmer, for example, sank 44 ships, totalling 266,629 tons, earning both the Kriegsmarine's submarine badge (*left*) for multiple patrols and the prestigious Knight's Cross.

1943 The tide turns
By May 1943, the British had developed new anti-submarine weapons, such as the forward-firing Hedgehog mortar (*pictured in use, left*). They had also extended their aerial patrols and improved their radar and intelligence capabilities. This combination forced the U-boat wolfpacks to retreat from the North Atlantic.

A U-boat commander looks into his submarine. Conditions were incredibly cramped for the crew of around 45 officers and men in the standard Type VII U-boat, which carried 14 torpedoes and had a range of 15,700 km (9,800 miles).

Finland ceded 12 per cent of its population to Russia at the end of the Winter War

1867–1951
CARL GUSTAF MANNERHEIM

Leader of Finland's army since the country gained independence in 1917, Mannerheim masterminded a superb defensive strategy during the Winter War of 1939–40, until the Red Army's superior strength forced him to accept Soviet peace terms.

18 March 1940
HITLER AND MUSSOLINI MEET

In their first meeting since Munich in 1938, Hitler held talks with Italian dictator Benito Mussolini at Brenner, on the Austro-Italian border. Mussolini failed to persuade Hitler to delay his western offensive to allow Italy time to prepare its armed forces, but declared his readiness to join Germany's war against Britain and France "at the decisive hour".

▷ **Hitler and Mussolini** at the Brenner Pass

1940

13 MARCH

21 March Paul Reynaud forms a new French government after Edouard Daladier resigns over criticism of his Finland policy

16 March The first British civilian is killed in a German bombing raid on Scapa Flow in the Orkney Islands

△ **Finnish foreign minister Väinö Tanner** announcing the end of the Winter War

13 March 1940
CEASEFIRE IN FINLAND

The Winter War between the USSR and Finland ended as a ceasefire came into effect at 11am. The USSR had suffered 200,000 fatalities, while Finland had lost 25,000 along with a tenth of its territory, including the Karelian isthmus, with its key industrial cities of Viipuri and Vuoksi and the Hangö naval base.

21 March 1940
FIRST GERMAN MERCHANT SHIP SUNK

The British submarine *Ursula* sank the 4,947-ton freighter carrier *Heddernheim* with a torpedo 13 km (8 miles) off the Danish coast. This first sinking of a German merchant vessel, which was carrying Swedish iron ore, demonstrated the Royal Navy's capacity to intercept supplies for Germany's war effort.

▷ **British U-class submarine** HMS *Ursula*

30 March 1940
PRO-JAPANESE GOVERNMENT ESTABLISHED IN CHINA

Wang Jingwei, an opponent of Chiang Kai-shek's government, established a Japanese-controlled government at Nanjing. He hoped to broker a lasting peace between China and Japan but had little influence and was recognized only by the Axis Powers. His Central Government was thus rapidly marginalized.

◁ **Wang Jingwei's supporters** at the start of his regime

27 March French and German artillery engage in duels in the Saar and Vosges sectors as the Phoney War continues

3 April Operation Wilfred, Britain's plan to mine Norwegian waters to prevent Germany transporting iron ore from Scandinavia, is approved

8 April British destroyer *Glowworm* is sunk by the German cruiser *Hipper* while laying mines off the coast of Norway

1940

8 APRIL

7 April The British Home Fleet leaves Scapa Flow en route for the Norwegian Sea

28 March 1940
BRITAIN AND FRANCE UNITE AGAINST GERMANY

Meeting in London, the Allied Supreme War Council declared that Britain and France would not conclude an armistice or treaty with Germany without the other's consent. But it failed to agree joint plans to float mines up the river Rhine or to mine Norwegian waters off Narvik.

◁ **Members of the Supreme War Council,** including Winston Churchill (*left*) and Paul Reynaud (*right*)

DENMARK SURRENDERS

Although the Royal Guard in Copenhagen resisted the invaders, the Danish king, Christian X, concluded that there was little chance of defeating the Germans and ordered a ceasefire just two hours after the invasion began. The Danish government continued in place but had to accept German supervision and German occupation troops.

△ **A German officer** tells Denmark's General Jakobson the terms of Denmark's surrender

▽ **Narvik Shield,** a German campaign award

10 April 1940

THE BATTLE OF NARVIK

Five British destroyers arrived too late to stop a German landing at Narvik but surprised a flotilla of ten enemy destroyers, sinking two of them. Two British warships were sunk before the arrival of reinforcements that helped sink the remaining German destroyers.

15–18 April British troops land in the Lofoten Islands and then at Namsos and Andalsenes in Norway in a bid to retake Trondheim

1940

9 APRIL

13 April British troops land in the Faroe Islands after their government accepts British protection

9 April 1940

GERMANY INVADES DENMARK AND NORWAY

In Norway, Bergen and Trondheim swiftly fell to German troops who had landed on the coast. Airborne troops seized airfields at Oslo and Stavanger, and German destroyers sank the Norwegian warships *Eidsvold* and *Norge*. In Denmark, two German divisions crossed the border, facing only light opposition in southern Jutland and Copenhagen.

◁ **German troops** landing at Trondheim, Norway (hand-coloured image)

29 April 1940
NORWAY'S KING HAAKON IS EVACUATED

The British cruiser *Glasgow* transported King Haakon VII, Crown Prince Olav, and the Norwegian government from Molde to Tromsø. They remained there until 7 June, when they were evacuated to Britain aboard HMS *Devonshire*. During the operation, HMS *Glorious* was sunk, but the Norwegian royal party arrived safely in England and established a government-in-exile in London.

◁ **King Haakon** aboard a Norwegian ship in the UK, 1940

26 April Norwegian and British troops halt the German advance at Kvam in the Gudbrandsdal valley, Norway

2 May British troops evacuate Namsos, abandoning the defence of southern Norway

5 May German spy Hermann Goertz tries to secure the Irish Republican Army's support for a planned German invasion of Britain

1940
9 MAY

3–4 May Norwegian forces around Trondheim surrender, opening the way for the Germans to advance to northern Norway

△ **Franz Halder** (*left*) with Walther von Brauchitsch

Norway resisted Germany's invasion for two months; Denmark resisted for just two hours

1 May 1940
HITLER ORDERS THE INVASION OF WESTERN EUROPE

After months of delay, Hitler finally gave the go-ahead to Fall Gelb (Case Yellow), a long-planned attack on Belgium, the Netherlands, and France. Overseen by Franz Halder, the plan was originally to simply neutralize Allied forces and reach the Channel coast ports, with a main thrust through the Netherlands and northern Belgium. However, this was modified by General Erich von Manstein's *Sichelschnitt* ("sickle cut"), an attack through the Ardennes aimed at destroying the Allied armies completely.

△ **Wehrmacht troops** in Belgium, May 1940 (hand-coloured image)

10 May 1940

GERMANY INVADES IN THE WEST

Germany launched its attack on Luxembourg, Belgium, and the Netherlands. Paratroops seized Dutch river crossings, and a glider-borne force assaulted the Belgian fortress of Eben Emael. As German ground troops poured across the frontiers, the British Expeditionary Force (BEF) and French armies moved into Belgium to counter their advance.

▷ Winston Churchill

10 May 1940

CHURCHILL BECOMES PRIME MINISTER

Criticized for his failure to defend Norway and hearing of Germany's invasion of Western Europe, the British prime minister, Neville Chamberlain, resigned. He was immediately replaced by Winston Churchill, who headed a coalition government of Conservative, Labour, and Liberal MPs.

12 May Internment begins in Britain with the confinement of 3,000 enemy and 11,000 non-enemy aliens

1940

10 MAY

10–19 May 1940

THE INVASION OF FRANCE

With the Germans advancing west across Belgium and making for France, the Allies concentrated their forces at the river Dyle, creating a defensive line running south to the densely forested Ardennes region, which they believed protected the French border. However, on 12 May, General Paul Ludwig von Kleist led a surprise panzer attack through the Ardennes towards Sedan. On 14 May, the French defence there collapsed. North of the Ardennes, the Germans breached the Dyle Line and reached the French border by 16 May, tying up Allied forces, while von Kleist advanced with little opposition towards the French coast.

A surprise attack

The Allies believed that the Ardennes was inpenetrable and left it weakly defended. The German tanks simply punched through at Sedan, destroying eight French divisions in four days and moving deep into France.

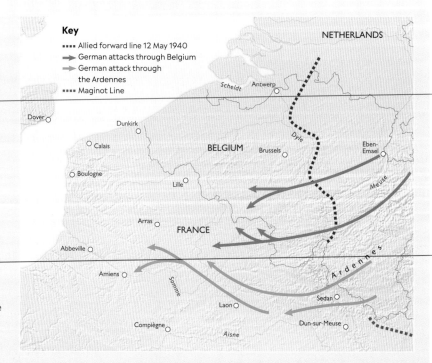

Key

- ···· Allied forward line 12 May 1940
- → German attacks through Belgium
- → German attack through the Ardennes
- ···· Maginot Line

NETHERLANDS

Scheldt · Antwerp

Dover

Dunkirk

Calais

BELGIUM · Brussels

Dyle

Eben-Emael

Boulogne

Meuse

Lille

Arras

FRANCE

Abbeville

Amiens

Somme

Ardennes

Laon

Sedan

Compiègne

Aisne

Dun-sur-Meuse

◁ **Destruction in Rotterdam** caused by the German bombing, 14 May 1940

15 May 1940
THE NETHERLANDS SURRENDERS
As Dutch forces continued to resist in the Amsterdam-Rotterdam-Utrecht area, on 14 May, the Germans launched a bombing raid on Rotterdam that destroyed much of the city. The following day the Dutch Army capitulated. Queen Wilhelmina and the Dutch government had already been evacuated to the United Kingdom.

19 May Maxime Weygand replaces Maurice Gamelin as commander of France's land forces

21 May A British counterattack at Arras in France meets with initial success

17 May German troops enter Brussels, jeopardizing Belgium's capacity to resist

1940

22 MAY

22 May 1940
CRACKING THE ENIGMA CODE
Cryptanalysts working at the British code-breaking centre at Bletchley Park cracked the code created by the German Luftwaffe's Enigma code machines. They broke the codes almost daily from then on, providing vital intelligence for the British war effort, although some Enigma codes, such as that of Germany's military intelligence service, proved harder to break.

△ **German combat patrol** in Amiens

▽ **Code breaking** at Bletchley Park

20 May 1940
THE GERMANS RACE ACROSS FRANCE
General Heinz Guderian's German panzer forces advanced rapidly to the Channel coast. The 1st Panzer Division took Amiens, while the 2nd Panzer Division captured Noyelles, at the mouth of the river Somme. As a result, the Allied armies were split in two, with the bulk of the BEF in danger of being encircled around Calais and Dunkirk.

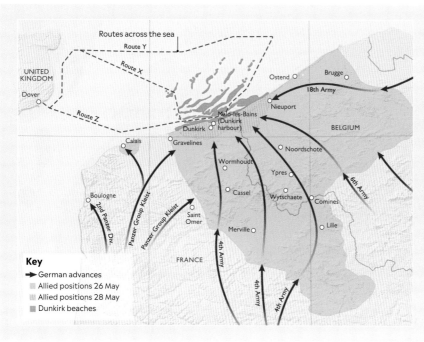

Routes across the sea

Route Y

UNITED KINGDOM

Route X

Dover

Route Z

Ostend

Brugge

18th Army

Nieuport

BELGIUM

Malo-les-Bains (Dunkirk harbour)

Dunkirk

Calais

Gravelines

Noordschote

Wormhoudt

Ypres

6th Army

Boulogne

Cassel

Wytschaete

Comines

2nd Panzer Div.

Panzer Group Kleist

Panzer Group Kleist

Saint Omer

Merville

Lille

FRANCE

4th Army

4th Army

4th Army

Key

➤ German advances
◻ Allied positions 26 May
◻ Allied positions 28 May
◼ Dunkirk beaches

26 May–4 June 1940
THE EVACUATION OF DUNKIRK

With the remaining British forces in France hemmed into an ever-decreasing perimeter around Dunkirk, on 26 May Winston Churchill launched Operation Dynamo, the evacuation of Allied forces from the town. Using Royal Naval vessels and a flotilla of 850 private "little ships", the evacuation removed more than 330,000 Allied troops, including 113,000 French soldiers, from Dunkirk's beaches and harbour. Carried out under heavy fire from the Luftwaffe and with the harbour area congested with troops awaiting evacuation, the operation helped prevent the collapse of the Allied cause.

Flight under fire

The Allied perimeter covered a small area around Dunkirk's centre by 28 May. The Allied troops were evacuated via three routes to Dover.

1940

23 MAY

23 May In Belgium, the Germans cross the river Scheldt at Oudenarde

24 May The Germans halt at the Gravelines-Lens line, southwest of Dunkirk, giving Allied troops time to organize their escape

26 May Operation Dynamo, the mass evacuation of Allied troops from Dunkirk, begins

338,226 French, British, and Belgian troops were evacuated from Dunkirk during Operation Dynamo

23–27 May 1940
THE CHANNEL PORTS FALL

After the Battle of Sedan, German panzers raced towards the Channel ports. British troops were evacuated under heavy fire from Boulogne, whose citadel fell on 24 May. Resistance in Calais was fiercer, but by 25 May, the defenders were confined to the citadel. After the Luftwaffe threatened to pulverize Calais' defences, the French commander surrendered.

▷ **Ruined buildings in Calais** after German bombing (hand-coloured image)

27–28 May 1940
BELGIUM CAPITULATES

On 24 May, the Germans broke through the last Belgian defence line at Courtrai. Vigorous counterattacks held them back but exhausted the Belgian forces. After ordering the destruction of the river Yser bridges and the blocking of Ostend and Zeebrugge ports, King Leopold decreed the unconditional surrender of the Belgian Army at 4am on 28 May. This left a 32-km (20-mile) gap in the Allied front at Nieuport.

△ Norwegian troops in winter dress

△ Germany's General von Brauchitsch congratulating a German officer in Ypres (hand-coloured photo)

28 May 1940
THE CAPTURE OF NARVIK

After a protracted siege, French Foreign Legion troops and Norwegian forces finally took Narvik. But the German commander, Major-General Dietl, extricated the garrison in a fighting retreat towards the Swedish border. The victory was a hollow one, as Allied troops were soon evacuated from Norway to be redeployed elsewhere.

3 June The Luftwaffe launches Operation Paula, its first major raid on Paris, involving 200 bombers; 254 people are killed

1940

4 JUNE

27 May German SS troops massacre more than 90 captured British soldiers of the Royal Norfolk Regiment in the French village of Le Paradis

29 May The Germans capture Ypres and Ostend, completing the occupation of Belgium and pushing the French back from Lille

> "We shall defend our island whatever the cost may be, we shall fight on the beaches... we shall never surrender."

WINSTON CHURCHILL, SPEECH, 4 JUNE 1940

4 June 1940
THE GERMANS TAKE DUNKIRK

German forces finally entered Dunkirk, capturing the remaining 40,000 French defenders, who had stayed to cover the Allied evacuation, which ended just hours before. They also captured huge quantities of abandoned heavy equipment, including 2,450 guns and around 75,000 vehicles, and a number of British stragglers.

▷ **German soldiers** during the fighting for Dunkirk

9 June 1940
THE GERMANS CAPTURE ROUEN

After routing the French 10th Army on the Somme and reaching the river Aisne at Soissons, General von Bock's Army Group B captured Rouen. The remnants of the 10th Army retreated towards the Channel coast. This created a breach in the French lines, opening the way for a German advance on Paris.

▷ **The city of Rouen** during the German invasion

9 June An armistice ends the fighting in Norway, which becomes occupied territory. Most Allied troops have already been evacuated

1940

5 JUNE

5 June The Battle of France begins when the Germans cross the river Somme and the Oise-Aisne canal in an offensive aimed at Paris

10 June 1940
ITALY ENTERS THE WAR

Mussolini declared war on Britain and France. Initially there were only light skirmishes on the French border, but on 11 June, 55 Italian bombers raided Malta, beginning an aerial siege of the island that lasted until November 1942. During that time, Malta endured over 3,000 air raids in a stubborn defence that earned the whole island the British George Cross medal.

△ Illustration of **Italian bombers** over Malta in June 1940

1883-1945
BENITO MUSSOLINI

Mussolini founded the Fascist Party in 1919, leveraging fears of communism to gain power in 1922. Aiming to build an Italian empire, he invaded Ethiopia in 1935. His alliance with Hitler ended in disaster, and he was deposed in 1943 after the Allies invaded Italy.

"Italy cannot remain neutral for the whole of the war without... reducing herself to the level of a tenfold Switzerland."

BENITO MUSSOLINI, 31 MARCH 1940

15–18 June 1940
SOVIET TROOPS MOVE INTO THE BALTIC STATES

The USSR took advantage of German advances in Poland to annex Estonia, Latvia, and Lithuania, despite having mutual assistance pacts with each of them. On 15 June, Soviet forces crossed into Lithuania. After an ultimatum to their governments, the Red Army occupied Estonia and Latvia on 17 June. Pro-Soviet regimes were installed, and all independent opposition was suppressed.

△ **Red Army forces** on the streets of Vilnius, Lithuania

▽ **1st Royal Tank Regiment** in North Africa

11 June 1940
THE WAR IN NORTH AFRICA BEGINS

In reponse to Italy's declaration of war, the British RAF bombed Italian airfields in Libya. A convoy of British armoured cars crossed the Libyan–Egyptian border to ambush Italian troops near Fort Capuzzo, capturing 62 of them and taking the fort itself three days later.

13 June Operation Cycle, the evacuation of British and Allied troops from northwest France, ends

1940

15 JUNE

11 June France withdraws its forces across the river Marne, and the government evacuates from Paris to Tours

12 June The Japanese capture the port and air base at Ichang on the river Yangzi, east of Chungking in China

14 June 1940
PARIS FALLS TO THE GERMANS

After the fall of Rouen, German armies advanced rapidly on Paris, crossing the Marne and capturing Rheims on 12 June. The following day, the French government declared Paris an open city and withdrew all troops, allowing the German 18th Army to enter the capital unhindered. Nine days later, a triumphant Hitler visited the city to savour his triumph.

▷ **Adolf Hitler,** with architect Albert Speer (*left*) and artist Arno Breker (*right*), in Paris, June 1940 (hand-coloured image)

18 June 1940
CHERBOURG AND BREST FALL

As France's last defensive lines crumbled, Rommel's 7th Panzer Division took Cherbourg. The next day, the 5th Panzer Division captured Brest, ending French hopes of fighting from a defensive redoubt in Brittany. Its position hopeless, the French government sought an armistice with Germany.

▷ **The German swastika flag** raised over Cherbourg

21 June 1940
ITALY INVADES SOUTHERN FRANCE

Italy launched a general offensive across its Alpine frontier, hoping to secure territory in southeast France. General Olry's troops mounted a highly effective defence, and the Italians, pinned in the mountain passes, failed to advance more than a few kilometres before an armistice on 25 June.

△ **Italian Alpini mountain troops** in the French Alps

> ## "France has lost a battle! But France has not lost the war!"

GENERAL DE GAULLE'S APPEAL, 18 JUNE 1940

1940

16 JUNE

16 June German troops breach the Maginot Line in Champagne, France, and push towards the river Loire

16 June France's prime minister, Paul Reynaud, resigns and is replaced by Marshal Philippe Pétain

18 June Broadcasting from London, French general, Charles de Gaulle, calls for the French to continuing resisting Germany

1940–42
VICHY FRANCE

The armistice's terms left the southern third of France under the control of a French regime. Based in the spa town of Vichy and headed by Marshal Pétain, this collaborated openly with the Germans, passing anti-Jewish legislation and restricting trade unions. Meanwhile, Free French forces under General de Gaulle continued to fight, particularly in France's colonies in Africa and the Middle East. The Vichy regime essentially became part of the German state when German soldiers occupied southern France in November 1942 (see p.165).

Collaborationist propaganda
This poster contrasts the Vichy government's self-proclaimed values of hard work, patriotism, and the family with the alleged chaos of previous regimes.

△ **Scene from Jersey's Occupation Tapestry,** created in 1995

30 June 1940
GERMANY OCCUPIES THE CHANNEL ISLANDS

After killing 44 people in a bombing raid on Jersey and Guernsey two days before, German troops landed in the Channel Islands, which Britain was responsible for defending. Half the civilian population had been evacuated, but the remaining 30,000 stayed under German occupation until May 1945.

28 June The USSR forces Romania to cede Bessarabia and part of Bukovina after threatening to invade

29 June At the Battle of Moyale, Italian troops attack a British garrison of King's African Rifles on the border between Kenya and Ethiopia

3 July The British Royal Navy bombards the French fleet at Mers-el-Kebir, in Algeria, to stop it falling into German hands

3 July Channel convoys through the Straits of Dover end after suffering high losses to the Luftwaffe

1940

8 JULY

1,297 French naval personnel were killed in the British attack on the French fleet at Mers-el-Kebir

22 June 1940
FRANCO-GERMAN ARMISTICE SIGNED

With defeat imminent, Pétain's French government began negotiations for an armistice. To add to France's humiliation, the talks took place at Compiègne, the site of the 1918 armistice. In the agreement reached, France's army and navy were demobilized and Germany was allowed to occupy two-thirds of France in the north and west.

◁ **The railway carriage in Compiègne** where the 1918 and 1940 armistices were signed

10 July 1940
THE BATTLE OF BRITAIN BEGINS

A raid by 70 German aircraft on docks in South Wales marked the beginning of an intense aerial campaign aimed at achieving air superiority over Britain as a prelude to a planned invasion. The attacks peaked on 13 August, known as *Adlertag* ("Eagle Day"), and London was targeted for 57 successive days from 7 September. The RAF put up a determined defence. By the time the campaign ended on 31 October, the Luftwaffe had lost 1,294 aircraft, the RAF only 788.

▷ **RAF pilots scramble** to their Hawker Hurricanes during the Battle of Britain

1882–1970
HUGH DOWDING

Head of Fighter Command from 1936, Dowding masterminded the country's defence in the Battle of Britain, ensuring fighter groups and radar operators worked together to head off German attacks.

9 July The Battle of Punta Stilo off Italy's coast is the first major clash between British and Italian fleets

11 July Pétain becomes France's head of state after the resignation of President Lebrun

14 July Elections in Soviet-controlled Lithuania, Latvia, and Estonia produce governments that vote for union with the USSR

1940

9 JULY

> "The English air force must be so reduced morally and physically that it is unable to deliver any significant attack against the German crossing."

ADOLF HITLER, DIRECTIVE NO. 16, 16 JULY 1940

16 July 1940
HITLER PREPARES TO INVADE BRITAIN

Hitler issued Directive No. 16 ordering preparations to be made for Unternehmen Seelöwe (Operation Sealion), an invasion of Britain. The plan was that the RAF would be defeated by mid-August, after which, elements of Army Group A would land in Britain and install a pro-Nazi regime. However, the RAF's success in the Battle of Britain meant that the invasion was postponed.

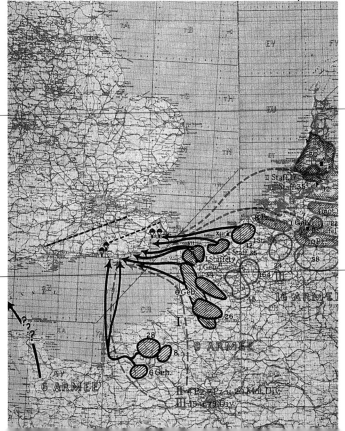

△ **German map from 1941** detailing the planned

27 July 1940

THE GREATER EAST ASIA CO-PROSPERITY SPHERE

Japan declared the establishment of a region of Asian solidarity, opposed to Western imperialism and influence. In reality, it was a means to secure Japanese political and economic control over allies, such as Thailand, and puppet regimes in China and Manchuria.

◁ **A 1944 Japanese board-game** based around the countries of the Co-Prosperity Sphere

19 July Hitler makes his "Last Appeal to Reason" speech to the Reichstag, calling on Britain to make peace

1940

14 AUGUST

11–15 August At the Battle of Tug Argan in Somaliland, a small British force holds a pass for five days against Italian attacks

3–19 August 1940

ITALY INVADES BRITISH SOMALILAND

Around 25,000 Italian troops crossed the border from Italian to British Somaliland in East Africa. The small British garrison fought a delaying action but was forced to retreat. British Somaliland was the first British colony to fall to Italy; its capture allowed the Italians to dominate the southern Red Sea.

△ **USS Yorktown,** one of the US Navy's new aircraft carriers

19 July 1940

THE USA INCREASES ITS NAVY

As concerns grew about the USA's military preparedness for war, President Roosevelt pushed for massive programmes of military expansion. The Two-Ocean Navy Expansion Act mandated an increase in naval tonnage to 3 million tons. This included 18 new aircraft carriers and enabled the USA to keep self-sufficient battle fleets in both the Atlantic and the Pacific Oceans.

▽ **A column of Italian tanks** in British Somaliland, August 1940

25 August 1940
JAPAN ENCROACHES ON INDOCHINA

Under intense pressure, the Vichy French government conceded to a Japanese request to station military forces in northern French Indochina. However, the Japanese then increased their demands. They issued an ultimatum on 20 September stipulating that they be granted the use of air bases and the port of Haiphong, and free passage for troops moving into China. Fighting broke out on 23 September, when the French garrison at Da Nang in Vietnam resisted the arriving Japanese occupation forces.

▷ **Japanese soldiers advance** on Liang Son, in French Indochina

1940

17 August Germany announces a total blockade of British ports

24 August The first daytime bombing of central London by the Luftwaffe badly damages the church of St Giles' Cripplegate

25 August In China, the small British garrisons at Shanghai and Tianjin are withdrawn in the face of a Japanese blockade

15 AUGUST

19 August Italian forces occupy Berbera, the capital of British Somaliland, two days after its garrison evacuates

15 August 1940
THE HELLE INCIDENT

The Greek cruiser *Helle* sank mysteriously while at anchor off the island of Tinos in the Aegean Sea. Torpedo fragments of Italian origin were found in the wreckage. Italy denied responsibility, but it later emerged that the Italian submarine *Delfino* had carried out the attack.

◁ **A Greek stamp** commemorating the sinking of the *Helle*

△ **West African Free French troops**

27 August 1940
FREE FRANCE IN WEST AFRICA

After the fall of France, the French colonies rallied to either the Vichy government or Free France. In Equatorial Africa, Chad declared its support for Free France on 26 August. On 27 August, Free French forces took over Duala, in Cameroon, and the next day secured Brazzaville, in French Congo. Only Gabon adhered to the Vichy cause, and then only until November 1940.

30 August 1940
THE SECOND VIENNA AWARD

Hitler imposed a territorial settlement on Romania that, by the transfer of northern Transylvania, rewarded his ally Hungary with a population of over 2 million. In return, Hungary allowed German troops free passage through its territory. Hungarian troops entered the region on 5 September, and a humiliated King Carol of Romania abdicated the next day.

◁ **The Romanian foreign minister,** Mihail Manoilescu, signs the Vienna Award

◁ **American dock workers** prepare a destroyer for transfer to Britain

3 September 1940
THE DESTROYERS FOR BASES DEAL

President Roosevelt signed an agreement with Britain for the transfer of 50 old destroyers. In return, the USA was granted 99-year leases on British Empire naval and air bases in St Lucia, the Bahamas, Bermuda, British Guiana, Jamaica, Trinidad, and Newfoundland.

1940

9 SEPTEMBER

1.1 million houses and flats were damaged or destroyed during the Blitz

1940–41
THE BLITZ

On 7 September 1940, the Luftwaffe launched its first major raid on London: 350 bombers caused huge fires in the docks and more than 400 people were killed.

28 September 1940 The British government orders the mass evacuation of more than 480,000 mothers and children from London.

14–15 October 1940 The largest raid to date sees 400 German bombers start 900 large-scale fires; 67 people are killed when a bomb penetrates Balham Underground Station.

14–15 November 1940 In Operation Moonlight Sonata, bombs kill 568 people and devastate much of Coventry city centre, destroying the cathedral.

10–11 May 1941 On the last night of the Blitz, German bombers launch their heaviest raid on London. The Luftwaffe is then sent to attack the USSR.

10 September 1940
OPERATION SEALION POSTPONED

With the Luftwaffe having failed to gain air superiority in Britain, Hitler postponed the invasion of Britain to 24 September; it was deferred again to 27 September just four days later. Mounting Luftwaffe losses led to preparations for Operation Sealion being paused, and a decision was made on 12 October to put off the invasion until spring 1941. When the focus shifted in December 1940 to planning Operation Barbarossa on the Eastern Front, Sealion was abandoned altogether.

◁ **British coastal defences** against a German invasion

1940

10 SEPTEMBER

13 September In London, Buckingham Palace is hit by five bombs during a German air raid; part of the Royal Chapel is damaged

16 September Italian forces occupy Sidi Barrani, 60 km (40 miles) from the Egyptian border

17 September British ocean liner *City of Benares* is sunk by a German U-boat while evacuating 90 children to Canada; such evacuations are then suspended

13 September 1940
JAPAN'S ZERO FIGHTER

The Mitsubishi A6M2, codenamed "Zero", Japan's most advanced fighter aircraft and feared by Allied pilots for its agility, made its major combat debut over Chungking, China. Thirteen Zeros accompanying Japanese bombers on a raid destroyed at least 20 Chinese fighters; only four Japanese aircraft were damaged.

▷ **Italian rifleman** on a motorcycle in Egypt

13 September 1940
ITALY INVADES EGYPT

Five divisions of the Italian 10th Army under General Mario Berti launched an invasion of Egypt from Libya. As the Italians reached Sollum, 10 km (6 miles) from the border, the British Western Desert Force, with only two lightly equipped divisions, retreated east towards Mersa Matruh.

△ A Japanese Mitsubishi A6M2 Zero fighter

77 children, 64 other passengers, and 131 crew died in the sinking of the *City of Benares*

23–26 September 1940
RAID ON DAKAR

In an attempt to capture the Vichy stronghold in West Africa, 4,200 British and 2,700 Free French troops landed in Dakar, Senegal. Security breaches had alerted the Vichy governor to the force's arrival, so the Allies met with unexpected resistance, including from the battleship *Richelieu*. This and bad weather caused the operation to be called off. The Allies suffered more than 550 casualties.

◁ Vichy anti-British propaganda poster featuring Winston Churchill as a ghoul-like figure

18 September The Italian Army halts its advance near Sidi Barrani owing to supply difficulties

19 September The French colony of New Caledonia, in the South Pacific, ousts its pro-Vichy governor

30 September The Luftwaffe makes its last major daylight raids on England, bombing London and towns in southern England

1940

2 OCTOBER

25 September US cryptanalysts discover Japan's top-secret codes in Operation Magic

27 September 1940
THE TRIPARTITE PACT

Signed in Berlin by Germany, Italy, and Japan, the pact was primarily aimed at preventing US intervention, and promised assistance to any signatories attacked by a power not already engaged in the European war or the Sino-Japanese War. The USSR was invited to join in November 1940, but refused. As other powers joined the pact, it became a general military bloc set against the Allies.

◁ A Fascist demonstration in Italy celebrating the pact

1939-45
COMMUNICATIONS

World War II coincided with the development of reliable long-range radio. Although wireless equipment had been used at sea in World War I, it was too heavy, bulky, and unreliable for land operations, where the wired telegraph and telephone were favoured.

New radio technology allowed WWII commanders on both sides to engage in spoken two-way communication with infantry, aircraft, ships, and tanks. This allowed the development of tactics that relied on swift response times, notably the German *blitzkrieg*. Smaller pack radios carried by infantry meant that a platoon of around 30–40 men had the means to communicate with their company or battalion, or to ask for fire support from artillery. Western Allied infantry radios had a typical range of around 6–10 km (4–6 miles), but the Soviets were poorly equipped with radio until near the end of the war, and this was a factor in their often clumsy tactics. Radio communication also allowed officers and diplomats to send messages around the globe, transforming military exchanges at the strategic level. Radio signals could, however, be intercepted by the enemy with relative ease. The solution was to encode messages, leading to the development of code breaking, at which the Allies excelled.

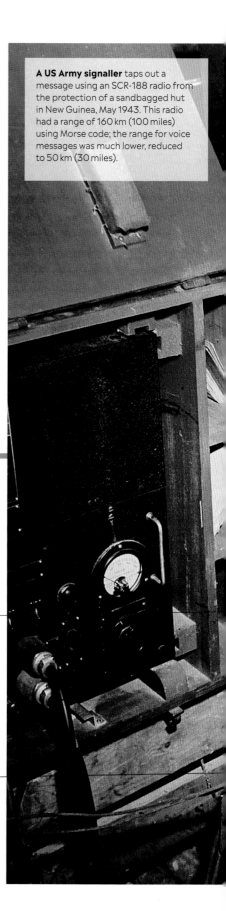

A US Army signaller taps out a message using an SCR-188 radio from the protection of a sandbagged hut in New Guinea, May 1943. This radio had a range of 160 km (100 miles) using Morse code; the range for voice messages was much lower, reduced to 50 km (30 miles).

KEY MOMENTS

1940 **Enigma and the Wehrmacht**
Some 30,000 Enigma coding machines were used to encode radio messages by the German armed forces and diplomatic service. Polish and British code breakers began to crack the Enigma codes – believed by the Germans to be secure – from 1940 onwards.

1942 **US intelligence at Midway**
Captain Joseph J. Rochefort (*pictured far left*) played a key role in breaking Japanese diplomatic and naval codes. This gave the US Navy reliable knowledge of Japanese ship movements, vital to American success at the pivotal Battle of Midway in June 1942.

1942 **Indigenous American code talkers**
In the Pacific, US Marines deployed more than 400 Navajo-speaking soldiers to send uncoded messages that the Japanese – who had no knowledge of the Navajo language – could not understand. This system proved far quicker than using the US Army's SIGABA electromechanical coding machine.

OUR NAVY ATTACKS—*Vivid Pictures and Full Story*

THE WAR WEEKLY

RUMANIAN OIL-WELLS BLAZE AS NAZIS MARCH IN

7 October 1940

GERMANY SECURES ROMANIA'S OIL

To cement his position after seizing power in September, Romania's leader, Ion Antonescu, invited a German military mission to enter the country. The first of what would eventually total 500,000 German troops arrived on 7 October. They took control of the Ploesti oil fields, securing vital supplies for Germany's war effort and preparing the area as a springboard for an eventual campaign against the USSR.

◁ **1940 magazine cover** showing burning Romanian oil wells

16 million men registered for military service in the United States in October 1940

12 October Hitler postpones Operation Sealion until spring 1941, releasing forces for other fronts

1940

3 OCTOBER

4 October Hitler and Mussolini meet again at the Brenner Pass between Italy and Austria to discuss their strategy following France's fall

"We are waiting for the long-promised invasion. So are the fishes!"

WINSTON CHURCHILL, SPEAKING OF THE POSTPONEMENT OF OPERATION SEALION, 21 OCTOBER 1940

8 October 1940

THE BURMA ROAD REOPENS

The Burma Road, a mountainous route that linked Lashio in the British colony of Burma with Kunming in China, was a vital lifeline for Chiang Kai-shek's forces in their fight against the Japanese (who had blockaded China's coast). Churchill had closed the road in July 1940, under pressure from Japan and fearing that Britain would be unable to fight Japan and Germany simultaneously. It was reopened as tensions with Japan mounted and China began asking for greater support.

▷ **A convoy of military trucks** on a section of the Burma Road

17–20 October 1940
CARNAGE AT SEA

In the Battle of the Atlantic, Allied Convoys SC-7 and HX-79 were attacked by eight German U-boats, which sank 32 ships totalling 152,000 tons and damaged a further four ships. That month, German submarines wrought a terrible toll on the Allies, sinking a further 266,000 tons of shipping.

◁ **The Allied tanker** *Dixie Arrow* after being torpedoed in the Battle of the Atlantic

16 October The US draft begins when all males aged 21 to 35 are required to register for military service by the Selective Service System Act

20 October Italian bombers fly 4,500 km (2,800 miles) from the Dodecanese Islands to bomb oil installations in Eritrea

23 October Hitler and General Franco meet on the French–Spanish border at Hendaye

1940

24 OCTOBER

21 October The Italian Navy forms a new Mediterranean naval command in preparation for an impending invasion of Greece

◁ **Japanese observation post**

13 October 1940
CHINESE FORCES SHELL YICHANG

Captured in June after a fierce battle in which the Japanese used gas shells to drive out the Chinese, Yichang was the furthest point west that Japan advanced in China. Chinese artillery, secretly transported behind Japanese lines, shelled Yichang's airfield, jeopardizing its use as a base for an attack on China's wartime capital, Chongqing.

24 October 1940
HITLER MEETS PÉTAIN

Hitler and the the new French leader met to discuss Franco-German cooperation. The Vichy regime issued a communiqué on an "Agreement in principle on collaboration" with Germany. On 30 October, Pétain declared in a radio broadcast, "I enter today on the path of collaboration."

▷ **Marshal Pétain** shaking hands with Hitler in October 1940

ΟΙ ΗΡΩΙΔΕΣ ΤΟΥ 1940

"*Ochi*" ("No") was General Metaxas's one-word reply to Italy's ultimatum

28 October 1940
ITALY INVADES GREECE

After issuing an ultimatum to Greece demanding free passage for Italian troops, which was brusquely dismissed by the Greek prime minister, General Metaxas, Mussolini ordered Italian troops to advance into Greece from Albania. Twenty-seven Italian divisions faced 16 divisions of Greek defenders, but they made slow progress in the Pindus Mountains.

◁ **A Greek poster** showing peasant women taking supplies to troops in the mountains

1884–1944
FELIX EBOUE

Made governor-general of French Equatorial Africa in 1940, Eboué was the first Black person to reach such high rank in the French colonial administration. His support for the Free French cause in Africa was crucial.

1940

25 OCTOBER

31 October The first British forces land on Crete as Britain increases its military support for Greece

31 October The Battle of Britain ends. During the final raids, the Luftwaffe loses 116 bombers and escort fighters; the RAF loses 190 fighters

5 November In the Atlantic, Germany's *Admiral Scheer* sinks fives ships and their only escort ship, the Royal Navy's HMS *Jervis Bay*, from an eastbound convoy

5 November Franklin D. Roosevelt is re-elected US president for a record third term

28 October 1940–11 April 1941
THE GRECO-ITALIAN WAR

Mussolini launched his invasion of Greece against Hitler's advice. Poor weather, the mountainous terrain, and rapid Greek mobilization hampered the Italians' advance from Albania. A general Greek counteroffensive from 4 November pushed the Italians back into Albania and captured northern Epirus by early 1941. Mussolini ordered a spring offensive in Epirus, but this petered out when a massive artillery bombardment on 9 March 1941 failed to dislodge the Greeks near Mount Trebeshina.

Italy outmatched
The Italians achieved only limited bridgeheads in Greece before being forced back and losing territory in Albania, an Italian protectorate.

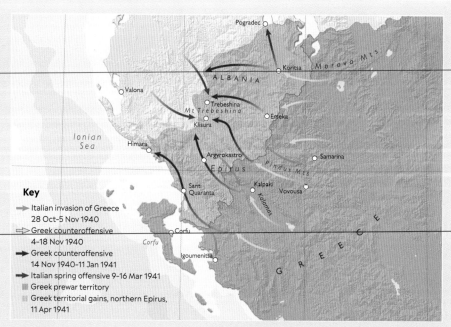

Key

→ Italian invasion of Greece 28 Oct–5 Nov 1940
⇨ Greek counteroffensive 4–18 Nov 1940
➡ Greek counteroffensive 14 Nov 1940–11 Jan 1941
➡ Italian spring offensive 9–16 Mar 1941
▪ Greek prewar territory
▪ Greek territorial gains, northern Epirus, 11 Apr 1941

11–12 November 1940
THE BATTLE OF TARANTO

Twenty-one Fairey Swordfish biplanes from Britain's HMS *Illustrious* attacked the Italian fleet at anchor in Taranto harbour, in Italy. The planes attacked in two waves an hour apart; their aerial torpedoes badly damaged three battleships and a cruiser. These losses and the withdrawal of the Italian fleet to safer ports on Italy's western coast tilted the naval balance in the Mediterranean in the Allies' favour.

◁ **Aerial torpedo entering the water** after being launched by a Fairey Swordfish aircraft

10 November British forces under Brigadier Viscount Slim recapture Galabat in Sudan, held by the Italians since July

14 November The Greek Army launches a counteroffensive in Epirus and Macedonia, inflicting a major defeat on the Italians

1940

14 NOVEMBER

▽ **Molotov (left)** and Hitler in Berlin

12 November 1940
MOLOTOV VISITS BERLIN

The Soviet foreign minister, Vyacheslav Molotov, visited Berlin to discuss the USSR joining the Tripartite Pact and closer cooperation with Germany. The talks foundered over the Soviet Union's ambition to have a sphere of influence in the Balkans, while Germany wanted to direct Soviet influence away from Europe toward East and Southeast Asia.

12 November 1940
FRENCH EQUATORIAL AFRICA SIDES WITH FREE FRANCE

By November 1940, all but one of the French colonies in Equatorial Africa had declared support for the Free French cause, most having followed the example of Chad and its governor, Félix Eboué. Only Gabon remained loyal to the Vichy government. On a visit to Africa, General de Gaulle authorized a land and naval attack on Gabon, which quickly capitulated. Control of the colonies gave de Gaulle access to substantial resources.

◁ **Félix Eboué** with Charles de Gaulle

20 November 1940
THE TRIPARTITE PACT EXPANDS

The alliance between Germany, Italy, and Japan expanded when three more countries added their names to the pact: Hungary on 20 November, Romania on 23 November, and Slovakia the following day. The new members significantly strengthened Germany's position in Central Europe and the Balkans.

▷ **A Hungarian recruitment poster** exhorts, "You also do your duty!"

23 November 1940
BELGIUM DECLARES WAR ON ITALY

The Belgian government-in-exile declared war on Italy. This allowed Belgium to deploy the only major force under its control, the 15,000-strong Force Publique in Congo, to support the British campaign in East Africa. The Congo troops, many of them conscripted, played a key role in the siege of Italy's headquarters at Saio, in Ethiopia (March–July 1941).

△ **Force Publique Fusiliers** leaving for Ethiopia

> "We have thrown away our honour. We have allied ourselves to scoundrels"

HUNGARIAN PRIME MINISTER PAL TELEKI REFLECTING ON HUNGARY JOINING THE TRIPARTITE PACT IN 1941

1940

15 NOVEMBER

18 November The Italians in Epirus are driven back over the river Kalamas

19 November A Luftwaffe night raid on Birmingham, UK, involving 350 aircraft causes widespread damage

28 November Liverpool, UK, suffers a major raid. The Luftwaffe drops 350 tons of bombs, killing almost 300 people

15 November 1940
TRAPPED IN THE GHETTO

Ludwig Fischer, the German governor of Warsaw, ordered the sealing of the city's ghetto. Around 400,000 Jewish people were enclosed by a wall, 3 m (10 ft) high and topped with barbed wire, into an area measuring just 3.4 sq km (just over 2 sq miles). Conditions were intolerably cramped, and the residents were forbidden to leave without a permit on pain of death. Malnutrition, cold, and disease had claimed 92,000 lives by July 1942, when the Germans began "liquidating" the ghetto.

◁ **Jewish stonemasons** building walls around the Warsaw Ghetto, 1940

30 November 1940
COLLABORATON IN CHINA
A treaty was signed between Japan and the Reorganized National Government (RNG) of China, a puppet regime headed by Wang Jingwei. It committed the RNG to supporting Japan against the Kuomintang regime headed by Chiang Kai-shek and against the Communists, to closer economic cooperation, and to recognizing Manchukuo, another Japanese puppet state in northern China (*see p.29*).

◁ **The RNG's flag** being raised at a military school in Nanjing, home to the Wang Jingwei regime

8 DECEMBER

4 December Greek soldiers capture Premeti in southwestern Albania; four days later, the Greeks advance into the Albanian-held area of northern Epirus

5 December Plans for a German invasion of the USSR, codenamed Operation Otto, are presented for the first time

An estimated 85,000 children under 14 lived in the Warsaw Ghetto at the peak of its population in April 1941

6 December 1940
BADOGLIO RESIGNS
Marshal Pietro Badoglio, chief of staff of the Italian Army and architect of Italy's victorious 1936 Ethiopia campaign, resigned after Italy's defeat in Greece and over disagreements with Mussolini about strategy. He was replaced as chief of staff by General Ugo Cavallero, a former commander of the army in Italian East Africa.

△ Marshal Badoglio

9 December 1940
OPERATION COMPASS

The first major British offensive in North Africa, Operation Compass consisted of a two-pronged attack. While the 6th Australian Division marched along the coast road towards Sidi Barrani, the 7th Armoured Division, supported by the 4th Indian Division, drove through the desert, then swung north to capture the town.

△ **A fort south** of Sidi Barrani under attack by the British

△ **Column of Italian prisoners** on the march from Sidi Barrani

11 December 1940
SIDI BARRANI CAPTURED

Virtually cut off after the British captured camps further west, an Italian pocket at Maktila was easily neutralized and the Catanzaro Division was annihilated near Sollum as it tried to flee west. The fall of Sidi Barrani left Bardia in Libya as the last major Italian position before Tobruk.

17 December The British capture Sollum and Fort Capuzzo near the Libyan–Egyptian border

1940

9 DECEMBER

9 December In Egypt, British Indian Army forces capture the Italian camps at Nibeiwa and Tummar East and West

18 December Germany's Führer Directive No. 21 confirms plans for Operation Barbarossa (the invasion of the USSR) to begin by 15 May 1941

1940–43
DESERT WARFARE

Harsh desert conditions meant that much of the fighting in North Africa was confined to a narrow coastal strip and a limited number of strategic roads and positions. The long distances and the logistical difficulties this posed meant that advances were often very rapid once a breakthrough was made. In such terrain, tanks were vital, but forces able to operate over long distances in the desert itself were also important. For example, Britain's Long Range Desert Group, founded in June 1940, became expert in penetrating deep beyond enemy lines.

Matilda tank
Britain's Matilda infantry-support tanks outgunned the Italian tanks in the early phases of the North Africa campaign. However, they could not match the speed and firepower of the German tanks that arrived in 1941 with Rommel's Afrika Korps and were replaced by the Valentine.

29 December 1940
THE SECOND GREAT FIRE OF LONDON

In one of the worst nights of the Blitz, 136 German bombers dropped tens of thousands of incendiary bombs on central London. Several churches were gutted, but St Paul's Cathedral survived in spite of being hit by 28 bombs; it became a symbol of London's resistance.

◁ **St Paul's shrouded by smoke and flames** during the 29 December raid

23 December Anthony Eden becomes Britain's foreign minister again, two years after resigning over appeasement

3 January 1941 Italy launches a counteroffensive against Greece; it proves unsuccessful

1941

5 JANUARY

◁ **Murzuk raid** commemorative stamp

4 January 1941
THE MURZUK RAID

Free French officers, their Tuareg allies, and the British Long Range Desert Force began a week-long march across nearly 500 km (310 miles) of desert from Chad to attack an Italian air base at the Murzuk oasis in southern Libya. The Italians were caught by surprise, and the airfield was destroyed.

35,949 Italian soldiers had been taken prisoner in the Western Desert Campaign by 23 December 1940

▽ **Australian soldiers** at the Battle of Bardia, 1941

5 January 1941
BARDIA FALLS

After two days of bitter fighting, and with the support of a naval bombardment by the British Mediterranean Fleet, the Australian 6th Division took Bardia. A further 38,000 Italian prisoners fell into Allied hands and the way was opened for an attack on Tobruk.

The USA supplied military equipment worth US$50.1 billion under Lend-Lease in 1941–45

7 January 1941
THE ALLIES BESIEGE TOBRUK

Advancing west from Bardia in eastern Libya, the British 7th Armoured Brigade and Australian 16th Brigade bypassed Tobruk to cut it off from the west, while the Australian 19th Brigade completed the encirclement of the city from the east. Defended by a 22,000-strong Italian garrison, Tobruk was the only deep-water port in eastern Libya and a vital and heavily fortified stronghold, the capture of which was essential for victory in the Western Desert Campaign.

◁ **British infantry** during the advance on Tobruk

1941

6 JANUARY

6 January President Roosevelt's "Four Freedoms" speech to Congress heralds the supply of US weapons to the Allies

11 January German Condor planes and Italian and German submarines carry out combined operations near Malta, sinking 33 ships

January Allied shipping losses in the Battle of the Atlantic reach 300,000 tons per month

15 January The Ethiopian emperor Haile Selassie crosses the border back into Ethiopia

10 January 1941
LEND-LEASE

The First Lend-Lease Bill was introduced into Congress, beginning a programme through which the USA could provide aid to nations at war with Germany and Italy without intervening directly. Providing military equipment in exchange for a repayable loan, Lend-Lease aid provided vital support at a time when Britain's capacity to resist Germany was fragile. Thirty-eight nations eventually took part in Lend-Lease, which continued after the USA entered the war.

▷ **Members of the Auxiliary Territorial Service** unloading American rifles sent to Britain under Lend-Lease

△ **Australian tanks and infantry** waiting to advance into Tobruk, January 1941

5–7 February 1941
THE BATTLE OF BEDA FOMM

As the Italian 10th Army tried to retreat westward from eastern Libya, British forces looped through the desert to cut them off at Beda Fomm. Caught between the British and the Australians advancing south down the coast from Benghazi, the Italians made desperate attempts to break out, but were forced to surrender with the loss of more than 100 tanks; 25,000 prisoners were taken.

22 January 1941
THE ALLIES CAPTURE TOBRUK

After a pre-dawn artillery barrage on 21 January, Australian troops cleared a way through the minefields outside Tobruk and rapidly overran Italian positions in the east of the city. The garrison surrendered early the next day, delivering 20,000 prisoners into Allied hands. Despite Italian attempts to destroy the harbour facilities, the Allies had it operational again within 48 hours.

▽ **Italian tanks** captured at Beda Fomm

21 January The Fascist Iron Guard mounts a coup against Romanian dictator General Antonescu, during which 121 Jews are murdered in a pogrom in Bucharest

3 February Allied forces occupy Cyrene in Libya, continuing their rapid advance westward after taking Tobruk

1941

5 FEBRUARY

17 January In the Battle of Koh Chang, Vichy French naval forces in Indochina attack the Thai Navy, sinking three ships

26 January British forces capture Biscia in Eritrea and begin their advance south towards Agordat

> "To manufacture... any defense article for the government of any country... vital to the defense of the United States."

THE LEND-LEASE ACT, 1941

1941
THE ERITREAN CAMPAIGN

On 19 January, Indian Divisions under Britain's General Platt crossed the Sudanese border to begin the Allied offensive against Italy in Eritrea.

28–31 January Allied forces take the garrison town of Agordat, forcing the Italians to retreat towards the coast.

3 February–27 March Italian operations in the mountainous terrain around Keren hold up the British advance for eight weeks.

1 April The Eritrean capital Asmara surrenders, leaving the port of Massawa as Italy's only significant remaining stronghold.

18 May South African and British troops trap the last large Italian force in East Africa at the mountain stronghold of Amba Alagi.

1939-postwar
RATIONING

Every major nation involved in World War II introduced rationing at some stage, with the aim of preserving stocks of essential goods and raw materials, such as food, fuel, rubber, and textiles. These were desperately needed by the armed forces and in shorter supply as the war continued to disrupt supply chains. Rationing usually relied on books or coupons that allocated set amounts of goods to households. Foods that were limited included meat, dairy products, alcohol, tea, coffee, eggs, sugar, and confectionery; and commodities such as clothing, shoes, paper, tobacco, petrol, coal, and even soap were often rationed.

Civilian experiences varied. In Britain, rationing was an inconvenience that resulted in a rather monotonous diet. In the Soviet Union, however, it was an essential measure that sustained a population that was often on the point of starvation. In Germany, supplies were supplemented by the Nazis' "Hunger Plan", which diverted resources from occupied territories in the Soviet Union. Food shortages became severe only when Germany was in retreat in 1944. Despite the efforts of the authorities and the risk of punishment, black markets for goods were commonplace as people sought to get round restrictions. In the USA, for example, 20 per cent of all meat was sold on the black market.

Do with less— so they'll have enough!

RATIONING GIVES YOU YOUR FAIR SHARE

KEY MOMENTS

1939–45 Leading the way
Rationing was often presented as a communal form of self-sacrifice that bound the nation together in support of the armed forces, for whom supplies were also limited. Civilians were encouraged not to waste food or complain about shortages, not to make unnecessary journeys, and to donate scrap rubber, metal, and rags to conserve resources for the war effort.

1940–45 The Japanese experience
Rationing officially began in Japan in 1940, with families allocated food based on their number, occupations, and gender and age make-up. At first, the government managed to preserve prewar levels of consumption, although shortages of basic goods were common in the territories conquered by Japan. However, in 1945, Allied blockades and the bombing of Japan led to severe food shortages, and only Japan's surrender prevented mass deaths from famine.

Rationing made day-to-day transactions time-consuming because shopkeepers had to ensure goods were fairly distributed. As this image from wartime New York shows, people were issued with books of stamps that had to be exchanged for rationed items.

"I would rather have four of my teeth pulled out than deal with that man again."

ADOLF HITLER SPEAKING ABOUT SPAIN'S GENERAL FRANCO, FEBRUARY 1941

6 February 1941
SPANISH–GERMAN DIPLOMACY

Adolf Hitler wrote to Spanish dictator Francisco Franco, asking him to allow German troops to pass through Spain to carry out Operation Felix, an attack on British-held Gibraltar. Despite being offered grain and military supplies, Franco was unenthusiastic and did not even reply for three weeks, infuriating the German Führer. He was equally dismissive when he met Mussolini on 12 February.

◁ **Adolf Hitler and Francisco Franco**
meeting at Hendaye, October 1940

1941

6 FEBRUARY

6 February Hitler issues Directive No. 23, outlining operations against the British war economy

9 February Forces under British general Archibald Wavell (*see p.101*) reach El Agheila, 265 km (165 miles) southwest of Benghazi

6 February 1941
THE FALL OF BENGHAZI

In the culmination of Operation Compass, Australian troops entered the Cyrenaican capital of Benghazi, which was virtually undefended after the Italian defeat at Beda Fomm. The rapid Allied advance threatened Axis control over Tripolitania to the west, but German reinforcements were soon to arrive.

△ **A crowd in Benghazi watching** as the city is handed over to the Allied military authorities

6 February 1941
ROMMEL IN COMMAND

Having made his name as the commander of the 7th Panzer Division during the invasion of France, Erwin Rommel was appointed commander of German forces in North Africa. He would twice drive the British back to the borders of Egypt, before defeat at El Alamein in October 1942 helped end the war in North Africa.

◁ **Erwin Rommel, 1941** (hand-coloured image)

10 February 1941
THE STIRLING DEBUTS

The new British-made Stirling four-engine bomber made its operational debut in a raid against Hanover. Although highly manoeuvrable, the Stirling's low operating ceiling (which kept it at low altitudes) made it vulnerable to enemy ground fire. Within a year, it was supplanted by the newer Halifax and Lancaster bombers, and for the last years of the war, it was relegated to transport duties.

◁ **The Stirling** was the first heavy bomber to enter service with the Royal Air Force

17 February Free French Forces under General Philippe Leclerc attack the Kufra oasis in Libya

1 March Bulgaria joins the Axis powers by signing the Tripartite Pact

6 March In a series of attacks, German mine-laying aircraft block the Suez Canal for three weeks

25 February Allied forces capture Mogadishu in Italian Somaliland

4 March In Operation Claymore, British and Norwegian commandos raid the Lofoten Islands

1941
6 MARCH

14 February 1941
THE AFRIKA KORPS ARRIVES IN TRIPOLI

Two days after Rommel, their commander, arrived in North Africa, elements of the German 5th Light Division began disembarking in Tripoli. They were the first units of what would become the Afrika Korps, ready to support their Italian allies and stem the Allied advance, which threatened to overrun Tripolitania. They first clashed with the British on 24 February, at Nofilia, west of El Agheila.

△ **Afrika Korps equipment,** including a private's belt and buckle, a gas protection blanket, and protective motorcycle goggles

1891–1944
ERWIN ROMMEL

Rommel led the Afrika Korps from 1941 to 1943. He was transferred to Greece, then to command Army Group B in France. He died by suicide in October 1944 after being implicated in a plot against Hitler.

24 March 1941
ROMMEL DRIVES THE BRITISH OUT OF EL AGHEILA

Rommel began his first offensive in North Africa with a drive eastward from Tripoli. At this time, the battle-hardened British 7th Armoured Division and Australian 6th Division had been withdrawn for refitting. Their inexperienced replacements were unable to hold back Rommel's attack on El Agheila (taken by the Allies just six weeks earlier). This heralded the rapid unravelling of most of the Allied gains made since January.

▷ **The German flag** flying over the desert fort of El Agheila after its capture by the Afrika Korps

25–27 March 1941
COUP IN YUGOSLAVIA

After Yugoslavia signed the Tripartite Pact, joining the Axis powers, a coup in Belgrade saw the overthrow of the pro-Axis prime minister. An anti-Nazi government, which repudiated the Pact, was formed under General Simovic, and the 17-year-old Yugoslavian crown prince was proclaimed King Peter II. This led Hitler to accelerate plans to invade Yugoslavia.

◁ **King Peter II** in exile in London, May 1943

1941

7 MARCH

9 March Italian forces launch an offensive against the Greeks in Albania that is repelled by 16 March

19 March The Luftwaffe launches its heaviest bombing raid on London since December 1940

21 March The Italian garrison at Jarabub in southern Libya surrenders after a 15-week siege

German submarine *U-99* sank 244,658 tons of Allied shipping

17 March 1941
THE ALLIES SINK U-99

U-99, one of the most successful German U-boats, sank southeast of Iceland after being struck by depth charges dropped by HMS *Walker*. During its eight Atlantic patrols, the submarine had sunk 38 Allied vessels, including three warships, without suffering a single casualty among its crew until its final day of operations.

◁ **German submarine *U-99*** (hand-coloured image)

28 March 1941
THE BATTLE OF CAPE MATAPAN

A British squadron intercepted a group of 22 Italian warships on a mission to attack Allied supply lines southwest of the Peloponnese, Greece. Gunfire from three British battleships and air attacks by Fairey Swordfish and Albacore torpedo bombers sank three Italian heavy cruisers and two destroyers. This action tipped the naval balance in the Allies' favour in the Eastern Mediterranean.

◁ **HMS** *Valiant* **firing a broadside** as the Allies pound the Italian fleet during the Battle of Cape Matapan

31 March In the Battle of Mersa Brega in Libya, Rommel attacks the British 2nd Armoured Division, forcing the British to withdraw

1 April Rice rationing is introduced in Tokyo and five other major Japanese cities; it is extended to all Japan in February 1942

1941

2 APRIL

1 April In Iraq, Rashid Ali al-Gaylani seizes power and installs a pro-German regime

1883–1950
ARCHIBALD WAVELL

Wavell led the British forces in North Africa from 1939 to 1941, when he was replaced by Auchinleck because of his poor performance. The loss of Singapore and Burma further damaged his reputation.

2 April 1941
THE HE 280 TAKES FLIGHT

After several unpowered glides, the world's first purpose-built jet fighter, the German-made He 280, made its maiden fully powered flight. Several prototypes of the aircraft were built, some reaching speeds of more than 800 km/h (497 mph), but its development was halted in 1944 in favour of the Me 262 fighter-bomber.

△ **The Heinkel He 280** turbo-jet fighter

"Belgrade will be destroyed from the air."

ADOLF HITLER, ON HEARING OF THE ANTI-GERMAN COUP IN YUGOSLAVIA ON 27 MARCH 1941

6 April 1941
LUFTWAFFE BOMBING DEVASTATES BELGRADE

In Operation Bestrafung ("Punishment"), German bombers and dive-bombers flew hundreds of sorties against the Yugoslavian capital of Belgrade as German ground forces began their invasion of the country. Around 17,000 people died amid huge fires that devastated the centre of the city, destroying government buildings, hospitals, and the Royal Palace. With fewer than 80 fighters based around Belgrade, the Yugoslav Air Force was almost powerless to resist.

◁ **Ruins of the New Palace in Belgrade** after the German bombing

1941

3 APRIL

4 April The Germans enter Benghazi after Rommel's panzers advance 960 km (600 miles) in two weeks

5 April Yugoslavia and the Soviet Union sign a Friendship and Non-Aggression Pact

8 April The Allies capture Massawa, the last Italian stronghold in Eritrea

12 April US troops land in Greenland after the Danish envoy there signs a protectorate agreement with the USA

5 April 1941
THE ITALIANS SURRENDER ADDIS ABABA

Having advanced rapidly westward from Harar and Dire Dawa, the Commonwealth troops of 11th (African) Division crossed the gorge of the river Awash, where the Italians had destroyed the bridge, to advance on Addis Ababa. By the time the first Allied forces arrived 16 km (10 miles) outside the Ethiopian capital on 5 April, the Italians had already negotiated their surrender, and the Allies faced no resistance when they entered Addis Ababa the next day. The Ethiopian emperor, Haile Selassie, returned to the city on 5 May.

△ **Haile Selassie's triumphant entry** into Addis Ababa

"Yugoslavia... must be regarded as an enemy and beaten down as soon as possible."

ADOLF HITLER, FÜHRER DIRECTIVE NO. 25, 27 MARCH 1941

6-27 April 1941
THE AXIS INVASION OF YUGOSLAVIA AND GREECE

Furious at Yugoslavia's withdrawal from the Tripartite Pact following the March coup (*see p.100*), Hiltler ordered the invasion of Yugoslavia. Fifty Axis divisions crossed the border on 6 April, overwhelming Yugoslavia's poorly equipped army spread along the 1,500-km (930-mile) frontier. Within a week, the Germans had occupied Belgrade, and the Yugoslavs capitulated on 17 April. Axis forces also invaded the thinly defended northeast of Greece on 8 April, making rapid advances there and forcing the British W Force to retreat south, before capturing Athens on 27 April.

▷ **German troops advancing** in Serbia during the invasion of Yugoslavia (hand-coloured image)

13 April Japan and the USSR sign a neutrality pact in Moscow

17 April Yugoslavia surrenders and King Peter goes into exile

18 April An Indian army brigade arrives in Iraq to protect RAF bases in the country

18 April The Messerschmitt Me 262 German jet fighter has its first flight

1941

20 APRIL

13 April 1941
THE GERMANS BESIEGE TOBRUK

Having been ordered not to bypass Tobruk, on Libya's coast, Rommel encircled the town. The Australian 9th Division repelled an initial assault by German panzers and four further attacks over the next 11 days. The Allied garrison settled in to resist a siege that would last eight months.

1892-1975
HAILE SELASSIE

Ethiopian emperor from 1930, Haile Selassie led economic, social, and educational reforms, but was forced into exile in 1935 after the Italian invasion. He returned in 1941 and ruled until his deposition in a revolution by Marxist army officers in 1974.

20 April 1941
THE GREEK EPIRUS ARMY SURRENDERS

Left isolated in Albania by the Axis invasion of Greece, the commander of the Greek forces in Epirus, Lieutenant General Georgios Tsolakoglou, surrendered to Sepp Dietrich, commander of the SS Leibstandarte Division. With the Greek defences shattered and the British W Force withdrawing south, the Germans were free to advance on Athens.

▽ **German soldiers in Epirus**, April 1941

27 April 1941
GERMAN TROOPS ENTER ATHENS

German Army forces arrived at Athens on 27 March and reached the southern coast of Greece just three days later. This was the culmination of a campaign in which 15,700 Greeks died and 10,000 Allied soldiers were taken prisoner. The fighting in Greece and Yugoslavia delayed Germany's planned invasion of Russia.

▷ **Luftwaffe Dornier Do 172** light bombers flying over Athens, June 1942

1941

21 APRIL

21 April Japanese forces occupy the strategic port of Fuzhou in Fujian province; they hold it until September

23 April The number of German divisions deployed to the Eastern Front reaches 59 in preparation for the invasion of the Soviet Union

25 April Rommel's advance in North Africa continues as he drives the British from Halfaya Pass, east of Bardia

22–28 April 1941
THE ALLIES LEAVE GREECE

With the Germans advancing rapidly southward, Allied forces began evacuating from mainland Greece, via the Peloponnese, to Crete. A plan to fight a rearguard action to protect withdrawing troops was abandoned when German paratroopers landed at Corinth on 25 April and crossed into the Peloponnese, threatening the retreating forces.

◁ **Exhausted British** soldiers being evacuated on a Greek coastal steamer

"The German Reich has had no territorial or selfish political interests in the Balkans."

ADOLF HITLER, SPEECH TO THE REICHSTAG, 1 MAY 1941

10 May 1941
RUDOLF HESS'S PEACE MISSION

Hitler's deputy, Rudolf Hess, believed that he could negotiate peace between Germany and the UK. A trained pilot, he secretly flew to Scotland hoping to meet British representatives. Injured while parachuting from his Messerschmidt BF 10, he was arrested, and it soon became clear that his mission was not authorized by Hitler. Hess was detained in Britain and held as a prisoner of war; back in Germany, *Der Führer* newspaper claimed he was confused and deluded.

▷ **Soldiers inspect the wreckage** of the plane ditched by Hess over Scotland

29 April Iraq's prime minister, Rashid Ali, lays siege to the British RAF base at Habbaniya. The base is relieved on 6 May by the 10th Indian Division, advancing from Basra

5 May Major General Bernard Freyberg is appointed commander of the British forces in Crete

1941

10 MAY

28 April The last Allied forces leave mainland Greece aboard Royal Navy warships

29 April Intelligence from Allied code breakers indicates that the Germans plan to land on Crete

1894–1987
RUDOLF HESS

An early Nazi Party member, Hess became Hitler's deputy in 1933 but was disenchanted by 1941, when he flew to Britain on a personal peace mission. He was condemned for war crimes in 1945 and held in Spandau Prison until his suicide at the age of 93.

1939–45
THE SINGING SPY

American-born singer and dancer Josephine Baker built a successful career in France from the 1920s. Recruited by French military intelligence in 1939, her access to Japanese, German, and Italian officials allowed her to feed information to her handlers. After the Germans took Paris, she fled to the Dordogne, where she helped refugees escaping the German occupation. In 1941 she moved to Algiers, where she continued to perform and to provide the Resistance with intelligence on Axis movements, which she often hid in song-sheets or in her underwear. After the war, she was awarded the Croix de Guerre for her espionage work.

▷ Josephine Baker

18 May 1941

HABFORCE ARRIVES AT HABBANIYA

Churchill ordered Habforce – a unit assembled from British forces in the Middle East – to strike rapidly through Iraq to relieve the RAF base at Habbaniya, which was under siege by the pro-Nazi Iraqi regime of Rashid Ali. An advance column left Haifa on 11 May under the command of Brigadier Kingstone. By the time it reached Habbaniya, the Iraqi attackers had already fled. Kingstone pressed on towards Baghdad, reaching the Iraqi capital 12 days later.

▷ **Members of Habforce** in a Fordson Armoured Car outside Baghdad, May 1941

1941

11 MAY

10–11 May In the last night of the Blitz, German bombers launch a heavy raid on London

11 May German forces complete the occupation of the Aegean Islands, taking over from former Italian garrisons

19 May In Ethiopia, the 5th Indian Division takes Amba Alagi, the last major Italian position in East Africa

15 May The Gloster E.28/39, the first British jet, makes its first test flight at RAF Cranwell

△ **A British barricade** on the road between Fort Capuzzo and Bardia

15 May 1941

OPERATION BREVITY

In a new British offensive in North Africa aimed at relieving pressure on besieged Tobruk, Churchill ordered General Gott to advance on Halfaya Pass, Sollum, and Fort Capuzzo. If successful, he was to move towards Tobruk. Overcoming strong Italian resistance, which destroyed seven Matilda tanks, the British 22nd Guards Brigade took Halfaya Pass, but the other arms of the offensive along the coast stalled, and German reinforcements prevented further progress.

MAY 1941
THE BATTLE OF CRETE

After Germany's conquest of Greece, Britain's General Freyberg resolved to defend Crete, but suffered another Allied defeat as the island's defences crumbled.

20 May Germany's attack on Crete begins with airdrops of thousands of paratroopers on Maleme and other airfields. They encounter stiff resistance.

24 May 1941
THE BISMARCK SINKS HMS HOOD

The German battleship *Bismarck* and heavy cruiser *Prinz Eugen*, which had been raiding Allied Atlantic convoys, were intercepted by the Royal Navy between Iceland and Germany. A shell from the *Bismarck* hit the British battleship HMS *Hood*, exploding its ammunition stores. *Hood* sank, with the loss of all but three of its 1,400-strong crew.

◁ **The last picture of HMS** *Hood*, taken from the deck of HMS *Prince of Wales*, 1941

27 May 1941
THE BRITISH SINK THE BISMARCK

After HMS *Hood* was sunk, the surviving British ships shadowed the *Bismarck* while they waited for reinforcements. On 26 May, torpedo bombers from HMS *Ark Royal* disabled *Bismarck*'s steering equipment. With *Bismarck*'s guns also out of action, *King George V* and *Rodney* peppered it with shells, scoring around 400 hits. The *Bismarck* soon sank, and 2,200 of the ship's crew died.

△ **Model of German battleship** *Bismarck*

1941

28 MAY

27 May The 20th Indian Division marches north towards Baghdad after securing Basra in southern Iraq

27 May Rommel's Afrika Korps attacks Halfaya Pass, forcing the British Coldstream Guards to abandon the position

27 May 1941 The first convoy to have continuous protection across the Atlantic sails from Canada

1,856 German paratroopers were killed during the initial airdrop on Crete

22 May Hesitation by Freyberg and communications difficulties allow the Germans to take Maleme and Souda in northern Crete. The Allies begin retreating to the south.

26 May The Germans break through the perimeter held by New Zealand troops around Maleme and advance rapidly, taking Hania, the island's capital.

27 May Freyberg decides Crete cannot be held. Evacuations begin of the Allied troops through the small harbour at Sphakia on Crete's southern coast.

1 June Out of 32,00 Allied troops, 19,000 are evacuated; the rest are forced to surrender and taken prisoner, although a few hundred escape to join the Cretan resistance.

2 June 1941
THE TUSKEGEE AIRMEN

Discriminatory laws meant that the US Army Air Force had no African-American pilots until 1941, when a programme was set up to train Black air personnel at Tuskegee air base in Alabama. In all, 922 pilots were trained there, forming first the 99th Fighter Squadron and then the 332nd Fighter Group. They flew their first combat mission in Sicily in June 1943 and fought in the Italian campaign and in raids on Germany and occupied Europe. Members of the Tuskegee units won 96 Distinguished Flying Crosses.

▷ **Tuskegee airmen study a map** before a training mission at the flying school in Alabama

1941

29 MAY

30 May Iraq's Prime Minister Rashid Ali flees to Iran

31 May German aircraft aiming for Bristol and Liverpool accidentally bomb Dublin, killing 28 people

1 June Clothes and footwear rationing is introduced in the United Kingdom

10 June In Operation Chronometer, Indian troops of the 15th Punjab Regiment occupy the Eritrean port of Assab

8 June 1941
THE ALLIES IN SYRIA AND LEBANON

Aiming to prevent Germany establishing a presence in the Middle East, General Henry Wilson led a 34,000-strong Commonwealth and Free French force in a three-pronged assault towards Beirut and Rayak in Lebanon and Damascus in Syria. He wrongly assumed that the Vichy garrisons would offer little resistance, but counterattacks held up the Allies in Lebanon, and progress was made only towards Damascus.

▷ **Members of the 21st Australian Brigade** in action during the Syria–Lebanon campaign against the Vichy French

"Our infantry tanks... are too slow for a battle in the desert."

GENERAL WAVELL, BRITISH COMMANDER IN NORTH AFRICA, 28 MAY 1941

21 June 1941

FREE FRENCH FORCES CAPTURE DAMASCUS

In the Battle of Damascus, the Allied advance on the city had stalled, and the Indian unit that took Mezzeh to the southwest had been captured. The arrival of British and Australian reinforcements allowed the Free French to take the defensive ring of forts around Damascus and, at 11am on 21 June, its Vichy commander finally surrendered.

△ **Insignia of Free French Forces** in World War II

14 June 1941

THE LUCY SPY RING

Established in Switzerland by Rudolf Roessler, a refugee German publisher, the Lucy spy ring provided Moscow with a date of 14 June for the German invasion of the Soviet Union. Roessler's intelligence was ignored, but proved to be almost correct when Operation Barbarossa began on 22 June. From then on, intelligence from Lucy was given top priority; it gave advance warning of German attacks on Stalingrad in 1942 and Kursk in 1943.

◁ **Major General Hans Oster,** one of the high-ranking German intelligence officers who leaked information to Lucy

1941

21 JUNE

14 June President Roosevelt freezes all German and Italian assets in the USA

15 June The Australian 21st Brigade captures Sidon on the Lebanese coast

17 June Finland secretly begins to mobilize in preparation for an attack on the Soviet Union

100 out of 180 British tanks were lost during Operation Battleaxe

15 June 1941

OPERATION BATTLEAXE LAUNCHED

Under pressure from Churchill to relieve Tobruk, General Wavell planned an operation to smash through Axis defences at Halfaya, Sollum, and Fort Capuzzo and advance beyond Tobruk to Derna. Almost immediately, the British tanks were ambushed and decimated by German artillery. The Allies took Capuzzo, but were forced to withdraw, just escaping encirclement by the German panzers.

◁ **Indian forces at Halfaya Pass,** June 1941

GLOBAL WAR

Hitler's great ambition was to carve out new lands in Eastern Europe to provide the German people with the *Lebensraum* ("living space") that he believed essential to the survival of the "Aryan race". Thus, on 22 June 1941, more than 3 million Axis troops smashed their way through the Soviet border at the start of Operation Barbarossa – the invasion of the USSR. The war on the Eastern Front was the most ferocious in the history of warfare. Not only were tens of millions of soldiers involved in a conflict that stretched from the Baltic to the Black Sea, but also the nature of the fighting was pitiless.

A war of extermination

For Hitler, this was a war of extermination, and the German armed forces were instructed to behave accordingly. Jews, communists, and Soviet officials were to be killed on the spot, while other civilians would be starved to death. Ordinary Soviet prisoners were treated so badly that out of approximately 6 million of them, well over half died of starvation, disease, and casual killings.

In the initial phase of Operation Barbarossa, the Germans scored a remarkable series of victories against the poorly deployed and cumbersome Red Army. At one point it seemed that Moscow might fall to a German thrust late in 1941, but this represented the high-water mark of Hitler's invasion. In December 1941,

Germany's exhausted armies began to falter, while the arrival of reinforcements from Siberia tipped the scales in favour of the Red Army.

A winter offensive by the Soviet forces came as a shock to the German invaders, although they were eventually able to hold their positions and await the arrival of mechanized reinforcements for the coming campaign in the spring of 1942. Then, instead of renewing the assault on Moscow, Hitler decided to strike southwards in a move that was aimed at capturing the oil-rich region around the Caucasus Mountains. This decision would lead the German forces to the extraordinary confrontation at the city of Stalingrad that became the defining battle of the war on the Eastern Front.

Conflict in North Africa

The arrival of Rommel's Afrika Korps transformed the conflict in North Africa into a see-saw battle between the Axis and the Allies that saw first one side and then the other gaining temporary ascendancy. However, following the Axis victory at Gazala and the fall of Tobruk in June 1942, it seemed that Germany's Afrika Korps had broken the desert stalemate. During July, Rommel's forces surged into Egypt, but fuel shortages and the arrival of British reinforcements brought the advance to a halt. While the Axis prepared defensive positions, the Allies brought up further reinforcements in readiness for a new offensive at the town of El Alamein – a place that would prove to be of vital significance in the war in North Africa.

Japan enters the war

Unable to gain direct access to vital raw materials and faced by opposition from the West, Japan's government felt trapped and believed war to be the only solution to its problems. Its military planners hoped that a swift naval campaign would destroy American might in the Pacific, and that conquests in southern Asia would form the basis for a "Greater East Asia Co-prosperity Sphere" that would provide Japan with the economic self-sufficiency it desired.

This was, however, a reckless strategy. It was based on the hope that superior Japanese martial spirit would somehow overcome the greater economic and military might of the Western powers. The audacious attack on Pearl Harbor on 7 December 1941 and the assaults on the Dutch East Indies, the Philippines, and Malaya – which brought the USA into the war and threatened the Western Allies' colonies in Asia – provided Japan with stunning military victories; the progress it made across the Pacific was rapid. Yet, at the Battle of Midway in June 1942 – just six months after the Pearl Harbor attack – the Japanese suffered their first military setback. From then on, they would find themselves fighting a defensive war in the Pacific.

▽ **Red Army troops** based in Russia's border garrisons surrendering to the Germans (hand-coloured image)

3.6 million Axis troops crossed into the USSR at the start of Operation Barbarossa

22 June 1941

OPERATION BARBAROSSA BEGINS

After months of preparation, 120 German divisions crossed into the USSR along a 2,900-km (1,800-mile) front stretching from the Black Sea to the Baltic. Despite intelligence warnings, the 2.5 million Soviet defenders were unprepared and caught in exposed advance positions. River bridges were rapidly captured, and 1,000 Soviet planes destroyed in the first day as the German forces advanced more than 80 km (50 miles).

23 June In Syria, the British 4th Brigade reaches Palmyra, where the Vichy garrison resists for 12 days before surrendering

24 June Hitler arrives at the Wolf's Lair in East Prussia, his military headquarters on the Eastern Front. "Wolf" was a nickname Hitler gave himself

1941

22 JUNE

23-30 June German and Soviet forces clash at the Battle of Brody in a massive engagement involving 4,000 tanks that holds up the German 1st Panzer Division's advance into Ukraine for a week

22 June–16 October 1941

OPERATION BARBAROSSA

Originally planned for May 1941, Barbarossa's launch was delayed for six weeks by Germany's campaign against Yugoslavia and Greece. It was the largest military offensive in history, involving more than 6 million German and Soviet troops. Initial progress spearheaded by the German panzer divisions was rapid, and hundreds of thousands of Red Army troops found themselves trapped in pockets. By October, however, the German supply lines were overstretched, and the onset of a bitter winter, for which the German Army was ill equipped, halted the offensive outside Moscow.

A three-pronged attack
Army Group North's objective was Leningrad via the Baltic. Army Group Centre advanced on Moscow, but was diverted south to support Army Group South, advancing on Kyiv, the Crimea, and the Donbas region.

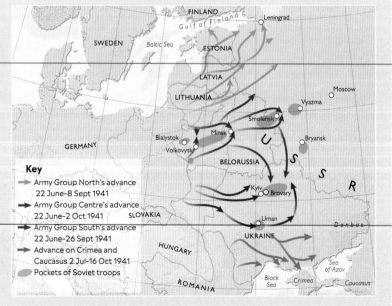

Key
➤ Army Group North's advance
  22 June–8 Sept 1941
➤ Army Group Centre's advance
  22 June–2 Oct 1941
➤ Army Group South's advance
  22 June–26 Sept 1941
➤ Advance on Crimea and
  Caucasus 2 Jul–16 Oct 1941
⬭ Pockets of Soviet troops

28 June 1941
THE GERMANS CAPTURE MINSK

The armoured spearheads of Germany's Army Group Centre – the 2nd and 3rd Panzer Groups – advanced rapidly towards Moscow. They covered 300 km (190 miles) within a week and met east of Minsk, trapping more than 500,000 men of the Red Army's Western Front in pockets at Novogrudok and Bialystok. Minsk itself fell on 28 June. Soviet counterattacks to relieve the trapped men were blunted by the German 9th and 4th armies. By the time the pockets finally collapsed on 9 July, the Russians had suffered catastrophic losses.

▷ **The ruins of Minsk** after its capture by the Germans during Barbarossa

26 June Finland declares war on the USSR and allows German troops stationed in Finland to conduct offensive action against the Soviet army

29 June Stalin takes direct control of the Soviet Defence Ministry

1 July In Latvia, Riga falls to the German Army; German panzers cross the river Berezina

1941

1 JULY

26 June Türkiye refuses permission for Vichy French supplies and forces to cross its territory

27 June Hungary declares war on the USSR; Hungarian troops join Germany's Army Group South

△ **German troops entrenched** in the centre of Kaunas

24 June 1941
GERMAN FORCES CAPTURE KAUNAS AND VILNA

In Lithuania, a Soviet counterattack at Raseiniai destroyed 150 German panzers from Army Group North. Finally, however, Marshal Kuznetsov ordered a Soviet retreat towards Riga – for which he was removed from command of the Soviet Northwestern Front – and the Germans took Kaunas and Vilna without a fight.

△ **German guards** stationed in front of Lviv's town hall, 1941

30 June 1941
GERMAN FORCES CAPTURE LVIV

Germany's Army Group South made slow progress at first through Galicia towards Kyiv, gaining just 10 km (6 miles) a day. But by 29 June it had taken Rovno, and a day later, it entered Lviv. Pogroms broke out against Lviv's large Jewish population, in which around 5,000 were killed, while German SS death squads (the Einsatzgruppen) murdered thousands more in organized mass killings.

△ **Soviet propaganda poster** showing Joseph Stalin and Kliment Voroshilov saluting a military parade

11 July 1941
NEW SOVIET COMMANDERS APPOINTED

Dissatisfied with the Red Army's initial performance against Germany's Operation Barbarossa, Stalin appointed new frontline commanders: Kliment Voroshilov was to head the Northern Front, Semyon Timoshenko the Central Front, and Semyon Budyonny the Southern Front. Continued failures against the Germans saw both Voroshilov and Budyonny demoted just eight weeks later.

8 July 1941
ITALO-GERMAN AGREEMENT

◁ **Dagger for senior officers** of the Independent State of Croatia

Following its capitulation, Yugoslavia was dismembered by the Axis powers. Germany annexed northern Slovenia and occupied much of Serbia; Hungary was given Vojvodina in northern Serbia; Bulgaria took Macedonia; and Italy annexed the Dalmatian coast and southern Slovenia and occupied Bosnia, Herzegovina, and Montenegro. Croatia remained as an independent, pro-Axis puppet state.

3 July **The British 4th Cavalry Brigade** captures Palmyra in Syria after advancing north from Iraq

9 July **In Belorussia, the German 3rd Panzer Army** takes Vitebsk, opening the way to move on Smolensk

1941
2 JULY

12 July **The USSR and the UK sign** a mutual assistance pact, pledging that neither will seek a separate peace with Germany

3 July 1941
STALIN'S "SCORCHED EARTH" BROADCAST

Speaking in a radio broadcast, Joseph Stalin exhorted the Soviet people to resist the German invasion and employ guerrilla tactics to disrupt the German forces. Subsequently, hundreds of factories were dismantled and moved eastwards, as were hundreds of thousands of vehicles. What could not be transported was destroyed, while crops and other materials useful to the Germans were burned.

◁ **A German soldier** in a Russian village set on fire by its inhabitants (hand-coloured image)

> "The enemy must not find a single railway engine, not a wagon, not a pound of bread or a glassful of petrol."

JOSEPH STALIN, "SCORCHED EARTH" SPEECH, 3 JULY 1941

21 July 1941
THE MOSCOW BLITZ

The first major German air raid against Moscow was carried out by more than 220 Heinkel He 111 and Dornier Do 217 bombers, which dropped more than 100 tons of bombs on the city. Some 130 people were killed, but heavy anti-aircraft fire prevented greater casualties. The "Moscow Blitz" lasted until June 1943. In that time, the Luftwaffe attacked the Soviet capital 122 times, hitting the Kremlin on six occasions.

▷ **Children shelter in a trench** during a German air raid on Moscow

14 July The Convention of Acre ends the Syrian campaign. Surrendering Vichy troops can choose between joining the Free French or repatriation to France

20 July Stalin becomes People's Commissar for Defence, taking direct control of the Soviet war effort

26 July All Japanese assets in the USA are seized in retaliation for the occupation of Indochina

1941

26 JULY

16 July Stalin's son, Jacob Dzugashvili, is captured by the Germans during the Battle of Smolensk

△ **Russian women in the ruins** of Smolensk, following the battle, August 1941

1895–1970
SEMYON TIMOSHENKO
A former Tsarist officer, Timoshenko was head of the Stavka (Soviet Supreme Military Command) when the Germans invaded. He commanded various fronts in 1941–43 and ended the war directing the Soviet advance into Hungary and Austria.

15 July 1941
THE BATTLE OF SMOLENSK

Germany's 2nd and 3rd Panzer Armies began to envelop large Soviet formations east of Smolensk. By 27 July, they surrounded them completely. Although some Soviet troops broke out a few days later, the German armies gradually constricted the pocket, eliminating it by 5 August and capturing around 310,000 Russian soldiers.

5 August 1941
THE SIEGE OF ODESA

The 4th Romanian Army began a 73-day siege of the strategic Black Sea port of Odesa, in Ukraine. The Soviet garrison stubbornly defended the city, repelling a series of Romanian assaults. A Soviet counteroffensive to relieve Odesa failed on 21–22 September, and the Romanians finally took the city on 16 October. While the Soviet Navy managed to evacuate 350,000 soldiers and civilians during the siege, the Romanians lost 18,000 soldiers.

◁ **Children helping erect barricades** in Odesa during the siege in 1941

1941

27 JULY

31 July Hitler's deputy, Hermann Göring, orders plans to be made for the "final solution to the Jewish question"

4 August Polish general Wladyslaw Anders is released from a Soviet prison to organize a Polish army in Russia

8 August In China, Chongqing, is hit in a series of 40 Japanese air raids, in the ongoing bombing campaign against the city

4 August South African forces bomb Gondar, in Ethiopia, the last Italian stronghold in East Africa

5 August Britain announces that it will reinforce the garrison in Singapore

"All of the nations of the world… must come to the abandonment of the use of force."

THE ATLANTIC CHARTER, 14 AUGUST 1941

12 August 1941
HITLER POSTPONES THE GERMAN ADVANCE ON MOSCOW

Hitler halted Army Group Centre's advance on Moscow and redirected its forces to encircle 500,000 Soviet troops near Kyiv, to the south. After Kyiv was captured on 19 September, Army Group Centre was able to focus once more on its original objective, but the delay meant it was forced to attack Moscow in the harsh conditions of winter.

▷ **German infantrymen** in Russia, 1941 (hand-coloured image)

August 1941–May 1945
THE ARCTIC CONVOYS

Allied convoys carrying military aid to the Soviet Union began sailing through Arctic waters to the north of Norway in August 1941. By the end of the war, they had transported 4.4 million tons of supplies, but had suffered heavy losses: almost 8 per cent of the vessels were lost to German submarine, naval, and air attacks. Sailors on board the convoy vessels suffered extreme cold and faced great dangers, especially when sea ice forced the convoys close to land. Escort by Royal Navy destroyers helped, but disasters such as the attack on convoy PQ-17 in July 1942 – when failure to act on intelligence led to the loss of 24 ships (*see p.152*) – caused the convoys to be suspended periodically.

▷ **Ice forming on a 20-inch signal projector** on the cruiser HMS *Sheffield* while escorting an Arctic convoy to Russia, 1941

16 August Britain and the USSR sign an agreement in Moscow on the exchange of war goods and credit

17 August German forces capture Novgorod, after the Red Army evacuates it the previous day

21 August The first Allied Arctic convoy to northern Russia sets out from Reykjavik

1941
23 AUGUST

△ **Roosevelt and Churchill** at the Atlantic Conference, August 1941

14 August 1941
THE ATLANTIC CHARTER

After a series of meetings in Newfoundland, Churchill and Roosevelt signed the Atlantic Charter, outlining British and American political aims for the postwar period. These included global cooperation on international trade and social conditions, no border changes against the wishes of the people, and no territorial aggrandizement. The Charter paved the way for the United Nations.

19 August 1941
RELIEF FORCES ARRIVE AT TOBRUK

Although besieged by the Germans since April 1941, Tobruk was still accessible by sea. Royal Navy ships evacuated 6,000 Australian troops of the 9th Division and replaced them with British, Polish, and Czech units. Further successful replacements of the beleaguered Australian garrison took place in September.

▷ **Australian and Polish soldiers** meeting at Tobruk, 1941

8 September 1941
THE SIEGE OF LENINGRAD BEGINS

As Germany's Army Group North pushed east from Estonia to reach Lake Ladoga (east of Leningrad), it severed the last rail route and the final road into the city. Meanwhile, Finland's army sealed the Karelian Isthmus, which connected Finland and Soviet Russia, from the north. Leningrad was almost totally surrounded, and the city's 2.5 million civilians and 200,000 defenders could be supplied only via a narrow land corridor around Lake Ladoga. The siege of the city lasted more than two years.

▷ **Leningrad inhabitants** constructing anti-tank ditches in 1941

1941

24 AUGUST

24 August A British minelayer disguised as a French naval vessel lays 140 mines off Livorno, Italy

28 August The German army takes Tallinn in Estonia after a nine-day offensive

11 September President Roosevelt announces the exclusion of German and Italian ships from US waters

△ **Indian soldiers** taking over an oil refinery, Iran, 1941

25 August 1941
ANGLO-SOVIET OCCUPATION OF IRAN

Fears about growing Axis influence over Iran, with its strategically important oil fields, prompted Britain to attack from Iraq and the Soviet Union to invade from the north. Iran's outnumbered army resisted for four days before its ruler, Reza Shah, surrendered. British and Soviet troops remained in Iran until 1946.

30 August 1941
THE SHETLAND BUS

British and Norwegian intelligence established the "Shetland Bus", using fishing boats to transport agents and supplies to and from Norway under cover of darkness. The first "Bus" departed from Lunna Ness in Shetland on 30 August; by the end of the war, the programme had transported nearly 200 agents.

▽ **The Shetland Bus memorial** at Scalloway in Shetland, UK

△ Roadblocks being removed in Kyiv, 1941

19 September 1941
THE GERMANS CAPTURE KYIV

As the German 1st and 2nd Panzer Groups advanced, they met east of Kyiv on 16 September, trapping three Soviet armies. The Soviet forces were methodically reduced, and three days later, the Germans entered Kyiv. By 26 September they had captured more than 500,000 enemy soldiers.

11 September General Zhukov replaces Voroshilov as commander of the Leningrad Front and begins strengthening the city's defences

24 September 1941
GENERAL DE GAULLE FORMS THE FREE FRENCH NATIONAL COMMITTEE

De Gaulle announced the formation of the Free French National Committee and Advisory Council to coordinate Free French activities globally. It formed the nucleus of a provisional government, although tensions with other Free French leaders, such as General Henri Giraud, and with communist resistance groups in France hampered its work.

△ **Recruitment postcard** for the Free French Army

"AUX ARMES" CITOYENS"!..

UN SEUL COMBAT POUR UNE SEULE PATRIE

1941

25 SEPTEMBER

17 September British and Soviet forces reach Tehran, the day after Iran's ruler, the Shah, abdicates

25 September German ground forces supported by paratroopers attempt to break through the Isthmus of Perekop into Crimea

1890–1970
CHARLES DE GAULLE

A veteran soldier, de Gaulle escaped to Britain and became a rallying figure for the Free French and leader of France's Provisional Government in 1944. He served as president of France from 1959 to 1969.

8 September 1941–27 January 1944
SIEGE OF LENINGRAD

The siege was at first a loose blockade, but the German capture of Tikhvin in November 1941 left the city cut off. An ice road built over the frozen Lake Ladoga became the city's sole viable supply route. It was woefully inadequate, and the population suffered terribly, with rations reduced to just 125 g (4 oz) of bread daily in winter 1941–42. Ultimately, more than a million people died from starvation, exposure, or military action. A Soviet offensive in January 1942 opened a new route into the city, though the Germans closed it six months later. Another Red Army offensive in January 1943 succeeded in reopening the rail route, and in January 1944, the siege was finally broken.

▷ **Russian Defence of Leningrad medal**

A female worker trains on a lathe at the Douglas arms factory in California. Around 30 per cent of adult women in the USA were engaged in war work; more than in the Axis nations but lower than the 70 per cent figure for Britain.

1939-45
WAR AND INDUSTRY

World War II was arguably the ultimate "total war", in which the mobilization of industry and the civilian population was as important as the deployment of the armed forces. The three principal Axis countries – Germany, Italy, and Japan – shared similar economic problems and adopted similar approaches to find a solution. They all suffered from a shortage of raw materials, especially oil, the "black gold" that powered both armies and industry. Rather than rely on trade to gain access to these vital commodities, they turned instead to coercion and conquest. A growing demand for workers was supplied by forced labour from the countries they had occupied.

Of the Allied nations, Britain was the first to mobilize its economy for total war, with the government given broad powers to direct both the people and industry towards the war effort. In the Soviet Union, the dictatorial power of Stalin's Communist Party allowed total control of the war economy that was brutal but effective. The large and flexible industrial base of the United States made it possible to upscale to a war economy with relative ease. The industrial output of the Allies, especially the Soviet Union and the United States, dwarfed that of the Axis nations – a major factor behind the Allied victory in 1945.

KEY MOMENTS

1943 Rosie the Riveter
This iconic poster was produced to boost morale in US arms factories. The figure of "Rosie the Riveter", symbolizing female determination and war work, was often seen in photographs and posters during the war.

1944 Disabled soldiers at work
During World War I, some 8 million men were seriously injured. Many of them were amputees. During World War II, significant efforts were made to bring those with disabilities into the war effort. Here, a British ex-soldier (*right*) uses his own artificial arm to work a lathe producing artificial limbs for other people with disabilities.

1945 Japanese female workers
While the Allies employed large numbers of women in war work from the outset of the conflict, Japan – far more socially conservative than many Allied nations – was reluctant to draw upon its potential female workforce until near the end of the war.

2 October 1941
THE ME 163 ROCKET-PROPELLED FIGHTER

A German Me 163 Komet, the only rocket-propelled fighter ever produced, set an air speed record of 1,005 km/h (625 mph) at Peenemünde research station. The fighter went into operation in May 1944, but technical difficulties – notably its eight-minute flight capability – meant that the 370 aircraft produced had almost no impact on the air war.

△ **Me 163 V1 Komet** rocket-propelled aircraft

30 September 1941
OPERATION TYPHOON BEGINS

The German Army launched a strategic offensive designed to reach Moscow before the winter. The 3rd and 4th Panzer Groups were to strike from the north, and the 2nd Panzer Group from the south via Tula, forming a pincer movement. The operation was one of the war's largest offensives and involved around 2 million men and 2,000 tanks.

26 September The Italian garrison at Wolchefit, in Ethiopia, surrenders

1 October The USSR begins deporting the German population in the North Caucasus to Kazakhstan

1941

26 SEPTEMBER

28 September Reinhard Heydrich, Himmler's deputy, is appointed *Reichsprotektor* ("governor") of Bohemia and Moravia

30 September 1941
THE BABYN YAR MASSACRE

In the aftermath of the capture of Kyiv, German SS Einsatzkommandos and local auxiliary police murdered more than 33,000 Jews at the Babyn Yar ravine outside the city. The victims believed they were being evacuated to safety; only 29 survived.

"[Russia] has already been broken and will never rise again."

JOSEPH GOEBBELS, GERMAN PROPAGANDA MINISTER, 3 OCTOBER 1941

7 October 1941
THE BATTLE OF VYAZMA–BRYANSK

In the campaign to take Moscow, the German 2nd Panzer Group encircled four Soviet armies near Vyazma, and the 3rd Panzer Group surrounded two further armies at Bryansk. More than 600,000 Red Army soldiers were captured, but their resistance slowed the German advance for a critical two weeks.

▷ **German convoy** during the combat for Vyazma, 1941

16 October 1941
PANIC IN MOSCOW

The arrival on 13 October of the German Army at Mozhaisk, on Moscow's outermost defence line, provoked a crisis in the city. The Soviet government evacuated east to Kuybyshev, on the river Volga, and law and order broke down in Moscow as the roads and railways became clogged with fleeing civilians. Stalin himself, however, refused to leave, and the panic subsided.

◁ **Barricade at the intersection** of Balchug Street and Lubochny Lane, Moscow, built to protect the Kremlin, 1941

18 October In Japan, General Tojo forms a new government dominated by the military, with himself as prime minister and minister of war

1941
23 OCTOBER

16 October Romanian forces capture the Black Sea port of Odesa after a two-month siege

18 October Romania's General Antonescu announces the annexation of Transnistria (part of Ukraine)

21 October General Zhukov takes command of the Moscow garrison to prepare the city for the impending German assault

18 October 1941
SOVIET SPY ARRESTED

Communist sympathizer Richard Sorge was recruited by Soviet intelligence in 1925. Posing as a journalist and Nazi supporter, he set up a spy ring in Japan and used contacts in the German embassy to obtain secret information, including about preparations for Operation Barbarossa. He was arrested after a Japanese member of his spy ring was detained, and was executed in November 1944.

◁ **Soviet spy Richard Sorge** featured on a 1965 commemorative stamp from the USSR

663,000 Soviet soldiers were taken prisoner from the Vyazma and Bryansk pocket in October 1941

6 November 1941
STALIN'S RALLYING CRY
Speaking at a parade in Red Square commemorating the anniversary of the October 1917 Bolshevik Revolution, Stalin called on the Allies to open a second front and exhorted his people to defend "Mother Russia". He predicted the liberation of occupied territories and "doom" for Germany, which he claimed had already lost 4.5 million men.

△ **Soviet poster showing Mother Russia** holding the Red Army Oath of Allegiance

30 October 1941
VON MANSTEIN BESIEGES SEVASTOPOL
The German and Romanian troops of Field Marshal von Manstein's 11th Army attacked Sevastopol after capturing the rest of Crimea. They were beaten back in two days of bitter fighting by 20,000 Soviet marines under Admiral Oktyabrsky, crushing German hopes of a rapid victory. The Russians reinforced their defences, and von Manstein settled in for a prolonged siege.

△ **Romanian troops** during the siege of Sevastopol (hand-coloured image)

1941

24 OCTOBER

24 October German forces advance in Ukraine, capturing Kharkiv on 24 and Kramatorsk on 27 October

5 November Admiral Yamamoto issues Top Secret Operations Order No. 1, the plan for Japan's entry into the war.

27 October Roosevelt denounces German attacks on US shipping and an alleged Nazi scheme to carve up Latin America

9 November The Germans capture Tikhvin, cutting off the last overland supply route to besieged Leningrad

1 November–5 December 1941
GERMANY FALTERS AT MOSCOW
Delays to Barbarossa left the Germans equipped with light summer kit and vulnerable to the approaching winter. They captured Tula to the south of Moscow on 1 November, but the offensive was stalling. A last push reached Klin, north of the capital, on 23 November and tanks reached Khimki train station, just 20 km (12 miles) from central Moscow, before plummeting temperatures and Soviet reinforcements forced the Germans to withdraw.

◁ **German tanks and infantry** advancing on Klin in December 1941

The lowest temperature recorded by German troops near Moscow was -40°C (-40°F), on 27 November 1941

18 November 1941
THE ALLIES LAUNCH OPERATION CRUSADER

In an offensive to relieve Tobruk, the British 8th Army initially made good progress. Rommel soon fought back. He foiled an attempted breakout by the Tobruk garrison on 20 November, decimated the 5th South African Brigade on 24 November at Sidi Rezegh, and sent forces to the Egyptian border to attack the Allied rear. Even so, the 2nd New Zealand Division relieved Tobruk on 27 November. By then, Rommel was short of fuel and operational tanks.

▷ **Infantry of the 2nd New Zealand Division** with a German panzer crew, captured driving a commandeered British tank

13 November *U-81* **torpedoes and sinks HMS** *Ark Royal*, a British aircraft carrier, 40 km (25 miles) east of Gibraltar

16 November German forces take Kerch, leaving Sevastopol as the only Soviet stronghold in Crimea

21 November German forces enter Rostov-on-Don, opening the way for further advances into the Caucasus

1941
25 NOVEMBER

25 November Rommel sends a raiding force into Egypt to attack the Allies from the rear

12 November 1941
ITALY DEFEATED IN ETHIOPIA

In the concluding stage of the East African campaign, Allied troops surrounded Gondar in Ethiopia, having broken through Wolchefit Pass after a three-month siege. The Italian commander, General Nasi, defended strongly, but after outlying forts fell and Allied air strikes increased, he surrendered the 23,000-strong garrison on 27 November. The British had suffered just 220 casualties.

"If they want a war of extermination, they will get it."

JOSEPH STALIN, "MOTHER RUSSIA" SPEECH ON THE 24TH ANNIVERSARY OF THE REVOLUTION, 6 NOVEMBER 1941

◁ **Italian troops captured at Wolchefit Pass** near Gondar, Ethiopia, marching past an Allied guard of honour in September 1941

7 December 1941
JAPAN GOES ON THE ATTACK

On 7 December, the Japanese High Command initiated "Plan Z". It launched simultaneous attacks on the Dutch East Indies, British Malaya, and Singapore, and a surgical strike against the US Pacific Fleet base at Pearl Harbor, Hawaii, designed to neutralize American naval superiority. Despite some intelligence warnings, the Japanese fleet and its 20 warships, including six carriers, went undetected as it left the Kurile Islands and reached Hawaii.

◁ **Thick smoke from the burning USS** *West Virginia* **and USS** *Tennessee* during the Japanese attack on Pearl Harbor (hand-coloured image)

1941

26 NOVEMBER

26 November A counteroffensive by Marshal Timoshenko in Ukraine advances 100 km (60 miles), threatening German control of Rostov

8 December Japanese forces land in Thailand, at Singora and Pattani, and at Kota Bharu in Malaya, taking the airfield there on 10 December

8 December The UK and the USA declare war on Japan following the Japanese attacks on them the previous day

8 December Japanese aircraft bomb Singapore; the Japanese 38th Division lands at Hong Kong

7 December 1941
PEARL HARBOR

On the morning of 7 December, the Japanese launched two waves of air attacks on the island of Oahu, Hawaii, targeting both the US fleet at Pearl Harbor (but not the submarine base) and the oil tanks, dockyards, and air and naval bases on the island. The first wave of more than 170 Japanese bombers and accompanying fighters reached Pearl Harbor at 7:50am, having been sent up by Vice Admiral Naqumo 90 minutes earlier. The second wave, including 134 bombers, struck around 8:40am. In total, more than 2,400 US service personnel and civilians were killed in the attacks; 188 aircraft were destroyed and a further 159 damaged.

Key
- ■ Oil tanks
- ● US ships at anchor
- ● Destroyed or sunk ships
- ● Damaged ships
- ⚓ Submarine base
- → First-wave attacks
- → Second-wave attacks

Attack on the fleet
Among the damaged or destroyed ships were all eight of the Pacific Fleet's battleships. All but the USS *Arizona* were later returned to service. The fleet's aircraft carriers were on patrol, escaping the attack.

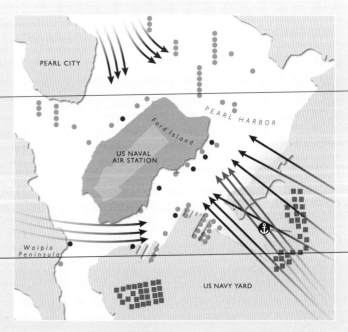

PEARL CITY

PEARL HARBOR

Ford Island

US NAVAL AIR STATION

Waipio Peninsula

US NAVY YARD

△ **A British soldier inspecting** German and Italian signs near Tobruk, December 1941

> "Yesterday, December 7, 1941 – a date which will live in infamy – the United States of America was suddenly and deliberately attacked by naval and air forces of the Empire of Japan."

FRANKLIN D. ROOSEVELT, SPEECH ON PEARL HARBOR AND DECLARATION OF WAR, 8 DECEMBER 1941

8 December 1941
ROMMEL RETREATS
Rommel withdrew his troops from Tobruk's eastern perimeter to attack the British around Bir el-Gobi. This assault failed, and part of the garrison linked up with the British 1st Tank Brigade and forced Rommel to withdraw.

9 December Japanese troops land on Tarawa in the Gilbert Islands and occupy Bangkok in Thailand

10 December Japanese aircraft sink HMS *Prince of Wales* and HMS *Repulse* 320 km (200 miles) east of Singapore

1941

10 DECEMBER

9 December Soviet forces restore the railway supply line to Leningrad, partially breaking the German siege of the city

◁ **Japanese propaganda poster** celebrating the invasion of the Philippines

8 December 1941
THE JAPANESE LAND ON THE PHILIPPINES
The Japanese began their invasion of the Philippines with a landing by naval infantry on Batan Island, off Luzon, securing the airfield there for use by their air force. Two days later, a small number of Japanese troops landed at Camiguin Island and Vigan and Aparri on northern Luzon; the main assault would not come for another two weeks.

△ **The ice road across Lake Ladoga** during the siege of Leningrad

10 December 1941
THE ICE ROAD TO LENINGRAD
Also known as the "Road of Life", the route was built over the frozen ice of Lake Ladoga and became Leningrad's lifeline. Trucks transported food and other goods – 350,000 tons in winter 1941–42 – into the city and brought more than 1.3 million civilian refugees back in return. The ice road was built again in winter 1942 and was in operation until Leningrad was relieved in January 1943.

1941

13 December 1941
COUNTEROFFENSIVE ON THE EASTERN FRONT

Soviet counteroffensive operations began on 5 December, as the German eastern advance stalled. From 6 December, Zhukov's West Front began attacking from the northeast and south of Moscow, putting increasing pressure on the Germans. Then, on 13 December, Timoshenko's Southwest Front struck the right flank of the German 2nd Army. A shaken German command began to make plans to retreat; the Soviet press trumpeted that the Germans had been repulsed from Moscow.

◁ **A Soviet poster** glorifying Stalin as a great military leader

Britain's Princess Elizabeth trained as a mechanic and driver with the ATS

11 December Germany and Italy declare war on the USA, and Congress reciprocates

16 December Japanese troops land in Borneo, at Sarawak and Brunei. The Allies set light to the island's oil fields

17 December The German and Romanian offensive to secure Sevastopol fails in the face of Soviet resistance

18 December 1941
HITLER'S "HALT ORDER"

Hitler was enraged when Walther von Brauchitsch, commander-in-chief of the Germany's army, ordered Army Group Centre to withdraw to more defensible lines west of Moscow. He countermanded the instruction, demanding that the German troops put up a "fanatical resistance" and refuse to retreat, even if surrounded. Disaster was avoided only because the local German leaders did not rigidly enforce the order.

▷ **German soldiers** at the Eastern Front, winter 1941

18 December 1941
BRITAIN EXTENDS CONSCRIPTION

With the demands of military service leaving many vital industries short of workers, the British Parliament passed a second National Service Act, introducing conscription for unmarried women and childless widows under the age of 30. The women could work in agriculture or industry, or join the armed forces. Among the units they could join were the Women's Land Army (*see p.53*) and the Auxiliary Territorial Service (ATS). By mid-1943, almost 90 per cent of single women were employed in war work.

◁ **ATS plotters working** at the 428 Battery, Coast Defence Artillery headquarters, 1942

19 December Hitler dismisses von Brauchitsch and takes personal command of military operations

23 December US troops begin withdrawing into the Bataan Peninsula on Luzon as the main Japanese landings take place

1941
23 DECEMBER

19 December The Japanese land at Davao on Mindanao in the Philippines to stop US reinforcements reaching Luzon

23 December Japanese forces capture Wake Island, providing Japan with a vital base in the Central Pacific

22 December 1941
THE FIRST WASHINGTON CONFERENCE

Roosevelt and Churchill met to discuss strategy following the USA's entry into the war. The Washington (or Arcadia) Conference established a Combined Chiefs of Staff in Washington and agreed a "Germany First" strategy, planning invasions of North Africa and northwest Europe for 1942–43.

▷ A **"Blood Chit"** issued to Flying Tiger pilots to identify them as allies of China

20 December 1941
THE FLYING TIGERS

Formed by Claire Lee Chenault, an American aviator in the service of Nationalist China, the American Volunteer Group (AVG), known as the Flying Tigers, used 100 donated Curtiss P-40 fighters flown by volunteer American pilots. Based at Kunming, between their first combat mission in December 1941 and July 1942, they downed 300 Japanese aircraft.

▷ **Roosevelt and Churchill** meeting the press at the Washington Conference

25 December 1941
HONG KONG FALLS TO THE JAPANESE

On 18 December, the Japanese landed in Hong Kong and cut the British defences in two by securing the Wong Nai Chung Gap in the middle of the island. They then captured the island's reservoirs, making resistance untenable. On 25 December the British governor, Sir Mark Aitchison Young, surrendered. The victorious Japanese troops perpetrated many atrocities, including bayonetting British troops in hospitals. Ten thousand British soldiers were captured in one of the country's worst military defeats.

◁ **Japanese soldiers cheering** their victory beside an enemy coastal artillery position, Hong Kong, December 1941

1941

24 DECEMBER

24 December The British 8th Army takes Benghazi, in Libya, as Rommel retreats from the Gazala line

29 December The Japanese capture Ipoh in Malaya and advance to Kuantan

2 January 1942 British and South African troops capture Bardia in Cyrenaica, east Libya, taking 8,000 prisoners

5 January The Japanese advance from landing points on the west coast of Malaya and take Kuala Lumpur on 12 January

1 January 1942
THE ALLIES UNITE

At the Washington Conference (*see p.129*), the USSR, Britain, France, and China signed the United Nations Declaration, with a further 22 nations adding their signatures the following day. In the declaration, the signatories pledged to devote all their resources to the defeat of the Axis, to not make separate peace treaties, and to acknowledge the common struggle to preserve human rights and justice. It became the basis for the United Nations Charter, created in 1945.

▷ **United Nations propaganda poster,** created by the United States Office of War Information

△ **A Japanese-issued** Philippines banknote

2 January 1942
JAPANESE FORCES OCCUPY MANILA IN THE PHILIPPINES

The Japanese advanced on Manila from two directions after landing along the Lingayen Gulf in central Luzon and the Lamon Gulf in the south on 22–23 December. US forces conducted delaying operations as they withdrew into the Bataan Peninsula, but they declared Manila an open city; the Japanese took it, and the neighbouring Cavite naval base, without resistance.

7 January 1942

THE BATTLE OF BATAAN BEGINS

On the 40-km-long (25-mile-long) Bataan Peninsula, 67,000 Filipino and 12,500 US troops began the defence of the last Allied position on Luzon. General Masaharu Homma expected a rapid Japanese victory, but the US commander, Douglas MacArthur, led a stubborn defence. Despite a Japanese breakthrough past the first line of defence on 9 January, the Allied forces finally surrendered only in April.

△ **Japanese artillery** position during the Battle of Bataan

1928–
LEE YONG SOO

Born in Korea, Lee was 16 when she was kidnapped by the Japanese and forced to become a "comfort woman" in Taiwan. Ostracized by her family after the war, she began campaigning in 1992 for recognition and compensation for the "comfort women".

10 January 1942 The Japanese invade the Dutch East Indies, landing on Tarakan island, off Borneo, and in the northern Celebes

17 January British forces recapture Halfaya Pass in North Africa, taking almost 6,000 Axis prisoners

1942

19 JANUARY

7 January Nationalist Chinese forces defeat the Japanese at the Battle of Changsha, in Henan province

19 January Soviet forces retake Mozhaisk, 110 km (70 miles) to the west of Moscow

1942–45

JAPAN'S "COMFORT WOMEN"

As Japanese forces advanced across the Pacific they coerced or forced women and girls into prostitution at military "comfort stations". Up to 200,000 women were taken. Most came from Korea, but there were also women from Indonesia, Taiwan, and the Philippines, alongside a few Dutch women. Brutalized by their captors and shamed, many of these women died by suicide, and the survivors suffered physical and psychological trauma. Postwar Japanese governments consistently refused to admit responsibility, although in 2015, Prime Minister Shinzo Abe, agreed to pay US$8 million in compensation to South Korea.

▷ Sculpture of "comfort women" at Sharing House, Gwangju, South Korea

Joseph Goebbels, seen here with German women in traditional dress, was head of Nazi Germany's Ministry of Public Enlightenment and Propaganda from 1933. He used a wide range of media to spread Nazi ideology, and particularly to cruelly dehumanize Jewish people.

1939-45
PROPAGANDA

Public support is key to success in a long conflict. In World War II, governments sought to persuade people that their cause was most just, their side morally superior, and their leaders wise and heroic, while reminding the audience of the perils of defeat. Various media were employed to carry such messages and to encourage patriotic behaviour, such as economizing on food. Most countries set up agencies to manage this messaging, or propaganda, such as the USA's Office of War Information (OWI), founded in 1942.

Racial and ideological overtones were often central to propaganda. Soviet propaganda stressed loyalty to Stalin and the motherland, while also vividly depicting Nazi atrocities. German propaganda demonized Jews as an existential threat to the German people, and the Allies frequently used racist tropes, particularly when depicting Japanese people.

Press, posters, and leaflets were essential channels for propaganda, as were the newer media of radio and cinema. Radio reached not only home, but also enemy, audiences. *Germany Calling*, for example, was an English-language programme broadcast to Britain by the Nazis. Cinema was a key propaganda tool in the USA, where content was checked by the OWI for its patriotism, and in Germany, where filmmakers such as Leni Riefenstahl became stars in their own right.

KEY MOMENTS

1941 **Hollywood goes to war**
The OWI worked closely with Hollywood to produce newsreels and films, often glorifying the Allied troops or demonizing the enemy (as in the film poster shown, *right*) to galvanize civilian and military audiences alike.

1941-45 **Airborne propaganda**
Propaganda leaflets were often loaded onto aircraft (*right*) for dropping over enemy troops in an attempt to demoralize them. They emphasized the danger and futility of war and sought to portray their leaders as uncaring and ineffective, as well as reminding soldiers of the comforts of home.

1945 **"Tokyo Rose" arrested**
Trapped in Japan when the USA entered the war, Iva Toguri (the American-born daughter of Japanese immigrants) became a host on a Japanese propaganda radio broadcast aimed at Allied servicemen, who nicknamed her "Tokyo Rose". After the war, she was found guilty of treason and imprisoned for six years.

20 January 1942
THE INVASION OF BURMA

After occupying airfields in Tenasserim in southern Burma as a base for air operations, the Japanese 55th Division began their main invasion of the country with a thrust west from Raheng in Thailand. Their objective was Moulmein, which would open the way to the Burmese capital, Rangoon. Advancing through the jungle, they outflanked the defending Indian 16th Brigade and forced them back into a perimeter around Moulmein at the river Salween.

◁ **Uniform of an Imperial Japanese Army officer** with jacket, service cap, military boots, puttees, trousers, and binoculars

440,000 Russians were evacuated from Leningrad on the Road of Life by April 1942

1942

20 JANUARY

22 January The Russians launch a mass evacuation from Leningrad along the Lake Ladoga ice road, known as the "Road of Life"

23–24 January In the Dutch East Indies, the Japanese land at Rabaul on New Britain and Kavieng on New Ireland, and at Balikpapan in the Celebes

22 January In a new offensive in North Africa, Rommel captures Agedabia, destroying 70 tanks of the British 1st Armoured Division

20 January 1942
THE WANNSEE CONFERENCE

Reinhard Heydrich gathered senior SS figures and Nazi bureaucrats in Berlin's Wannsee suburb to confirm the plan for "a final solution to the Jewish question". Heydrich had begun to oversee work on this in July 1941, but it was the Gestapo's head of Jewish Affairs, Adolf Eichmann, who devised the final plan. This called for the mass deportation of Jewish people to the east to be murdered in death camps. These death camps would operate alongside existing labour camps, where many Jews and other victims of the Nazi regime had already been killed (*see p.257*).

▷ **SS officer Reinhard Heydrich**

26 January 1942
US TROOPS IN NORTHERN IRELAND
As part of Operation Magnet, the plan for the build-up of US forces in the United Kingdom, the first contingent of 4,058 personnel, including 42 nurses, led by Major General Russell P. Hartle, disembarked at Belfast in Northern Ireland. Three further contingents arrived in the next four months, bringing the number of US troops based in Northern Ireland to more than 30,000. This provoked protest from Ireland's taoiseach, Eamonn de Valera, and Irish nationalists, who viewed the US forces as an occupation force.

◁ **American troops** and their pet dog in Northern Ireland, 1942

28 January Soviet forces under Marshal Timoshenko advance into Ukraine, taking Lozovo near Dnepropetrovsk

31 January The Japanese capture Moulmein in Burma as its garrison retreats across the river Salween in an attempt to protect Rangoon

1942

3 FEBRUARY

29 January 1942
ROMMEL RECAPTURES BENGHAZI
Rommel's forces, redesignated as Panzerarmee Afrika, advanced deeper into Cyrenaica in eastern Libya. Although the Italian high command refused to cooperate, halting at Mersa Brega, Rommel sent his panzers inland via Msus to outflank Benghazi and attack it from the east. The 4th Indian Division garrison withdrew, evading an attempted blockade by Rommel. The Germans took the city along with 1,000 prisoners and 300 military vehicles.

△ **Japanese armoured unit**, Malaya, 1942 (hand-coloured image)

△ **General Erwin Rommel** in the North African desert, 1942

30 January 1942
THE JAPANESE ADVANCE ON SINGAPORE
The Japanese completed their conquest of Malaya and were within 30 km (20 miles) of Singapore by 30 January. The British evacuated their forces across the causeway at Johore and then blew it up. With a garrison strength of 85,000 British and Commonwealth troops, Singapore's commander, Lieutenant General Arthur Percival, was confident he could defend Britain's last bastion in Southeast Asia against General Yamashita Tomoyuki and 35,000 Japanese soldiers.

5 February 1942

THE GERMANS STALL IN NORTH AFRICA

Between 28 January and 4 February, Rommel advanced nearly 400 km (249 miles) along the Libyan coast from Benghazi to Tmimi. However, the depleted British 8th Army was able to regroup and form a defensive line from Gazala to Bir Hakeim (an oasis held by the Free French). Rommel was by then critically short of fuel and hesitated to launch a direct assault, instead bringing his offensive to a halt.

◁ **The interior of Rommel's command vehicle,** used for military planning during the offensive of January–February 1942

1942

4 FEBRUARY

8 February The Japanese land on the west coast of Singapore Island and capture Tengah airfield

9 February The UK begins rationing soap – the first non-food item to be rationed. Each household is allowed 170 g (6 oz) a month

9 February In Burma, the Japanese cross the river Salween, threatening to outflank and surround the British 17th Division

11 February 1942

THE CHANNEL DASH

In Operation Cerberus, the German warships *Prinz Eugen*, *Scharnhorst*, and *Gneisenau* broke undetected out of Brest, their base since March 1941. British attacks with coastal artillery, motor torpedo boats, torpedo-carrying planes, and destroyers came too late to inflict much damage. The German ships escaped to berths in northern Germany, ready to counter a feared British invasion of Norway.

△ **The Grand Mufti and Rashid Ali in Berlin**

5 February 1942

ARAB NATIONALISTS IN EUROPE

Iraq's former leader, Rashid Ali al-Gaylani, and leading Muslim cleric Amin al-Husseini, the Grand Mufti of Jerusalem, arrived in Rome after visiting Berlin. Their trip was part of the Axis strategy to encourage anti-British sentiment in the Middle East and, if possible, to install pro-Axis regimes there.

▽ **The *Scharnhorst*** during the "Dash" through the English Channel

1892–1965
RASHID ALI AL-GAYLANI

Iraq's prime minister from March 1940, Arab nationalist al-Gaylani was deposed by the British in January 1941 for his pro-German sympathies. Restored after a pro-Nazi coup in April, he left Iraq when the British invaded in May, returning only in 1958.

15 February 1942
THE FALL OF SINGAPORE

Although 85,000 Allied troops were based in Singapore, its coastal defences were not designed to face a landward assault from Malaya. General Yamashita landed 35,000 troops in the west on 8–9 February, and by 13 February Japanese tanks were crossing the Johore causeway to Singapore Island. The Allied commander, Lieutenant General Arthur Percival, capitulated on 15 February. Japan took 85,000 military personnel prisoner in one of Britian's worst ever military defeats.

▷ **"For the King and Country – Singapore"**, propaganda poster

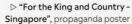

14 February Japanese paratroopers land in Sumatra, at Palembang, capturing one oil field and the airfield

19 February In the Battle of the Lombok Strait, an Allied naval squadron fails to prevent the Japanese landing on Bali

27 February In the Battle of the Java Sea, an Allied fleet fails to divert Japanese invasion fleets heading for Java

1942

27 FEBRUARY

18 February The RAF and RAAF withdraw their units from Sumatra to Java as the Japanese advance

23 February Russian forces capture Dorogobuzh, east of Smolensk, and reach the river Dnieper

19 February 1942
THE DARWIN RAID

In the first, and worst, Japanese air attack on mainland Australia, Kate bombers and Zero fighters struck in two waves against the unprepared northern port of Darwin. Sixteen ships in the harbour were sunk and 235 people were killed as the panicked civilian population fled. Although this was the precursor to more than 200 Japanese air raids by 1944, a feared Japanese invasion of northern Australia never materialized.

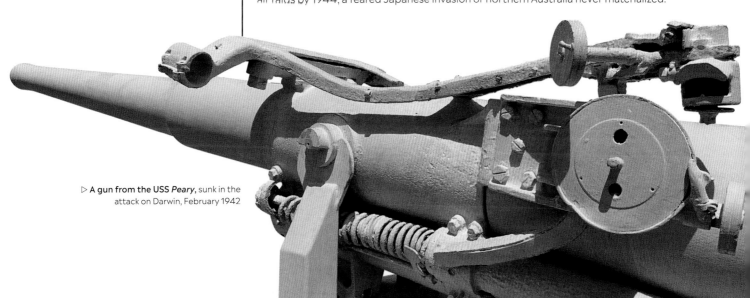

▷ **A gun from the USS *Peary*,** sunk in the attack on Darwin, February 1942

2 March 1942
JAPANESE AMERICANS ARE INTERNED

Fearing espionage by Japanese Americans, the US government announced the creation of two military zones in the western states from which people of Japanese ancestry were excluded. On 31 March, the newly established War Relocation Authority ordered 120,000 Japanese Americans to report to assembly centres, from where they were sent to internment camps around the USA. They were held until 1945, and their homes and businesses were often sold off.

◁ **The Granada War Relocation Center,** or Camp Amache, in Colorado, which held 7,300 Japanese Americans

1942

28 FEBRUARY

1 March The Soviets launch a counteroffensive in the Kerch Peninsula, Crimea but fail to advance

4 March The Japanese purge in Singapore ends; an estimated 25,000 Chinese men have been killed

6 March The Japanese occupy Batavia, in Java, after the Allied forces withdraw south to Bandung

28 February Japanese forces land at three places in northwest Java, in the Dutch East Indies

December 1941–June 1942
JAPANESE ADVANCES

The Japanese attack on Pearl Harbor in December 1941 was followed by a series of lightning land campaigns aimed at seizing the territories, oil, and other resources of the colonial powers. British-held Malaya, Singapore, and Hong Kong fell within weeks, and by February 1942, most of Burma and the Dutch East Indies had followed. After the collapse of the last US resistance in the Philippines, at Corregidor in May 1942, only southern New Guinea, northwest Burma, and some parts of China resisted Japan's advance.

Island conquests
A member of the Imperial Japanese Navy with a cache of bombs seized from the US Army on Wake Island, 1942.

△ **The Dutch surrender** to the Japanese at Kalidjata military airfield, West Java, 1942

9 March 1942
THE ALLIES ON JAVA CAPITULATE

By the end of February 1942, the island of Java was among the last remaining Allied strongholds in Southeast Asia. It was defended by a 25,000-strong garrison, which struggled to contain Japanese advances through Surabaya in the east and towards Batavia. After piecemeal counterattacks failed, the Dutch commander, General ter Poorten, surrendered.

10 March 1942
ALLIED–CHINESE COOPERATION

Lieutenant General Joseph "Vinegar Joe" Stilwell of the US Army was appointed by Chiang Kai-shek to be chief of staff of China's Nationalist armies. Stilwell's attempts to reform the armies by removing incompetent officers, and his opposition to Chiang's defence-in-depth strategy and insistence on sharing military aid with Communist units, eventually led to his recall in 1944.

△ Chiang Kai-shek and his wife, Soong Mei-Ling, with Joseph Stilwell

9 March In Burma, the Japanese cut the road at Taukkyan, north of Rangoon, blocking the line of retreat for British forces

14 March Hitler orders *Terrorangriffe* ("terror attacks") against provincial British cities and towns

1942

22 MARCH

△ **The burning docks** and oil refineries of Rangoon

8 March 1942
RANGOON FALLS TO THE JAPANESE

A British defeat at the river Sittang on 21–22 February had left the Burmese capital, Rangoon, fatally exposed. As Japanese spearheads approached the city, the Allies destroyed its oil facilities and evacuated north. The Japanese Army and its local ally, the Burma Independence Army, entered Rangoon unopposed, before advancing north towards the Indian frontier.

◁ **General Douglas MacArthur**, c. 1942

17 March 1942
GENERAL MACARTHUR TAKES CHARGE

Having escaped from Corregidor, in the Philippines, General Douglas MacArthur arrived in Australia, where he was nominated commander of the Allied forces in the Southwest Pacific. His command was formally instituted on 18 April. His immediate priorities were the defence of Australia and halting Japan's advances in the Philippines, New Guinea, and the Solomon Islands.

23 March 1942
THE ATLANTIC WALL

Hitler's Directive No. 40 called for the building of defensive fortifications along the coastline of occupied Belgium, the Netherlands, and France. *Festungen* ("fortress cities") were to be created at key ports such as Cherbourg, Antwerp, and Brest, and the coast defended by hundreds of gun batteries, a network of 15,000 concrete bunkers, and mines and anti-tank obstacles. The defences were built by 280,000 workers – many of them forced labourers – and were only just completed by the time the Allies invaded in June 1944.

◁ Atlantic Wall gun emplacement,
France, c. 1942 (hand-coloured image)

1942

23 MARCH

28 March A raid by 234 Allied bombers largely destroys the historic Baltic town of Lübeck

5 April A Japanese airstrike destroys 27 British aircraft at Colombo, Ceylon (now Sri Lanka), but the Allied Indian Ocean Fleet is not in port

6 April Japanese troops land on Bougainville in the Solomon Islands and Lorengau in the Admiralty Islands

27/28 March 1942
THE SAINT-NAZAIRE RAID

In a daring attack, Britain's HMS *Campbeltown* rammed the dock gates at Saint-Nazaire, on the river Loire, while a party of commandos set delayed-action torpedoes inside the dry dock – the only one large enough to service the German battleship *Tirpitz*. The high explosives with which *Campbeltown* was packed detonated hours later, killing almost 450 German soldiers who had boarded the ship. The torpedoes were set off the next day, putting the dock out of service for the rest of the war.

▷ HMS *Campbeltown* wedged
in Saint-Nazaire's dock gates
before it exploded

9 April 1942
THE US ARMY ON BATAAN CAPITULATES

A series of attacks by Japan's General Masaharu Homma's 14th Army had failed to dislodge the American and Filipino troops on the Bataan Peninsula. However, an offensive by reinforced Japanese force on 3 April finally saw the Allied defensive lines collapse. In the largest surrender in US military history, 75,000 American and Filipino troops were taken; at least 6,000 of them were executed by their captors in the ensuing Bataan Death March (*p.225*).

◁ **American and Filipino troops** surrendering to the Japanese during the fall of Bataan

1896–1993
JAMES DOOLITTLE

Aviation pioneer Doolittle rose from test pilot to general in the USAAF. Expecting to be court-martialled for losing his aircraft in the April 1942 raid on Japan, he was instead awarded the Congressional Medal of Honor and later led the US 8th Air Force.

16 April William Slim's Burma Corps destroys the Yenangyaung oil fields to stop them falling into Japanese hands

23 April The Luftwaffe launches the "Baedeker raids", reprisal attacks on the English cathedral cities of Exeter, Bath, Norwich, York, and Canterbury

1942

23 APRIL

◁ **George Cross medal**

15 April 1942
MALTA RECEIVES THE GEORGE CROSS

The island of Malta was awarded the George Cross, Britain's highest civilian award for gallantry, for having endured more than 3,000 German air raids since June 1940. Field Marshal John Gort presented the award to Sir George Borg, Malta's chief justice, in Valletta's ruined Palace Square.

18 April 1942
THE DOOLITTLE RAID

Sixteen US B-52 bombers commanded by Lieutenant Colonel "Jimmy" Doolittle launched a surprise raid against targets in Tokyo, Yokohama, Osaka, and Kobe. Although the raid caused only minor damage, sinking several patrol boats and killing 50 people, the attack demonstrated the vulnerability of Japan's home islands and severely dented morale. Fifteen of the raiding planes crashed or ditched in China; the remaining plane landed in the USSR, where its crew was detained.

▷ **B-52 bombers on the flight deck** of the US aircraft carrier *Hornet* just before their raid on Tokyo, April 1942

26 April 1942
TOTAL POWER IN GERMANY

Although most constitutional guarantees, such as the rights to assembly and free speech, had been suspended following the Reichstag Fire in February 1933 (*see p.31*), the Reichstag (German parliament) still – in theory – retained ultimate power in the country. On 26 April 1942, the body in effect abolished itself by appointing Hitler chief executive, legislator, and judge of the German nation, with the authority to make laws and all administrative decisions, and to mete out punishments at will.

◁ **Hitler at the Reichstag,**
26 April 1942

1942

24 APRIL

24 April The Japanese capture Taunggyi, in Burma, but lose it to Chinese forces the next day

29 April In Burma, the Japanese seize Lashio and sever the Burma Road (a vital supply route) as the Chinese withdraw from the Shan States

29 April Hitler and Mussolini meet near Salzburg to discuss war strategy, including sending Italian troops to the Eastern Front and a planned invasion of Malta

30 April Britain's Royal Navy establishes a secret meteorological and monitoring station on the remote Atlantic island of Tristan da Cunha

"Destiny has chosen me to lead the German nation in such a great period."

ADOLF HITLER, SPEECH TO THE REICHSTAG, 26 APRIL 1942

2 May 1942
MANDALAY FALLS

Advancing further into northwest Burma, General Iida Shojiro's Japanese 15th Army captured Mandalay, already devastated by a large-scale air raid on 3 April. The Japanese also took Monywa, on the river Chindwin, 80 km (50 miles) to the west, capturing the British 1st Burma Division's headquarters and threatening to cut off the remaining British forces' routes of retreat towards India.

▷ **The Japanese entering Mandalay,** from an Italian newspaper illustration

6 May 1942
THE JAPANESE TAKE CORREGIDOR

Further waves of Japanese infantry sent to reinforce the initial landing on Corregidor captured the key defensive point of Battery Denver. The US commander, General Wainwright, committed his reserves, but they failed to dislodge the attackers. With Japanese tanks beginning to land, Wainwright was forced to surrender both Corregidor and the remaining US and Filipino forces in the Philippines.

△ **Japanese soldiers** pull down the American flag after their capture of Corregidor

◁ **Vichy regime propaganda poster** denouncing the Allied invasion of Madagascar

5 May 1942
OPERATION IRONCLAD

Fearing that Vichy-French-controlled Madagascar might become a base for Japanese submarines, the Allies invaded. Their aim was to capture the harbour and airfield at Diego Suarez, in the north of the island. Allied Force 121 landed to the west of Diego Suarez on 5 May and advanced from the rear to capture the port in two days. Vichy resistance in Madagascar continued until November.

5 May Japanese troops land on Corregidor under the cover of an artillery bombardment and establish a beachhead

1942

7 MAY

△ **US naval personnel abanconing** the USS *Lexington* during the bactle

4–8 May 1942
THE BATTLE OF THE CORAL SEA

Alerted by deciphered Japanese transmissions, the US carriers *Lexington* and *Yorktown* moved to cut off a planned Japanese invasion of New Guinea. They unexpectedly encountered two Japanese aircraft carriers in the Coral Sea on 7 May, sparking the first ever carrier-to-carrier naval battle. The Japanese sank the *Lexington* but also lost one of their own carriers and suffered severe damage to another, among other losses, and were forced to cancel the invasion.

Seven Japanese warships were sunk at the Battle of the Coral Sea

1885–1966
CHESTER NIMITZ
Appointed commander-in-chief of the US Pacific Fleet after Pearl Harbor, Nimitz led it to victory at the battles of the Coral Sea and Midway in May/June 1942. He was aboard the USS *Missouri* to witness Japan's official surrender in September 1945.

Just 5.1 per cent of recruits to the Women's Army Corps were Black

▽ **German artillery gun** at the Eastern Front, May 1942

12–28 May 1942
THE SECOND BATTLE OF KHARKIV

Sending massive airstrikes against the Soviets, the Germans stalled an advance by Marshal Timoshenko's Southwestern Front towards Kharkiv. The German 6th Army and 1st Panzer Army then conducted a pincer counterattack, cutting off three Soviet armies by 22 May. In six days of relentless bombardment, the entire 250,000-strong Soviet force either surrendered or were killed.

1942

8 May The Japanese capture Akyab, the last British-held port in Burma

11 May Crossing the border from Burma into China, the Japanese take Tengyueh, in China's Yunnan province

8 MAY

9 May In Operation Bowery, an Anglo-American naval force delivers 60 Spitfire aircraft to Malta, forcing the Axis to abandon daylight raids on the island

9 May 1942
THE BRITISH RETREAT FROM BURMA

After withdrawing west of the river Chindwin, the British and Indian forces in Burma continued their retreat. The monsoon rains broke, hindering the pursuing Japanese. On 15 May, most of the remains of Burma Corps crossed the frontier into Assam. They were joined there by General Joseph Stilwell and 20,000 Chinese troops who had been cut off by the Japanese. Regrouping near Imphal, the Allies faced a real threat that the Japanese might advance into India.

△ **Japanese troops** occupying oil fields in Yenangyaung, near Mandalay, Burma, May 1942

> "We got run out of Burma, and it is as humiliating as hell."

GENERAL JOSEPH STILWELL AT A PRESS CONFERENCE, 24 MAY 1942

14 May 1942

THE US ARMY OPENS TO WOMEN

The US Congress approved the formation of the Women's Army Auxiliary Corps (WAAC), the first branch of the US armed forces open to women. It was joined by WAVES, a naval service for women, in July. The first 565 recruits arrived at Fort Des Moines, Iowa, on 20 July 1942. They were the vanguard of 150,000 American women who served as mechanics, radio operators, drivers, nurses, and more in all theatres of the war, including overseas from July 1943.

◁ **Members of the US Army Women's Army Auxiliary Corps (WAAC)** modelling uniforms, 1942 (hand-coloured image)

17 May A German counteroffensive forces the Soviets to abandon their attacks aimed at Kharkiv and the Donbas region

21 May The Japanese land in Leyte Gulf in the next stage in their occupation of the Philippines

1942

21 MAY

21 May Operation Herkules, the planned German invasion of Malta, is postponed after Rommel insists troops earmarked for it are needed in North Africa

◁ **Memorial to the Defence of the Adzhimushkay Quarry,** a suburb of Kerch

1905–95
OVETA CULP HOBBY

Chief of the women's division of the War Department's Public Relations Bureau, Hobby became the first director of the WAAC in 1942. Promoted to colonel, she oversaw its expansion into a regular army unit, the Women's Army Corps, in 1943.

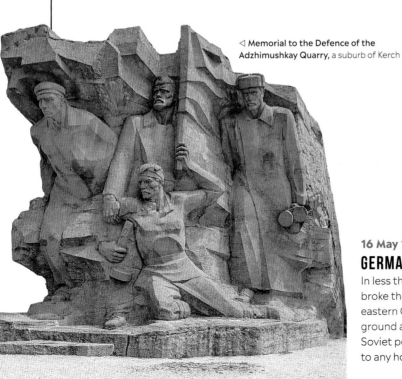

16 May 1942

GERMAN FORCES CAPTURE KERCH

In less than four hours on 9 May, Field Marshal von Manstein broke the Soviet defensive lines on the Kerch Peninsula, in eastern Crimea. Massive airstrikes, artillery bombardment, ground assaults, and amphibious landings overwhelmed the Soviet positions. Kerch itself fell a week later, putting an end to any hope of relieving the German siege of Sevastopol.

1942-45
THE US MILITARY

Over the course of the war, more than a million Black people were drafted into the US armed forces – forming around 10 per cent of its personnel. At that time, the US military was segregated: Black soldiers had separate units, training facilities, and accommodation. Black units included the Tuskegee Airmen (so called because they trained at the Tuskegee Army Airfield in Alabama, *see p.108*) and the 761st Tank Battalion, known as the "Black Panthers", both of which served with distinction in Europe. However, Black soldiers more often served in support roles, as mechanics and drivers, for example, or as stewards in the navy. Some 6,500 Black women also served in the US Army, for example in the 6888th Central Postal Directory Battalion, which managed postal services to soldiers in Europe (*see p.264*). Being stationed abroad gave many African Americans an insight into a life free of segregation that strengthened their determination to end discrimination and helped drive the postwar civil rights movement.

Other groups also served, including more than 500,000 Latinos, who were not placed in segregated units. Nor were the Native American recruits, many of whom worked as "code talkers" (*see p.84*), playing a vital role in the war. Another vital role was played by the 6,300 indigenous Alaskans who served in a home guard that helped secure supply routes to the USSR.

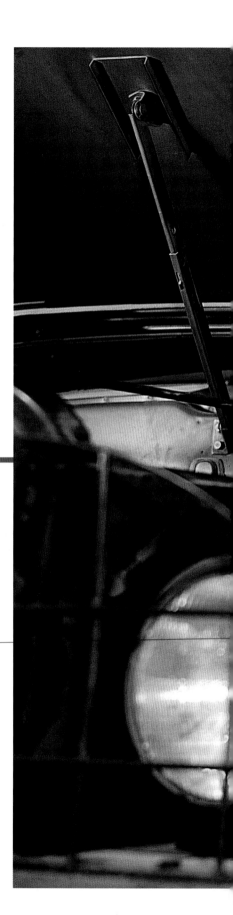

KEY MOMENTS

1942 **The Double V Campaign**
The African-American *Pittsburgh Courier* launched the "Double V" campaign to highlight that Black Americans were denied civil rights despite fighting for their country. It called for victory in the fight for democracy both overseas and at home.

1943 **America's *Nisei* soldiers**
More than 33,000 Japanese Americans volunteered for the US armed forces. Known as *Nisei* ("second generation"), they served largely in segregated units and saw the most action in Italy and France, suffering high casualties but becoming famed for their valour.

1944 **Native Americans**
Some 45,000 Native Americans enlisted, many of them leaving reservations and rural areas for the first time. Among them were more than 800 women, who served in auxiliary roles in the military. Like the Latinos, they did not fight in segregated units, but served alongside white Americans.

An African-American mechanic working on a truck at Fort Knox, 1942. In the early years of the war, 80 per cent of Black GIs were in the service forces, carrying out transport, repair, and maintenance work that helped keep the US war machine running.

30 May 1942
THOUSAND-BOMBER RAIDS BEGIN

The RAF launched a mass attack, involving 1,047 bombers, on the German city of Cologne. The planners employed a new tactic, the bomber stream, in which all planes flew the same route in various height bands to minimize exposure to German night-fighters and other countermeasures. The raid, in which 41 aircraft were lost, destroyed 13,000 buildings, devastating much of Cologne's centre.

▷ **The aftermath of the thousand-bomber raid** against Cologne, May 1942

1942

22 MAY

22 May **Mexico declares war** on Germany, Italy, and Japan following German submarine attacks on its shipping

26 May **The UK and the USSR sign** a Mutual Assistance Agreement, a military and political pact intended to last 20 years

1 June **A second thousand-bomber raid** targets Essen in the Ruhr industrial region; heavy cloud means few targets are hit

26 May 1942
OPERATION VENEZIA

Rommel outflanked the British at Bir Hakeim, Libya, while they waited for their depleted lines to be resupplied. He aimed to drive round the Gazala Line towards Tobruk. By 13 June, he had defeated the main British tank force, sparking an Allied retreat to the Egyptian border.

1884–1943
ISOROKU YAMAMOTO

Commander-in-chief of the Japanese Combined Fleet from 1939 and a great champion of carrier warfare, Yamamoto lost much of his carrier fleet at Midway in 1942, denting Japan's Pacific ambitions.

△ Heydrich's body lying in state watched over by an SS guard of honour

27 May 1942
THE ASSASSINATION OF HEYDRICH

In an operation code-named "Anthropoid", two Czech resistance agents – Jozef Gabcik and Jan Kubis – trained by the British Special Operations Executive, assassinated Reinhard Heydrich, governor of Bohemia–Moravia and chief of the Reich Security Main Office. As Heydrich travelled to Prague Castle, they threw a bomb at his car. Seriously wounded, Heydrich died eight days later.

△ **US propaganda poster** illustrating the Battle of Midway

4–7 June 1942
THE BATTLE OF MIDWAY

US intelligence detected a Japanese plan to attack the strategically important atoll of Midway (part of the Hawaiian chain). Aeroplanes from four Japanese carriers struck a blow against the US base on the morning of 4 June, but the ships were then attacked by torpedo bombers and dive bombers from two US carrier groups. The Japanese carriers *Soryu*, *Kaga*, and *Akagi* were soon crippled, and when the fourth carrier, *Hiryu*, was sunk on 5 June, Admiral Yamamoto ordered the Japanese fleet to withdraw.

7 June 1942
JAPANESE FORCES LAND IN THE ALEUTIAN ISLANDS

Around 500 Japanese naval infantry stormed ashore on Kiska, in the US-controlled Aleutian Islands; twice that number landed on neighbouring Attu. The virtually ungarrisoned islands could offer no resistance to the first invasion of the continental USA since 1812.

▷ **Japanese naval forces** raising the Imperial flag on Kiska in the Aleutian Islands, June 1942

5 June The Japanese fleet retreats from Midway towards the west with Admiral Spruance's task force in pursuit

7 June The USS *Yorktown* sinks after being hit by dive bombers and then torpedoed twice during the Battle of Midway

1942

7 JUNE

3 June The Japanese launch air raids on Dutch Harbor on Amaknak, in the Aleutian Islands

6 June Dive bombers from US carriers *Enterprise* and *Hornet* inflict severe damage on the retreating Japanese fleet, sinking the heavy cruiser *Mikuma* and damaging three other ships

4–7 June 1942
JAPAN'S PLAN AT MIDWAY

Intended to project Japanese naval power close to Hawaii, Admiral Yamamoto's "MI" plan for the attack on Midway involved a complicated feint north, with an attack on the Aleutian Islands by Admiral Hosogaya's 2nd Carrier Striking Force. Yamamoto hoped this would draw the US fleet north while a southern Carrier Striking Force and his own Fleet Main Body struck at Midway. Invasion troops were to follow from Saipan and Guam. However, Yamamoto's gamble merely divided the Japanese carrier force, making it easier to defeat.

The plan fails
Forewarned of the attack on Midway, the US fleet was directed to the island, where it met Yamamoto's depleted forces.

Key
- ➤ Japanese fleets
- ✗ Carrier-launched air attack
- ■ Japanese territory
- ➤ US fleets
- ✺ Air raid

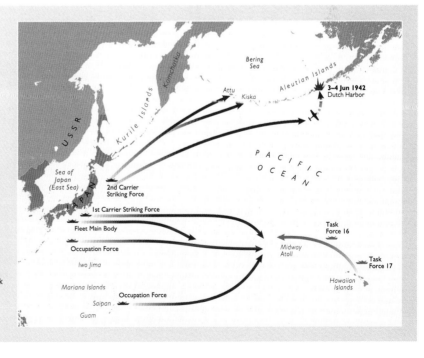

△ **Bronze statues** of the murdered children of Lidice

10 June 1942
THE LIDICE MASSACRE

As revenge for the assassination of Reinhard Heydrich (*see p.148*), German police and SS units murdered 173 Czech men and boys over the age of 15 at Lidice, a small town 20 km (12 miles) from Prague. The village was burned down and the women and children removed. Most of those children were taken to Chelmno extermination camp, where they were killed, and many of the women died in the camp at Ravensbrück.

10 June In Ukraine, Germany's 6th Army, under General Friedrich Paulus, advances on a broad front east of Kharkiv, capturing Kupiansk

17 June Nazi saboteurs land near Jacksonville, Florida, armed with explosives with which to disrupt US defence-related production; they are all arrested

1942

8 JUNE

15 June The German North African offensive reaches Sidi Rezegh, and the British withdraw east, leaving Tobruk isolated

18 June 1942 In Sevastopol, the German 11th Army breaks through Soviet defence lines to reach North Bay

21 June 1942
ROMMEL TAKES TOBRUK

Isolated and under siege from 18 June as the main British forces retreated to Egypt, Tobruk became vulnerable. Its protective minefields had been removed and its airfields lost to the advancing Germans. On 20 June, Rommel attacked from the southeast, piercing the perimeter and reaching the port. The next day, the Allied commander, Major General Klopper, surrendered his 33,000-strong garrison and thousands of tons of precious supplies.

▷ **Field Marshal Erwin Rommel** (*left*) with General von Bismarck during the siege of Tobruk, June 1942

25 June 1942
GENERAL AUCHINLECK TAKES COMMAND IN AFRICA

The relationship between General Neil Ritchie, commander of the British 8th Army, and General Claude Auchinleck, British commander-in-chief in the Middle East, became increasingly strained by the reverse at Gazala and the loss of Tobruk. Auchinleck took personal control of the 8th Army, but his retreat from Mersa Matruh to the El Alamein line and his reluctance to take the offensive against Rommel displeased Churchill, and in August, he in turn was replaced by General Harold Alexander.

▷ General Claude John Eyre Auchinleck

26 June 1942
ROMMEL IS PROMOTED TO FIELD MARSHAL

Formerly the head of the Führer's personal protection unit, and one of Hitler's favourites, Erwin Rommel was promoted to field marshal following his success as commander of Germany's Afrika Korps, and in particular his capture of Tobruk in June 1942. This was to be the summit of the career of the "Desert Fox". His last offensive in North Africa was in March 1943.

◁ Erwin Rommel's field marshal's baton (reproduction)

25 June A thousand-bomber raid on Bremen badly damages the Focke-Wulf aircraft factory

1942

26 JUNE

22 June Soviet ambassador Maxim Litvinov demands the immediate opening of a second front in Europe in a speech in New York

26 June 1942
THE BATTLE OF MERSA MATRUH

The British 8th Army was ordered to slow the German advance at Mersa Matruh, 240 km (150 miles) west of Alexandria. However, Rommel outmanoeuvred the British to reach Matruh on 26 June. In a disordered retreat, 6,000 British troops were captured as Auchinleck struggled to create a new defensive line at El Alamein.

△ A German fighter plane attacking Allied ground forces near Mersa Matruh, June 1942

"Soldiers of the Panzerarmee Afrika... we will not rest until we have shattered the last remnants of the British 8th Army."

SPEECH BY ERWIN ROMMEL , 21 JUNE 1941

4 July 1942
CONVOY PQ-17 DESTROYED

The Allied Arctic convoy PQ-17 sailed from Iceland for the USSR on 27 June, its 35 merchant ships guarded by a naval escort. On 4 July, the British Admiralty received intelligence that the German battleships *Tirpitz* and *Bismarck* were approaching and ordered the convoy to scatter. The escort fled, leaving the convoy an easy target for the German bombers and U-boats, which sank 24 vessels in one of the worst Allied naval disasters of the war.

◁ **Merchant ships and escorts** gather at Hvalfjörd, Iceland, before departing for Russia, 1942

1942

27 JUNE

29 June Rommel captures Mersa Matruh and 6,000 Allied POWs, together with large quantities of supplies

1 July The First Battle of El Alamein begins after Rommel crosses the Egyptian border

4 July The AVG Flying Tigers are incorporated into the USAAF as the 23rd Fighter Group

7 July The Germans attack Voronezh, east of Kursk, but the Soviet forces retreat intact southwards

△ German soldiers in Rostov, July 1942

4 July 1942
THE GERMANS CAPTURE SEVASTOPOL

After Kerch fell in May 1942, the 106,000 soldiers of the Soviet Coastal Army at Sevastopol presented the last barrier to German control of Crimea. Besieged since October 1941, the garrison had resisted waves of attacks. However, on 30 June, the Germans finally broke into the city. General Petrov, the Soviet commander, ordered an evacuation, but the Germans overran the last defensive line on 3 July and captured 90,000 Red Army soldiers.

▽ **German soldiers with a Soviet banner** after the capture of Sevastopol, July 1942

28 June 1942
CASE BLUE BEGINS

The Germans launched Fall Blau ("Case Blue"), driving some 1.5 million soldiers east of Kursk. Its objectives were to secure the Caucasus oil fields around Maikop and attack further north to seize Stalingrad. Stalin's belief that the Germans intended to make a direct assault on Moscow hampered the Soviet response.

1891–1980
KARL DÖNITZ

The architect of Germany's U-boat fleet, which he commanded from 1936, Dönitz was appointed commander-in-chief of Germany's navy in 1943. Dönitz succeeded Hitler as head of state after Germany's surrender in May 1945 until his arrest two weeks later.

1–27 July 1942
THE FIRST BATTLE OF EL ALAMEIN

Keen to exploit his recent successes and to seize Cairo and the Suez Canal before the 8th Army could recover, Rommel attacked the British defences at El Alamein in Egypt on 1 July. Sandstorms and resistance by the 18th Indian Infantry Brigade allowed General Auchinleck to regroup and attempt a counterattack from the Ruweisat Ridge the next day. The battle degenerated into a series of confused engagements, while Rommel's extended supply lines left him short of fuel. The battle had reached a stalemate by 30 July, but Rommel's failure to push on to Cairo meant that it was a strategic defeat for the Afrika Korps.

△ **A tropical visor cap** of the German Afrika Korps

23 July In Directive No. 45, Hitler orders simultaneous attacks on the Caucasus and Stalingrad, weakening the chances of success in either operation

26 July US general Dwight D. Eisenhower is made commander of Operation Torch (*see p.165*), the Allied invasion of North Africa

1942

26 JULY

21 July The Japanese land at Buna as they begin an advance towards Port Moresby in New Guinea

24 July The Germans capture Rostov, opening the way to the oil fields in the Caucasus

9 July 1942
THE OFFICE OF STRATEGIC SERVICES

The Office of Strategic Services (OSS), the forerunner of the CIA created by President Roosevelt in June, began its first major overseas operation. Carrying out the agency's remit to coordinate intelligence and espionage activities behind enemy lines, 21 SOE Agents of Unit 101 arrived in Nazira, Assam, close to the Burmese border. There, they recruited and trained local Kachin people to act as guides and conduct sabotage operations against the Japanese.

△ **A radio set** used by the American OSS

3,350 motor vehicles, 430 tanks, 210 bombers, and 99,316 tons of general cargo, including radar sets and ammunition, went down with the ships of PQ-17

8 August 1942
THE BATTLE OF SAVO ISLAND

Reacting to the US landing on Guadalcanal, Japan's Vice Admiral Gunichi Mikawa led a task force of five heavy cruisers and three other warships to destroy the US troop transports. He caught the Americans by surprise, penetrating their screen of cruisers and destroyers off Savo Island, north of Guadalcanal. The Japanese sank four Allied cruisers, but fearing air strikes, Mikawa withdrew without attacking the troop transports. The US commander, Admiral Kelly Turner, also pulled back, leaving the US troops on Guadalcanal isolated and without supplies.

▷ **The USS** *Quincy* before it was sunk during the Battle of Savo Island (hand-coloured image)

1942

27 JULY

30 July The Germans capture Proletarskaya, southwest of Stalingrad, on the river Don, cutting the Krasnodar–Stalingrad railway line

30 July Chinese Nationalist forces recapture Tsingtien, as a successful counterattack against the Japanese in eastern China continues

30 July In New Guinea, the Japanese capture Kokoda, 80 km (50 miles) south of Buna, seizing the only airfield between Buna and Port Moresby

7 August General Gott, the new commander of the British 8th Army, is killed in North Africa when his plane is shot down

1,170 Allied soldiers died and 2,190 were taken prisoner in the Dieppe Raid

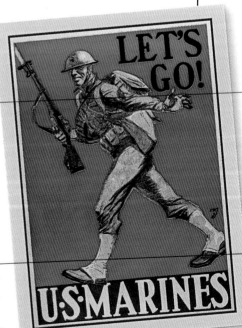

7 August 1942
THE ALLIES GO ON THE OFFENSIVE

To prevent the Japanese building an airstrip on Guadalcanal, in the Solomon Islands, the Allies launched Operation Watchtower. US Marines landed on Guadalcanal and on neighbouring Tulagi and Gavutu. The operation was a complete success on Guadalcanal, where 2,200 Japanese – mainly construction workers – fled inland. The garrisons on Tulagi and Gavutu, however, resisted fiercely for two days, and 95 per cent of the defenders were killed.

▷ **US propaganda poster** showing a rifle-bearing US Marine

9 August 1942
GERMAN FORCES TAKE MAIKOP'S OIL FIELDS

Pushing deeper into the Caucasus, von Kleist's 1st Panzer Army took Maikop and the surrounding oil fields – vital resources capable of producing 3 million tons of oil annually. However, as it retreated, the Red Army destroyed most of the oil installations and stocks of refined oil, which the Germans desperately needed to fuel their war effort.

◁ **Composer Dmitri Shostakovich,** whose Leningrad Symphony symbolized the city's resistance

▷ A German anti-tank unit advancing towards Maikop, with burning oil fields in the background

19 August–30 September 1942
FAILURE AT LENINGRAD

The Red Army began a third attempt to relieve Leningrad. The Leningrad Front quickly ran into German reinforcements brought from Crimea. An offensive by the Volkhov Front gained ground but was halted 6 km (4 miles) short of breaking the siege. The Red Army's actions, however, did forestall a planned German offensive, giving Leningrad breathing space.

9 August General Bernard Montgomery prepares to fly to Egypt to take command of the British 8th Army

16 August Carlson's Raiders, a submarine-borne force of US Marines, land on Makin, in the Gilbert Islands, to divert Japanese attention from Guadalcanal

1942
21 AUGUST

12 August At the Second Moscow Conference, Winston Churchill informs Stalin that there will be no second front in Europe until 1943

21 August At the Battle of Tenaru River, US Marines destroy a large contingent of Japanese reinforcements that had landed on Guadalcanal

19 August 1942
THE DIEPPE RAID

The Allies launched a commando-style attack, spearheaded by the 2nd Canadian Division, on the German-held port of Dieppe as a trial run for a wider European invasion. However, the invasion fleet was detected, intelligence about the strength of German positions was faulty, the tanks landed late, and German reinforcements swiftly pinned the Allied force down. Huge casualties incurred before the force was evacuated made the raid one of the Allies' most devastating failures.

◁ The aftermath of the **Dieppe Raid,** August 1942

1941–45

LATIN AMERICA AT WAR

While most Latin American countries remained neutral at the start of the conflict, the attack on Pearl Harbor shocked some into declaring war on the Axis powers. Brazil, in particular, proved a vital ally, sending an expeditionary force to Italy in 1944 and leasing several air bases and ports to the Allies. The huge air base at Natal, in northeast Brazil, became the launching point for planes flying across the Atlantic to join the Takoradi route in Africa – an air network carrying supplies from West Africa to the Middle East.

Mexican pilots

Mexico was the only Latin American nation other than Brazil to send troops to fight the Axis powers. Shown here (*right*) are pilots of Mexico's "Aztec Eagles" squadron, who fought in the Philippines in summer 1945.

1942

22 August German troops breach the Soviet lines at Vertyachi, north of Stalingrad, and raise the German flag on Mount Elbrus, the highest peak in the Caucasus

23 August In the Stalingrad terror raid, 600 German bombers drop 1,000 tons of high explosives on the city, devastating it and killing more than 40,000 civilians

22 AUGUST

23 August Japanese forces occupy the Micronesian island of Nauru, northeast of Australia

24 August In Operation Sinyavino, troops of the Soviet Volkhov Front almost manage to link up with Leningrad's defenders

◁ **President Getulio Vargas of Brazil** and President Roosevelt together in Brazil

▽ **Japanese bomb hitting the USS *Enterprise*** during the Battle of the Eastern Solomons, 24 August 1942

22 August 1942

BRAZIL DECLARES WAR

Brazil broke off diplomatic relations with the Axis powers in February 1942 and supplied vital war materials to the Allies. When attacks on Brazilian shipping reached a peak in August 1942, Brazil became the first South American country to declare war on Germany and Italy.

24 August 1942

THE BATTLE OF THE EASTERN SOLOMONS

A US scout plane spotted three Japanese carriers supporting the landing of reinforcements on Guadalcanal. The carriers reversed course, but a US air strike sank the *Ryujo*. Although Japanese planes crippled the US carrier *Enterprise*, the warships turned back and the landing craft also retreated after two of them were sunk.

30 August 1942

THE BATTLE OF ALAM HALFA

Rommel attempted to outflank the "Desert Rats" of the British 8th Army by capturing Alam Halfa Ridge, near El Alamein. Hampered by fuel shortages, he could only deploy a fraction of his 440 tanks. Pounded by air strikes and harassed by a New Zealand counterattack, the offensive, which Rommel halted on 4 September, achieved little.

▷ **Symbol of the British "Desert Rats"**

△ **Harro Schulze-Boysen (right)** with fellow Rote Kapelle members Marta Husemann and Günther Weisenborn

31 August 1942

SPY RING SMASHED

Gestapo agents arrested and later hanged Luftwaffe officer Harro Schulze-Boysen, a central member of the Rote Kapelle ("Red Chapel") resistance group and spy ring, who had provided information to the USSR about the Barbarossa invasion plans. Other resistance groups, including several run by Soviet agent Leopold Trepper, were also broken up.

26 August Japanese forces land at Milne Bay, southeast New Guinea, to establish a base for an attack on Port Moresby

1942

4 SEPTEMBER

30 August Germany annexes Luxembourg, which is already under its administration; 21 protesters are executed

▽ **German soldiers** prepare an attack in Stalingrad

3 September 1942

THE GERMANS CLOSE IN ON STALINGRAD

Hermann Hoth's 4th Panzer Army met Friedrich Paulus's 6th Army at Jablotchni on the outskirts of Stalingrad, cutting off the Soviet 62nd Army. A Red Army counterattack two days later failed to disrupt the German advance, and the fighting degenerated into urban warfare as the Soviets, reinforced by units hurriedly moved across the Volga, committed to a diehard defence. Casualties were extremely high on both sides.

> "We shall never surrender the city of our birth, every house of every street is to be transformed into an impregnable fortress."
>
> *STALINGRAD'S COMMUNIST PARTY COMMITTEE PROCLAMATION, 25 AUGUST 1942*

1900–82
VASILY IVANOVICH CHUIKOV

Demoted after his poor showing in the 1940 Finnish–Soviet War, Chuikov was rehabilitated as commander of the Soviet 62nd Army in the successful defence of Stalingrad in late 1942. He led it until the war's end, and received Berlin's surrender in May 1945.

▷ **Survivors from the *Laconia*** being rescued by a Vichy French cruiser

12 September 1942
THE LACONIA INCIDENT

The converted British liner *Laconia*, which was transporting 1,800 Italian POWs among its passengers, was sunk by the German submarine *U-156* off Ascension Island. Other U-boats began taking on survivors until attacks by an Allied Liberator bomber caused the rescue attempt to be called off. Admiral Dönitz subsequently issued the "Laconia Order", forbidding such rescue efforts. In total, 1,400 of the POWs and 130 crew lost their lives.

1942

5 SEPTEMBER

5 September Japanese fast destroyers, working at night as part of the "Tokyo Express", land reinforcements on Guadalcanal

5 September German forces capture Novorossisk, securing the northeast Black Sea and pushing aside resistance by the Soviet 47th Army

10 September Allied forces begin completing the occupation of Madagascar, which began in May; British and South African forces advance across the island

11 September On New Guinea, the Japanese advance is halted 50 km (30 miles) north of Port Moresby

13 September–19 November 1942
THE BATTLE OF STALINGRAD

By 13 September, the German 6th Army, supported by the 4th Panzer Army, had fought through Stalingrad's outskirts to trap the Soviet 62nd and 64th armies in the city's suburbs. After weeks of brutal hand-to-hand fighting though the streets, Vasily Chuikov's 62nd Army was left sheltering in the factory district alone, the 64th Army having retreated across the river Volga. Paulus's 6th Army pressed on with a massive assault that drove the remaining Soviet forces into a narrow strip of land by the river. There, Chuikov's soldiers clung on until the Red Army launched Operation Uranus on 19 November. This counterattack encircled Stalingrad, trapping the German 6th Army in the city.

Determined defence
The Soviet defenders at Stalingrad were gradually pressed into a narrow strip west of the Volga. There, they were able to hold out, with supplies brought by boat from the east bank and artillery support from the Stalingrad front.

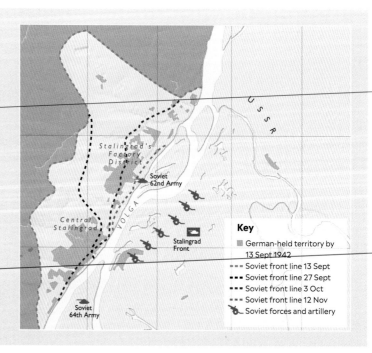

Key
- German-held territory by 13 Sept 1942
- --- Soviet front line 13 Sept
- --- Soviet front line 27 Sept
- --- Soviet front line 3 Oct
- --- Soviet front line 12 Nov
- Soviet forces and artillery

◁ **German soldiers of the 24th Panzer Division** in action during fighting for Stalingrad's southern station, 15 September 1942

13 September 1942

THE GERMANS' "FINAL OFFENSIVE" IN STALINGRAD

Commander of the German 6th Army at Stalingrad Friedrich Paulus unleashed a new attack intended to penetrate Stalingrad's centre and finally expel the Soviet garrison. However, the Germans were soon caught in desperate close-range combat, fighting the Soviets for every building and making little headway in the face of determined Soviet resistance. Paulus called off the attempt a week later.

14 September **Operation Agreement,** an Allied combined sea and land attack on Tobruk harbour, fails

21 September **British forces begin probing** Arakan, Burma, after a planned larger offensive is called off because of a lack of landing craft

1 October **Germany annexes Northern Slovenia,** which it has administered since April 1941

1942

1 OCTOBER

△ **The US Marine Raiders Monument** atop Bloody Ridge on Guadalcanal

13 September 1942

THE BATTLE OF BLOODY RIDGE

The Japanese attempted to expel the US Marines from Henderson Field, the air base they had constructed on Guadalcanal. Attacking across what came to be known as Bloody Ridge, General Kawaguchi's 35th Infantry Brigade engaged in two nights of bitter hand-to-hand fighting against Merritt Edson's 1st Raider Battalion. Finally repulsed, the Japanese retreated into Guadalcanal's interior, having lost more than 800 men.

27 September 1942

THE LIBERTY SHIPS

The Stephen Hopkins becomes the first "Liberty Ship" to sink a German vessel, though it itself sinks. Liberty ships were mass-produced vessels designed to fulfil the vast wartime need for transport and cargo ships; a total of 2,711 were built from 1941, many of them with the help of female construction workers. Some were built in a mere six weeks.

▽ **Construction worker Eastine Cowner** at work on a Liberty ship

3 October 1942

THE AGGREGAT ROCKET PROGRAMME

The first successful launch of an Aggregat 4 (A4) rocket was made from Peenemünde, on Germany's Baltic coast. Designed by Wernher von Braun, head of Germany's rocket programme, the A4 was propelled by liquid fuel and flew more than 190 km (120 miles). Renamed the V-2, the rocket could deliver a 1,000 kg (2,205 lb) high-explosive warhead.

▽ V-2 rocket

▽ **Sailor W.R. Martin pointing to the trophy flags** used as a scoreboard of enemy ships claimed sunk in the Battle of Cape Esperance, 11–12 October 1942

11 October 1942

THE BATTLE OF CAPE ESPERANCE

A US task force under Rear Admiral Norman Scott intercepted a Japanese reinforcement convoy northwest of Guadalcanal, sinking a Japanese cruiser and destroyer. With its commander, Aritomo Goto, mortally wounded, part of the Japanese force retreated. The other section landed the reinforcements, but lost two more destroyers to US planes. The battle aggravated Japanese supply problems on Guadalcanal.

18 October Hitler issues his "commando order", decreeing that all captured British commandos be summarily executed

1942

2 OCTOBER

8 October The Japanese rearguard makes a stand at Templeton's Crossing, New Guinea, delaying the Allied advance up the Kokoda Track

14 October 1942

THE GERMANS ADVANCE IN STALINGRAD

The Germans launched a second "final offensive" in Stalingrad. Preceded by a fierce artillery bombardment, the 14th Panzer Division pushed into the ruins of Volgograd Tractor Factory by the end of the day, but staunch resistance by the Siberian regiment defending the Red October Factory halted the German advance. Red October would resist 116 further attacks before the Germans called off the offensive in late October, frustrated by the lack of progress.

▷ **A platoon of German infantry** resting after capturing Volgograd Tractor Factory (hand-coloured image)

26 October 1942
THE BATTLE OF THE SANTA CRUZ ISLANDS

The Japanese Combined Fleet moved north of Guadalcanal, preparing to fly aircraft into Henderson Field airfield, which they expected their land offensive to capture. The subsequent battle, fought mainly between carrier-based planes, saw the defending US task force lose the carrier *Hornet*, while the Japanese suffered heavy damage to the carriers *Zuiho* and *Shokaku*. The Japanese failed in their primary objective of capturing the airfield to help alleviate their supply problems.

▷ A Japanese Type 99 shipboard bomber diving toward USS *Hornet* during the Battle of the Santa Cruz Islands, October 1942

19 October In Madagascar, King's African Rifle troops capture 800 Vichy French soldiers near Ivato

22 October The age of call-up for military service in the UK is reduced from 20 to 18

1942
31 OCTOBER

22 October Heavy raids on Italy's industrial heartland, the Turin–Milan–Genoa triangle, are carried out by 100 Lancaster bombers

23 October The Japanese launch a four-day offensive in a bid to take Guadalcanal's Henderson Field from US Marines

900 Allied guns took part in the preliminary bombardment at the Second Battle of El Alamein

23 October 1942
THE SECOND BATTLE OF EL ALAMEIN

General Bernard Montgomery launched Operation Lightfoot – the first stage of the pivotal battle that stopped Rommel at El Alamein, in Egypt, and forced his retreat to Tunisia. The battle began with a massive artillery attack on the north of the front line, and attacks by infantry and armoured divisions. It reached its peak on 2 November, when the Allies began Operation Supercharge (*see p. 164*).

◁ British Ordnance QF 25-pounder field gun

THE WAR IN THE BALANCE

In the closing months of 1942, the course of the war was in the balance; at many times, the Axis appeared to have the advantage. Despite their setback at Midway, the Japanese held swathes of territory that broadly fulfilled the demands of their original strategy; and on the Eastern Front, it seemed only a matter of time before Stalingrad fell to the hard-driving German Army. In North Africa, Axis forces had advanced deep into Egypt, with only one more push required before the fall of Cairo and the capture of the strategically vital Suez Canal, control of which provided access from the Mediterranean to the Indian Ocean, and thus a quick route to Asia and East Africa.

However, everything would change in the space of just a few months. The Germans suffered a disaster in the terrible winter conditions at Stalingrad. This was the first in a series of German defeats that would see them expelled from the Ukrainian heartland during 1943. In North Africa, the British victory in the Second Battle of El Alamein and the Allied Operation Torch landings in Morocco and Algeria in November 1942 left the Germans trapped between the desert and Allied forces advancing from east and west. This signalled the end of German hopes for an outright victory in the desert and was followed by the mass surrender of all Axis troops in North Africa. In the Pacific, the strategic initiative now lay firmly in the hands of the USA.

The Axis and Allied strategies

Whereas the Axis triumphs in the first part of the war had been characterized by their military brilliance, the Allies relied on superior numerical and material resources to grind down their opponents. And, reflecting their businesslike approach to the war, Allied leaders worked closely together, meeting regularly to resolve differences and develop a unified strategy. Members of the Axis, by contrast, operated independently, with no multi-combatant strategy in place. Despite the change in the balance of fortune between the two sides, the Axis powers would prove masters of defensive warfare, managing to hold off superior Allied forces far longer than anticipated.

Mastery of sea and air

The Allied strategy would culminate in the occupation of Germany and Japan, but this was contingent upon the domination of sea and air. In the war against Germany, an essential step was victory in the Battle of the Atlantic, which was achieved in mid-1943 with the defeat of the U-boat wolfpacks in the North Atlantic. This guaranteed British food and material supplies and made the Atlantic safe for the millions of US troops crossing over to Britain in preparation for the invasion of Europe. The ability of Allied shipyards to produce huge numbers of merchant and naval vessels was a decisive factor in Allied success. In the Atlantic, the steady flow of convoys was never interrupted by German U-boats, while in the Pacific, the might of the US Navy overwhelmed its Japanese opponents.

In the air, Britain mounted a nighttime strategic bombing offensive against Germany from as early as February 1942, intended to destroy its economic resources and undermine the will of its civilian population. Britain's RAF was joined by the US Army Air Force, which, in the summer of 1943, began to make its presence felt, flying in daylight from air bases in Britain and North Africa.

The invasion of Italy

The assault on Axis-held Europe began in earnest with the invasion of southern Italy in September 1943. Mussolini was deposed in a coup, and a new Italian government came to terms with the Allies. Furious at what it saw as betrayal by the Italians, Germany's reaction was swift and ruthless: its soldiers took over the country in a matter of days and introduced a defensive strategy that brought the Allied advance to a slow and painful crawl.

Most Anglo-American planners regarded the war in Italy as something of a sideshow, however. The main effort would come through a cross-Channel invasion of northern France. There, it was hoped, superior Allied resources at sea, in the air, and on land would be sufficient to defeat the Germans in open battle.

△ The 28th (Maori) Battalion

1 November 1942
THE MATANIKAU OFFENSIVE

US forces in Guadalcanal crossed the river Matanikau to attack Japanese troops on the island's northwestern coast. Despite inflicting heavy losses, the attackers withdrew 10 days later, when word arrived of Japanese reinforcements reaching the island.

△ **US Marines** crossing the Matanikau River

2 November 1942
OPERATION SUPERCHARGE

In the last phase of the Second Battle of El Alamein, British and New Zealand troops broke through the German lines, forcing Field Marshal Rommel to withdraw westward along the North African coast. Two New Zealand brigades, including the 28th (Maori) Battalion, led the attack.

5 November On the Eastern Front, Axis forces capture Alagir in the Caucasus; it is the southernmost town they will take in their invasion of the USSR

1942

1 NOVEMBER

1887–1976
BERNARD MONTGOMERY

Although a difficult and abrasive person, who often resented his US colleagues, "Monty" led the Allies to victories in North Africa, Italy, and France as one of Britain's most successful commanders.

4 November 1942–23 January 1943
ROMMEL'S RETREAT WESTWARD

The Allied forces of Operation Supercharge drove Rommel's forces from their positions around El Alamein on 4 November and pursued them along the Egyptian coast. The Axis troops initially planned to make a stand midway across Libya at the port town of El Agheila, but shortages of supplies, worsened by successful Allied attacks on Axis shipping, forced Rommel to continue the retreat. A second defensive line established at Wadi Zemzem also failed to hold, and Rommel withdrew to Tunisia.

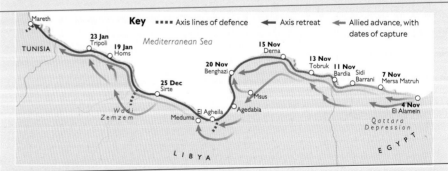

Escape along North Africa's Mediterranean coast
Within six days of the start of the retreat, Axis forces were crossing the Egyptian border into Libya. The pursuit continued westward, reaching the Tunisian frontier on 23 January 1943.

8 November 1942
OPERATION TORCH
Launching a campaign to win back all North Africa, Allied forces landed in Morocco and Algeria (then French colonies). There were three task forces – the Western, the Central, and the Eastern – which targeted Casablanca in Morocco, Oran in western Algeria, and the the city of Algiers, respectively. All three cities were in Allied hands within three days of the start of the operation.

◁ **Bombs being loaded onto the wing** of a Fairey Albacore torpedo bomber during Operation Torch

8 November French Resistance fighters stage a coup in Algiers to coincide with the Allied landings

10 November The Axis powers land troops in northeastern Tunisia to counter the Torch landings

10 November Casablanca falls to the Allies after putting up unexpected resistance

1942
11 NOVEMBER

10 November Oran surrenders to Operation Torch's Central Task Force after heavy fighting in the port

10 November Allied forces land unopposed at Bougie in eastern Algeria

> "This is not the end. It is not even the beginning of the end. But it is, perhaps, the end of the beginning."

WINSTON CHURCHILL, IN RESPONSE TO ALLIED PROGRESS IN NORTH AFRICA, 10 NOVEMBER 1942

▽ **Artillery in Marseille's** Place de la Major during the German occupation

11 November 1942
GERMAN FORCES OCCUPY VICHY FRANCE
In response to setbacks in North Africa, German forces took over the rest of France, until then nominally independent under the collaborationist Vichy regime, and disbanded its remaining military forces. The demarcation line separating "free" and occupied France disappeared, although day-to-day civil administration remained in the hands of a puppet ministry headed by Pierre Laval.

▷ **The Road to Victory!** A Soviet propaganda poster showing Russian troops, tanks, and aircraft advancing on the Stalingrad front

13 November 1942
THE NAVAL BATTLE OF GUADALCANAL

Japan sent a naval convoy in an attempt to land reinforcements on the island of Guadalcanal and retake the US-held Henderson Airfield. American warships and aircraft attacked the convoy and succeeded in sinking a heavy cruiser, two battleships, three destroyers, and most of the troop ships in a four-day battle. The encounter effectively ended Japanese attempts to win back control of Guadalcanal, swinging the Solomon Islands campaign in the USA's favour.

▷ **Killed at Guadalcanal,** Admiral Daniel Callaghan was posthumously awarded the Medal of Honor

19 November 1942
SOVIET FORCES ENCIRCLE STALINGRAD

Russian forces launched a pincer attack, code-named Uranus, aimed at encircling the Axis troops in and around Stalingrad. Deploying more than a million men, the Soviet offensive swept away two Romanian armies guarding the approaches to the city and, by 22 November, its two wings linked up, trapping 290,000 Axis troops within a ring of steel.

1942

12 NOVEMBER

12 November British paratroopers seize Bône near the Algerian–Tunisian border, pre-empting a German landing

14 November Changing sides, Admiral Darlan, Vichy France's military leader in North Africa, agrees to cooperate with the Allies

18 November Heavy fighting breaks out at Medjez el Bab as Allied forces from Bône meet Axis patrols moving out of Tunis and Bizerte

During its two-year siege, Malta endured more than 3,000 Axis bombing raids

1942–43
THE SIEGE OF STALINGRAD

The German 6th Army was trapped in the city in sub-zero temperatures. Many died of starvation or hypothermia as attempts to reach them failed.

19 November 1942 Soviet commander Zhukov bombards Stalingrad before overrunning the Romanian forces to the south of the city and completely encircling the 6th Army within.

22 November 1942 Hitler orders the 6th Army to remain in Stalingrad, incorrectly believing that the Luftwaffe can resupply the trapped Germans while they await reinforcements.

24 December 1942 With the German relief column in retreat, Germany's General Paulus orders the last horses in Stalingrad to be killed to provide Christmas dinner for his starving men.

27 November 1942
THE FRENCH NAVY IS SCUTTLED AT TOULON

In response to the German occupation of Vichy France, Admiral Gabriel Auphan, secretary of state for the French Navy, ordered the ships stationed at Toulon, the navy's principal base, to be scuttled to prevent them from falling into Axis hands. In all, 77 vessels were destroyed, including three battleships and seven cruisers.

▷ **Scuttled French ships** at Toulon, 27 November 1942 (hand-coloured image)

"SCUTTLE! SCUTTLE! SCUTTLE!"

MESSAGE SENT BY THE FRENCH FLAGSHIP, STRASBOURG, AS GERMAN TROOPS APPROACHED TOULON ON 27 NOVEMBER 1942

30 November Free French forces take control of the Indian Ocean island of Réunion from Vichy France

1942
30 NOVEMBER

23 November Russian troops destroy the Romanian 3rd Army outside Stalingrad

25 November In occupied Greece, British agents and Greek guerrillas blow up the Gorgopotamos railway bridge

26 November Colombia enters the war on the Allied side after a number of U-boat attacks on its shipping

△ **The damaged tanker** *Ohio* approaching the harbour in Malta

20 November 1942
THE SIEGE OF MALTA ENDS

With Axis air and naval forces in the Mediterranean theatre increasingly diverted to counter the Allied landings in Morocco and Algeria, a convoy of supply ships reached the island of Malta from the Egyptian port of Alexandria. Its arrival, virtually unscathed by Axis attacks, indicated that the two-year siege of Malta was over.

1896–1974
GEORGY KONSTANTINOVICH ZHUKOV
One of the USSR's greatest marshals, Zhukov played a key role in the major Soviet campaigns of World War II. After taking part in the defence of Leningrad, Moscow, and Stalingrad, he drove the Germans from Ukraine and Belorussia in 1943–44.

△ **A propaganda poster** showing Soviet troops advancing westward from Stalingrad

7 December 1942

THE COCKLESHELL HEROES

In Operation Frankton, British Royal Marines paddled by night in folding kayaks (the "Cockle" Mark II) up the Gironde estuary in southwest France to attack shipping around Bordeaux with limpet mines. Only two of the 10 men involved survived the raid.

△ **Commandos "walking"** their kayak into a river

16 December 1942

THE SOVIETS ATTACK ALONG THE DON

In response to the renewed German offensive near Stalingrad, Soviet forces launched a long-planned winter campaign intended to penetrate the German front line along the river Don to the southwest of the city. The aim was to retake Rostov, 450 km (280 miles) away near the mouth of the river, cutting off the Axis's southern front in the Caucasus.

22 December German forces start to withdraw from the Caucasus

1942

1 DECEMBER

13 December German forces under Erich von Manstein launch Operation Winter Storm, seeking to relieve the 6th Army in Stalingrad

24 December Vichy's military commander, Admiral Darlan, is shot dead in Algiers by a Resistance fighter who is himself executed two days later

17 December 1942

THE HOLOCAUST ACKNOWLEDGED

Responding to a report by the Polish government-in-exile, the Allied powers issued a Joint Declaration that was the first official statement to condemn the genocide of the Jews. The statement was read to Britain's House of Commons and printed on the front page of leading US newspapers.

▷ **Jewish prisoners arrive** at Auschwitz concentration camp, where around 1.1 million Jews were murdered

"The German authorities... are now carrying into effect Hitler's oft-repeated intention to exterminate the Jewish people in Europe."

FROM THE JOINT DECLARATION BY MEMBERS OF THE UNITED NATIONS, ISSUED ON BEHALF OF THE ALLIED POWERS, 17 DECEMBER 1942

31 December 1942
THE BATTLE OF THE BARENTS SEA
The northern sea lanes from Britain to Russia were key to the Allied war effort in the east. A German force of destroyers and heavy cruisers was sent to intercept convoy JW-51B, which consisted of 14 merchant ships carrying war materials to Murmansk. The Germans attacked in the Barents Sea but were repelled by Royal Navy warships and failed to inflict any significant damage.

◁ **HMS *Onslow*,** a Royal Navy destroyer involved in the Battle of the Barents Sea

28 December In East Africa, the governor of pro-Vichy French Somaliland surrenders to British and Free French forces

3 January 1943 On the Caucasus front, Russian forces enter Mozdok, held by German troops since the previous August

17 January In the north of Russia, Soviet forces recapture Velikiyi Luki, held by German troops for 17 months

1943

17 JANUARY

13–27 January Russian forces encircle and destroy the Hungarian 2nd Army near Svodoba, south of Voronezh

14–24 January 1943
CONFERENCE AT CASABLANCA
President Franklin D. Roosevelt and Prime Minister Winston Churchill met in Morocco, recently taken from Vichy French control, to discuss plans for the future conduct of the war. There, they agreed plans for an invasion of Italy, which would open a second front in Europe and relieve pressure on the USSR. They also approved the US Navy's "island-hopping" project (*see p.202*) for the war against Japan in the Pacific. On 24 January, the two leaders jointly endorsed a statement that demanded that the Axis powers surrender unconditionally.

▷ **President Roosevelt and Prime Minister Churchill** take questions from reporters during the Casablanca Conference

18 January 1943
THE WARSAW GHETTO FIGHTS BACK

Faced with a fresh round of deportations to concentration camps, Jews in the Warsaw ghetto took up arms for the first time against the German forces occupying the city. More than 1,000 resistance fighters were killed in the ensuing action, but they succeeded in delaying the deportations and reducing them in size.

◁ **Jewish civilians held at gunpoint** by German SS troops after being forced out of a bunker where they were sheltering during the Warsaw Ghetto Uprising (hand-coloured image)

1943

18 JANUARY

20 January Chile severs relations with Germany, Italy, and Japan

25 January Russian forces recapture the city of Voronezh, a key location guarding the northern approaches to Stalingrad

▷ **The first Allied armoured car** to enter Tripoli after the victory of the 8th Army

23 January 1943
TRIPOLI FALLS TO THE ALLIES

Driving westward out of Egypt into Libya, forces of the British 8th Army occupied Tripoli, Libya's capital, the morning after German troops had withdrawn to cross the border into southern Tunisia. From there, Rommel hoped to relieve pressure on Axis forces confronting the Allies in the north.

27 January 1943
US BOMBING RAIDS ON GERMANY BEGIN

Following agreements reached at the Casablanca Conference on the targeting of German military and industrial installations, the first all-American daylight bombing raid on Germany was launched. It focused on the naval base at Wilhelmshaven. In all, 55 bombers dropped 137 tons of explosives on warehouses and factories; the USA lost three aircraft in the raid.

▷ B-17 Flying Fortress

124485

A ★ DF

2 February 1943
RETREAT TO THE MARETH LINE

Retreating across the Libyan border, Rommel's troops entered Tunisia and reached the Mareth Line. This was a defensive position in the south of Tunisia originally created by the French in the 1930s to protect their forces against Italian forces in Libya. There, the Germans took a stand, opening a second front in the Tunisian campaign. They held their positions against the British 8th Army for seven weeks.

▷ **1943 contour map** of the Mareth Line in southern Tunisia

1890–1957
FRIEDRICH PAULUS
One of the planners of the invasion of Russia, Paulus led the German 6th Army to Stalingrad. Forced to surrender, he spent the rest of the war as a Soviet prisoner and became a vocal critic of the Nazi regime.

29 January President Roosevelt and Brazil's President Getulio Vargas issue a joint declaration of their determination to keep the Atlantic sea lanes open

3 February German radio officially announces the German defeat at Stalingrad

1943

3 FEBRUARY

28 January A new conscription law in Germany extends eligibility to men up to the age of 65

30 January Admiral Karl Dönitz is appointed commander-in-chief of the German Navy

2 February 1943
SURRENDER AT STALINGRAD

Faced with the prospect of annihilation, the last German troops in Stalingrad surrendered, ending a battle that had raged for more than five months. General Paulus, the Axis commander, had himself conceded defeat three days earlier, after Soviet forces succeeded in splitting his force into two main pockets of resistance. In all, some 91,000 sick, exhausted, and hungry men were taken prisoner by the Red Army.

◁ **Soviet medal** for the Defence of Stalingrad

"18,000 wounded without the slightest aid of bandages and medicines."

GERMAN COMMANDER FRIEDRICH PAULUS IN A RADIO REPORT TO HITLER, 24 JANUARY 1943

7 February 1943
RETREAT FROM GUADALCANAL

In a strategic move code-named Operation Ke, the last Japanese troops withdrew from Guadalcanal. In all, more than 10,000 men were moved from the island aboard destroyers from the country's 8th Fleet. The final troops left six months to the day after American forces had first arrived on the island. After the Japanese withdrawal, the US military used Guadalcanal as a major supply base for subsequent campaigns fought further up the Solomon Islands chain.

▷ **Japanese prisoners** in the Solomon Islands

1943

4 FEBRUARY

4 February Soviet forces land at the Black Sea port of Novorossiysk; they hold out at the port but fail to take the rest of the town

8 February Soviet forces regain Kursk after 15 months of German occupation

9 February A 48-hour working week is introduced by Roosevelt in US cities experiencing labour shortages

△ **Chindit fighters** crossing a river on their march into Burma, 1943

1903–44
ORDE WINGATE

After commanding the Gideon Force of guerrillas resisting the Italian occupation of Ethiopia, Wingate was transferred to Burma at the request of Winston Churchill. A year into the Chindit campaign, he was killed in a plane crash in northeast India.

8 February 1943
THE CHINDITS ENTER BURMA

Led by British Army brigadier Orde Wingate, British and Indian special forces and Gurkhas launched a guerrilla campaign against the Japanese in Burma. These special forces became known as Chindits, a corruption of *chinthe*, a Burmese mythical creature. Over the next two years until their disbandment, the Chindits were a thorn in the side of the occupying forces.

A quarter of a million German and Italian troops were taken prisoner in the Tunisian campaign

△ **General Jürgen von Arnim** speaking with soldiers

▷ **Medal awarded** to Heroes of the Soviet Union

14 February 1943
ROSTOV CHANGES HANDS

In February 1943, Soviet forces liberated the strategic port city and railway hub of Rostov-on-Don. Soviet access to the Sea of Azov and the Caucasus at the river Don's mouth was thereby restored. Red Army officer Ghukas Madoyan was made a Hero of the Soviet Union for his role in the city's recapture.

14–24 February 1943
OPERATION SPRING WIND

Seeking to win back the initiative from the Allied invaders in North Africa, four German battle groups under the command of von Arnim drove westward across central Tunisia. In a 10-day campaign, they captured Sbeitla and Sidi bou Zid, pushing the Allied front line back by more than 50 km (31 miles).

15–19 February Rommel's Afrika Korps attempts to link up with General Jürgen von Arnim's forces; it takes the Kasserine Pass, but its advance is halted by desert fighting

1943

16 FEBRUARY

10 February General Eisenhower's role as Supreme Commander of Allied Forces Headquarters (AFHQ) is extended across the Mediterranean to include the British 8th Army

16 February On the Eastern Front, Russian forces recapture the Ukrainian city of Kharkiv, which had been taken by German troops 16 months earlier

14 February–13 May 1943
VICTORY IN NORTH AFRICA: THE CAMPAIGN IN TUNISIA

The Tunisian campaign marked the final stage of the war in North Africa. Allied troops landed in Morocco and Algeria in November 1942 in Operation Torch (see p.165). They were countered by Axis forces ferried to northern Tunisia to reinforce Rommel's Afrika Korps as it retreated west along the coast after the Second Battle of El Alamein. Axis hopes, raised by the initial success of Operation Spring Wind (see above), were dashed by Allied counterstrikes, which culminated in the fall of Tunis in May 1943.

▷ **"Victors of the Mareth Line"**, 1943 (hand-coloured image)

> "His Majesty's enemies... have been completely eliminated from Egypt, Cyrenaica, Libya, and Tripolitania."

TELEGRAM MESSAGE FROM GENERAL ALEXANDER ON THE SITUATION IN NORTH AFRICA, FEBRUARY 1943

Armed resistance in Italy emerged soon after the German takeover in September 1943, although many people had previously opposed Italy's own Fascist leadership. Shown here is a group of Italian resistance fighters in Pistoia in 1944.

1939-45
RESISTANCE

The Axis occupation of much of Europe led to the rise of resistance movements, whose fighters were called partisans, across the continent. Their activities ranged from spreading propaganda, sabotage, and assassination to full-scale guerrilla attacks. Resistance members faced torture and execution if caught, and their actions often prompted broader reprisals against the local population, but their activities were vital in maintaining morale.

A large resistance movement emerged in Poland in September 1939, even before the country had officially fallen. In 1942, it was reorganized into the Home Army, which numbered up to 400,000 and launched many raids against German troops from bases in Poland's forests and marshes. Resistance to the Nazis in France was more fragmented, with several different cells and networks; moreover, tensions between communist and other groups hampered coordinated action. In contrast, the USSR closely controlled its partisans in occupied Soviet territory, linking their activities with those of the Red Army.

After the fall of France, the British government established the Special Operations Executive (SOE), with a brief to "set Europe ablaze" by assisting local resistance fighters and carrying out covert missions. The USA set up a similar espionage organization – the Office of Strategic Services (OSS).

KEY MOMENTS

1941-44 The Yugoslav Partisans
Josip Broz Tito, leader of the Communist Party of Yugoslavia, formed his Partisans in 1941. Fighting from their mountain bases, the Partisans continually harried Axis forces. In 1944, they joined the Red Army in Belgrade's liberation.

1940-43 Auschwitz infiltrated
Witold Pilecki, a member of the Polish resistance, allowed himself to be arrested and sent to Auschwitz in 1940. He smuggled out a series of messages from the camp in order to reveal the horrific conditions there, before escaping in 1943.

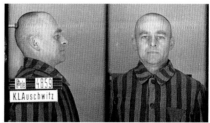

1945 The French Maquis fighters
Fleeing from the forced labour demanded of them by the Vichy regime in France, many young men sought refuge in the scrubland of southern France (the maquis). Banding together, they formed fighting groups; the name *maquisard* was later applied more broadly to the French resistance fighters.

△ **SS troops and a panzer** engaged in street fighting in Kharkiv, March 1943

20 February 1943

FIGHTBACK ON THE EASTERN FRONT

Having almost completely withdrawn from the Caucasus, German forces regrouped and launched a counteroffensive in eastern Ukraine. The aim was to win back Kharkiv and other cities between the rivers Donets and Dnieper, encircling the bulge in the front line created by recent Soviet advances.

> "Isn't it true that every honest German is ashamed of his government these days?"

FROM THE FIRST WHITE ROSE PAMPHLET, JUNE 1942

24 February Rommel withdraws German forces from central Tunisia back to the Mareth Line, allowing US troops to reoccupy the land around the Kasserine Pass

1943

17 FEBRUARY

21 February In Operation Cleanslate, US forces occupy the Russell Islands, beyond Guadalcanal's northern tip

5–6 March In the naval Battle of Blackett Strait, US warships destroy two Japanese vessels on a supply run in the Solomon Islands

2–4 March 1943

BATTLE OF THE BISMARCK SEA

In the South Pacific, US and Australian bombers, backed by fighter planes and torpedo boats, intercepted a convoy carrying troops from Rabaul, on New Britain, to reinforce the Japanese position in New Guinea. They sank all eight troop ships and four escorting destroyers, killing 2,900 men.

△ **Australian and US bombers** attack a Japanese battleship during the Battle of the Bismarck Sea

▽ **Sophie Scholl** (hand-coloured image)

18 February 1943

RESISTANCE INSIDE GERMANY

In Munich, Nazi authorities broke up the White Rose resistance group. Two of its leaders, Hans and Sophie Scholl, were arrested, then executed four days later. Other isolated anti-Nazi groups survived; one estimate suggests that the Gestapo arrested as many as 800,000 Germans for opposition activities during the war.

△ **A Lancaster bomber** in flight

6 March 1943

BOMBERS OVER THE RUHR

The Battle of the Ruhr – a strategic bombing campaign against Germany's industrial heartland – began with a 440-plane raid on the Krupp armament works at Essen. Over the next five months, Allied aircraft under the guidance of RAF Bomber Command attacked 21 cities in the region, including Duisburg, Mülheim, and Düsseldorf, inflicting critical damage on the Nazi war effort.

6 March In southern Tunisia, German forces unsuccessfully seek to seize the town of Medenine to protect the Mareth Line

1943

15 MARCH

15 March General Giraud restores representative government in French North Africa

15 March In eastern Ukraine, advancing German forces recapture Kharkiv four weeks after the city had been won back by Soviet forces

6 March 1943

CONFRONTATION ON THE NERETVA

In Yugoslavia, Case White, Germany's offensive against Tito's Partisan resistance fighters, failed in its main objective at the river Neretva. Having deceived his opponents by blowing up bridges across the stream and staging successful counterattacks against his pursuers, Tito changed course and made a strategic retreat across the river, using temporary spans improvised by his engineers.

◁ **Militiamen fighting** Tito's Partisans in the Bosnian mountains in Yugoslavia

16–19 March 1943
CRISIS IN THE MID-ATLANTIC

In the ongoing Battle of the Atlantic, changes to the German Enigma code made a week earlier temporarily blindsided code breakers at Bletchley Park. This led to disastrous Allied shipping losses to German U-boats. Almost 100 merchant ships making up convoys HX-229 and SC-122 were attacked by three German submarine wolfpacks; more than 300 Allied merchant seamen died and 22 ships were lost.

◁ **A US oil tanker** burning after being torpedoed by a U-boat in the Atlantic Ocean

1943

16 MARCH

17 March Forces of the US 1st Infantry Division occupy the town of Gafsa in Tunisia

18 March After German forces recapture Kharkiv, they attack Belgorod, 80 km (50 miles) to the north

19 March US forces striking east from Algeria battle Axis forces at El Guettar in Tunisia

21 March New Zealand troops moving to outflank the defences of the Mareth Line in Tunisia engage Axis forces in the Tabaga Gap

U-91 and *U-338* sank 10 of the 22 ships lost from convoys HX-229 and SC-122

19 March 1943
OPERATION PUGILIST

After the Germans failed to take Medenine in southeastern Tunisia as a protective bulwark against the advancing British 8th Army, Field Marshal Montgomery launched a direct assault on the defensive Mareth Line in the far south of the country. New Zealand and Free French troops conducted a flanking attack designed to force the Germans to withdraw.

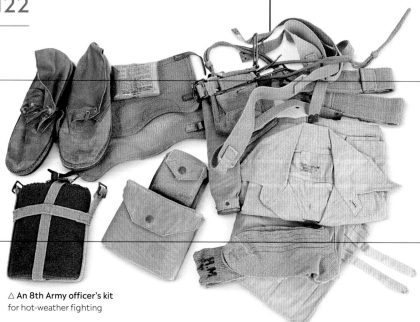

△ **An 8th Army officer's kit** for hot-weather fighting

△ A German soldier near Rzhev

22 March 1943

THE GERMANS WITHDRAW AT RZHEV

In the Eastern Front's central sector, German troops pursuing a scorched-earth policy completed a series of tactical withdrawals to the south of the town of Rzhev, 240 km (149 miles) west of Moscow. This operation effectively straightened and stablilized the front, shortening it by 370 km (230 miles).

28 March 1943

BREAKTHROUGH IN SOUTHERN TUNISIA

At the close of Operation Pugilist, Axis forces abandoned the Mareth Line in order to confront enemy troops outflanking them to the west. The British 8th Army forces were thereby freed to break through the fortifications and pursue the retreating enemy north through Tunisia, with the aim of joining up with troops from Operation Torch approaching from the northwest.

△ **British soldiers inspecting** the damage done by fighting in Mareth

1943

28 MARCH

26 March In an operation code-named Arsenal, Polish resistance fighters free 25 captives from a Nazi prison van in Warsaw

27 March In the Aleutians, a US naval force defeats a Japanese convoy in the Battle of the Komandorski Islands

28 March In the Battle of the Atlantic, U-boats sink four ships from convoy SL-126

1942–43

THE "FORGOTTEN WAR": THE BATTLE FOR THE ALEUTIAN ISLANDS

The Aleutian Islands campaign (June 1942– August 1943) saw a small Japanese force occupy US soil – Kiska and Attu, US islands in the remote chain that stretches west from Alaska. The Japanese took many of the indigenous inhabitants, the Unangax, as prisoners of war. The Japanese occupation went largely unchallenged for almost a year before the campaign to liberate the islands began. Harsh weather hampered efforts to retake the islands, but US forces prevailed in August 1943.

▷ **A monument in the Aleutian settlement of Unalaska** commemorating the forced internment and deaths of residents of the Aleutian Islands in World War II

△ **Los Alamos laboratory,**
main gate, 1943

1 April 1943
THE MANHATTAN PROJECT FINDS A HOME
By the spring of 1943, the US Manhattan nuclear research project, initially based in Manhattan, had been transferred to its new home in a former ranch school at Los Alamos, in a remote corner of New Mexico. It was here that the bombs dropped on the Japanese cities of Hiroshima and Nagasaki in 1945 were developed.

> ## "When man is willing to make the effort, he is capable of accomplishing virtually anything."

MAJOR GENERAL LESLIE RICHARD GROVES, HEAD OF THE MANHATTAN PROJECT, 1962

1943

29 MARCH

4 April News of the Bataan Death March reaches the West after 10 US POWs escape from the Davao penal colony on Mindanao, in the Philippines

10 April British forces enter the city of Sfax, previously a major Axis base, on the Tunisian coast

3 April The Battle of Manners Street erupts in Wellington, New Zealand, after white US servicemen try to prevent Maori soldiers from entering the Services Club

7 April Bolivia joins the Allies, having declared its solidarity with the USA following the Pearl Harbor attack

▽ **US tank crew** in Tunisia, 1943

7 April 1943
THE ALLIES JOIN FORCES
After penetrating the German defences on the Mareth Line in Tunisia, the British 8th Army advanced north. It finally linked up with other Allied forces, including the US II Corps, on 7 April, thus, effectively closing the cordon around the Germans in North Africa.

18 April 1943
OPERATION VENGEANCE

Operating on information gathered by US Navy intelligence, fighter aircraft were dispatched from Guadalcanal to intercept and shoot down the plane carrying Admiral Isoroku Yamamoto, commander-in-chief of the Japanese Combined Fleet, en route to an airfield off Bougainville Island. Yamamoto was specifically targeted because US leaders held him directly responsible for the attack on Pearl Harbor, which had brought the USA into the war. His death was a blow to Japanese morale.

▷ **A P-38G Lockheed Lightning fighter** of the type that carried out Operation Vengeance

17 April The Polish government-in-exile asks the Red Cross to investigate the reported massacre of its officers, but Stalin rejects the proposal, causing tensions in Polish–Soviet relations

18 April In the "Palm Sunday Massacre", US fighter squadrons shoot down large numbers of German transport planes on their way to rescue isolated German troops in Tunisia

13 April 1943
THE KATYN MASSACRE UNCOVERED

Radio Berlin announced the discovery of mass graves of Polish officers and members of the intelligentsia in the Katyn Forest, outside the city of Smolensk. The Germans accused the Soviet authorities of having carried out the atrocity. The Soviets denied this and blamed the Germans, but evidence showed that the victims, from a nearby Soviet prison camp, had been murdered in 1940, when the area was still under Soviet control.

◁ **French poster** by Austrian artist Theo Matjeko depicting Soviet officers carrying out the Katyn massacre

1908–40
JANINA LEWANDOWSKA

Having learned to fly two years before the war, Lewandowska was serving as an officer with Poland's 3rd Military Aviation Regiment when she was killed in the Katyn massacre – the only woman murdered in the atrocity. She died on her 32nd birthday.

Around 22,000 people, including 1 woman, were murdered in the Katyn massacre

22 April 1943
OPERATION VULCAN

In Tunisia, Allied forces launched Operation Vulcan, the final push to bring the Axis presence in North Africa to an end. The target cities were Bizerte, Cape Bon, and Tunis – the last German and Italian strongholds. Following strong resistance from the cities' defenders, the plan was revised, with fresh reinforcements and a new plan of attack.

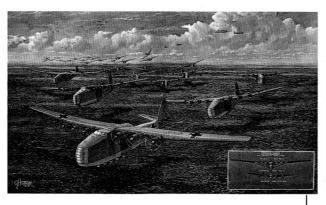

△ **German transport planes** sent to support the Axis forces in Tunis

△ **Officers of the British submarine** used in Operation Mincemeat

30 April 1943
OPERATION MINCEMEAT

In an elaborate deception operation, the British released a corpse bearing false documents from a submarine near the Spanish coast. Picked up by a local fisherman, the papers found their way to German intelligence operatives. They misled Axis planners into believing that the Allies were planning attacks on Greece and Sardinia rather than on their actual target – Sicily.

1943

19 APRIL

19 April At the Bermuda Conference, UK and US delegations discuss the situation of European Jews but fail to agree on measures to help

22 April Escort ships join Allied convoy ONS-5 at the start of what will be a climactic moment in the Battle of the Atlantic

19 April In Belgium, 236 Jews escape when the Belgian Resistance attacks a railway convoy destined for Auschwitz

27 April The Soviet authorities sever relations with the Polish government-in-exile in London over accusations of responsibility for the Katyn massacre

19 April 1943
THE WARSAW GHETTO REVOLT

An uprising began in the Polish capital when SS police and auxiliaries arrived to resume deportations, which had already seen more than 250,000 Jews transported to death camps. Resistance fighters took up arms to fight the police, starting a four-week revolt that ended with the total destruction of Warsaw's Jewish ghetto. By that time, 13,000 residents had died; 50,000 more were deported to the Treblinka and Majdanek extermination camps.

◁ **Nazi soldiers walking** past burning buildings during the revolt

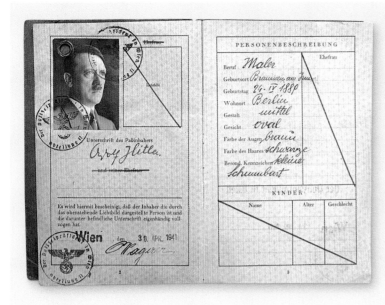

1940–45
FAKES AND FORGERIES

Both sides used deception in World War II. Britain's Special Operations Executive (SOE) faked a passport of Adolf Hitler, supposedly showing him to be Jewish. It also maintained a team of Polish exiles at Briggens House, in Essex, to forge fake identity papers for undercover agents in occupied Europe. Sometimes, more than forged documents were needed: the corpse in Operation Mincemeat was provided not just with official documents but also with love letters from a fiancée and a photo of the girl – in reality an MI5 clerk. Germany's Abwehr intelligence service employed similar tactics, once forcing a captured SOE operative to send misleading messages to Britain in a code supposedly known only to Dutch resistance fighters.

◁ **Faked passport** of Adolf Hitler

2 May Japanese aircraft again bomb Darwin, the capital of Australia's Northern Territory

6 May Stalin declares that, despite current difficulties, the USSR intends to have friendly postwar relations with an independent Poland

9 May The Chiangjiao Massacre begins in China: over four days, more than 30,000 civilians are killed by Japanese occupation forces

1943
9 MAY

▽ Office of War Information propaganda poster

OUR HIGH EXPLOSIVES
are beating the U-Boats

4–6 MAY 1943
THE FIGHT OVER ONS-5

The Battle of the Atlantic reached a climax when more than 40 U-boats attacked convoy ONS-5, carrying freight from Liverpool to Halifax, Nova Scotia. By the end of the confrontation, 13 ships had been sunk, but seven U-boats had also been destroyed and a similar number damaged – an unsustainable cost for the German Navy.

7 May 1943
THE ALLIES ENTER TUNIS

Two weeks after the launch of Operation Vulcan, troops from the British 1st Army entered Tunis. US forces took Bizerte on the same day, and Cap Bon fell a day later. There had been hard fighting, particularly for the strategic heights of Longstop Hill and Hill 609, before the British 1st Army and US II Corps finally broke through Axis defences.

▽ **Thousands of used shells** piled up in Bizerte

13 May 1943
SURRENDER IN NORTH AFRICA
Following the Allied capture of Tunis, Axis troops in Tunisia started to surrender en masse. The last to capitulate, on 13 May, was the 1st Italian Army under General Messe, trapped around the town of Enfidaville in the far northeastern corner of Tunisia. The Allied victory marked the end of resistance in North Africa. The Allies took almost a quarter of a million German and Italian soldiers prisoner.

◁ **Victory Day** parade in Tunis, May 1943

1943

10 MAY

12 May At a conference codenamed Trident, Roosevelt and Churchill meet in Washington to discuss plans for the invasion of Sicily and the Normandy landings

15 May Free French general Henri Giraud deposes Tunisia's ruler, Muhammad VII al-Munsif Bey, replacing him with Muhammad VIII al-Amin

15 May Axis forces launch a joint attack on Yugoslav partisans around the river Sujetska in southeast Bosnia

16 May The Warsaw Ghetto uprising is finally suppressed after four weeks of house-to-house fighting

△ Captured Japanese Daihatsu-class landing craft at Massacre Bay, Attu Island, 11 May 1943

11 May 1943
THE BATTLE FOR ATTU ISLAND
US and Canadian forces launched an assault on Attu, the westernmost of the Aleutian chain, in a move to drive out the Japanese occupying the island. The landings initiated 18 days of bitter fighting, culminating in a *banzai* charge (a suicide attack) that initially broke the Allied line before the Japanese troops involved were finally overcome in hand-to-hand combat. Even then, isolated survivors held out for another four months.

1930–
JONA LAKS
Aged 14 and following the deportation of their parents, Jona and her sister Miriam were sent to the Auschwitz concentration camp, where they were victims of Josef Mengele. After the war, Jona founded an organization for her fellow survivors.

3,000 twins were victims of the deadly genetic experiments of the "Angel of Death", SS camp doctor Josef Mengele

16–17 May 1943
THE DAMBUSTER RAIDS

RAF bombers led by Guy Gibson targeted three dams in the Ruhr industrial region of Germany, using "bouncing bombs" devised for the raid by the inventor Barnes Wallis. Two of the dams were breached, destroying or damaging several hydroelectric power stations and disabling factories and mines. The breaches also caused catastrophic flooding, resulting in the deaths of 1,600 civilians, including 1,000 mostly Russian enslaved labourers.

△ U-Boat under attack, 1943

▽ **Wing Commander Guy Gibson (*left*)** with members of 617 Squadron, the "Dambusters", 1943

23 May 1943
U-BOATS WITHDRAW FROM THE ATLANTIC

In "Black May", Germany lost 43 submarines, 34 of them in the Atlantic. In response to these spiralling losses – caused by the Allies' deployment of long-range bombers and anti-submarine hunting packs – Admiral Dönitz decided to cut German losses by temporarily withdrawing all U-boats from the mid-Atlantic region.

1943

27 MAY

27 May President Roosevelt establishes the Office of War Mobilization to coordinate the activities of all US government agencies involved in the war effort

24 May 1943
MENGELE AT AUSCHWITZ

Trained as a medical researcher, and with a background in genetics, Josef Mengele was appointed chief medical officer at Auschwitz concentration camp. Besides sitting on the panel that selected victims for the gas chambers, he also initiated a programme of cruel and often lethal experimentation on inmates, focused particularly on twins. The experiments performed included unnecessary limb amputations and infecting healthy patients with typhus and other pathogens; many victims died.

◁ **Prisoner identification photos** of child inmates of the Auschwitz-Birkenau concentration camp

1939-45
COLONIES AT WAR

At the onset of World War II, the major European powers, especially Britain, France, the Netherlands, and Belgium, directly ruled colonies around the world. The exploitation of the colonies' natural resources, such as rubber, oil, and minerals, was increased to feed the war effort, and (mainly) volunteers from their populations swelled the ranks of the armed forces. The largest contingents of recruits were from the British Empire, including 150,000 from West Africa, 10,000 from the Caribbean, and more than 2.5 million from the Indian subcontinent. Most were put in subordinate roles and denied leadership positions.

The French, Belgian, and Dutch surrender to Germany in 1940 left their colonial empires in a state of flux. Most of France's colonies recognized the collaborationist Vichy regime, although Félix Eboué (*see p.88*), the governor of Chad, refused to, establishing Free French Africa, which provided vital support for Charles de Gaulle's efforts. Similarly, Belgian Congo provided both military support and uranium to the Allies.

After the war, many colonies redoubled their prewar demands for independence. While this was sometimes achieved quickly, as in British India in 1947, the process was longer and bloodier in other places, such as Vietnam and Algeria.

KEY MOMENTS

1939-45 The Indian Army
By 1945, the British Indian Army had become the largest volunteer force in history. Fighting on three continents, its members won 18 Victoria Crosses. Pictured (*left*) is a cap badge from the Indian Medical Service.

1940 West Indians in the air war
From 1940, the RAF began recruiting air crew from British colonies in the West Indies. More than 6,000 Black Caribbean men volunteered for the RAF, as well as 80 women for the Women's Auxiliary Airforce. While most worked on the ground, around 450 men served as air crew (*left*).

1939-45 Africans fighting for empire
More than a million people were recruited from sub-Saharan Africa, particularly by the British. This image (*left*) shows men from West Africa in India, where they received jungle training before being deployed to fight in Burma.

The Auxiliary Territorial Service was the women's branch of the British Army. By the war's end, it included more than 200,000 women from across the empire. The first contingent from the West Indies, pictured here, arrived in Britain in 1943.

△ **A B-17 Flying Fortress** taking part in a raid on Marienburg

14 June 1943
OPERATION POINTBLANK

The Allied Combined Chiefs of Staff launched a new directive prioritizing the targeting of German aircraft manufacture in future bombing raids. A particular goal was the reduction of the Luftwaffe's fighter strength – something that was considered an essential preparatory step for an eventual invasion of continental Europe.

▽ **Generals Giraud and de Gaulle** shake hands at the Casablanca Conference, 1943

3 June 1943
THE FREE FRENCH UNITE

Under pressure from Allied leaders, Charles de Gaulle and Henri Giraud, who had succeeded the assassinated General Darlan as commander-in-chief of France's Army of Africa, jointly agreed to serve as co-presidents of a Committee of National Liberation, designed to unite the activities of Free French resistance groups.

8 June In the Aleutian Islands, Japanese forces begin to abandon Kiska in an evacuation that will take seven weeks

11–12 June British forces take Pantelleria, off the coast of Sicily; the island of Lampedusa also surrenders to the Allies

1943

28 MAY

3 June 1943
RACE RIOTS IN THE USA

On the home front in the USA, race riots broke out as white servicemen on leave and some civilians began searching out and beating the wearers of the flamboyant "zoot suits" favoured by young Mexican, Filipino, and Black Americans. For its wearers, the zoot suit signified style, swagger, and defiance of the discrimination they faced. Among America's racists, such defiance could not go unpunished, while others were offended by the unpatriotic use of so much cloth for a suit at a time when it was rationed. The worst of the riots took place in Los Angeles, but there were also incidents in Detroit, Michigan; Mobile, Alabama; and Beaumont, Texas.

◁ **Zoot suiters under arrest** outside a Los Angeles jail, June 1943

1939–45

THE NORTHWARD MIGRATION

In the USA, a long-term demographic change that had seen African-American families moving out of the southern states to seek a better life in the north was accelerated by the new opportunities offered to workers in the war industries. Shipbuilding proved particularly lucrative, especially on the Pacific Coast, and the Black population of Seattle tripled, while that of Portland quadrupled. The work these migrants undertook could be hazardous. For example, in 1944, a munitions explosion that happened while arms were being loaded onto a cargo ship at Port Chicago in California killed more than 200 African-American sailors.

▷ **Migrant workers** heading north from Florida to work picking potatoes in New Jersey

16 June Britain's Special Operations Executive sends its first female wireless operator, Noor Inayat Khan, to France

25 June In the USA, the Smith-Connally Act criminalizes strikes interfering with war production

30 June US troops land at Kula Gulf and other sites in New Georgia, an island group in the Solomon chain 800 km (500 miles) east of New Guinea

1943

30 JUNE

29 June In the course of Operation Cartwheel, a joint US-Australian force lands at Nassau Bay, in New Guinea, in preparation for a fresh assault on the major Japanese base at Salamaua

△ **US soldiers wading through water** on an island in the New Georgia group in the central Solomons

21 June 1943

OPERATION CARTWHEEL

In the Pacific, a long-planned major Allied offensive got under way, with the ultimate goal of taking out the main Japanese base in the region, at Rabaul, on New Britain. The plan called for a two-pronged attack that would strike westward across New Guinea from territory already held by the Allies and work up through the Solomon Islands chain to threaten Rabaul from the east.

14,203 bombs were dropped on Pantelleria before the Allies invaded

1914–44
NOOR INAYAT KHAN

Khan was a British special agent of Indian Muslim heritage who served as a wireless operator in occupied France. When the network she supported began to be rounded up, she stayed in post until she herself was caught. She was shot at Dachau.

7 July 1943
HITLER BACKS THE V-2

At a meeting with Wernher von Braun and other rocket scientists, Hitler agreed to give top priority in the German armaments programme to the Peenemünde research station and its V-2 rockets – so-called "Vengeance" weapons, designed to retaliate for the Allied bombing of German cities. At the time of the briefing, planned launch sites were already under construction near France's Channel coast.

△ V-2 rocket launch

> "If we had had these rockets in 1939, we should never have had this war."

HITLER TO WERNHER VON BRAUN, AT THE MEETING PRIORITIZING THE V-2 PROGRAMME, 7 JULY 1943

1943

1 JULY

4 July US troops secure Rendova, one of the islands in the New Georgia group of the Solomon Islands

5 July The Japanese government announces the cession of six Malay states to Thailand

6 July The Nassau Bay landings on New Guinea end; the troops provide support for the campaign against the Japanese bases at Salamaua and Lae

10 July Allied forces land in Sicily as a first step in the planned invasion of Italy

◁ Soviet T-34-85 medium tank

5–12 July 1943
THE BATTLE OF KURSK

German forces attacked from north and south in a massive assault on the Soviet salient at the southwestern city of Kursk. The Soviet forces had prepared a series of defensive lines that held back the initial German assault. Then, they counterattacked. The confrontation at Kursk developed into the largest tank battle in history. With planned reinforcements diverted to counter the Allied invasion of Sicily, the Germans lost the battle, along with an estimated 760 panzers; Soviet losses were even heavier.

25 July 1943

THE FASCISTS FALL IN ITALY

Italy's defeat in North Africa and the ensuing invasion of Sicily by the Allies were to prove fatal for the ruling Fascist Party. Following a vote by Italy's Grand Council, King Victor Emmanuel dismissed Mussolini as head of the government and placed him in custody. He was replaced as prime minister by Marshal Pietro Badoglio, a one-time colonial governor who had earlier served as chief of staff of the armed forces.

△ **The ruins of Hamburg** after Allied bombing, 1943

22-29 July 1943

THE HAMBURG RAIDS

An Allied campaign codenamed Operation Gomorrah unleashed a week of daytime and nighttime bombing raids on the German city of Hamburg. At the climax of the attack, on the night of 27 July, a force of 787 planes created a firestorm that killed an estimated 18,000 civilians.

22 July In Sicily, US forces under General George S. Patton capture the capital, Palermo

△ **An Allied leaflet** dropped over Italian troops in Tunisia urging them to boot out Mussolini

L'ITALIA FARÀ DA SE

1943

31 JULY

13 July Hitler calls off the German assault on Kursk, allowing Soviet forces, re-energized after their victory at Stalingrad, to go on the offensive

1912-77

WERNHER VON BRAUN

The leading figure in the development of the V-2 rocket, von Braun was smuggled out of Germany after the war to work on the US Army's ballistic missile programme. He later worked for NASA on the Apollo space programme.

July 1943–April 1944

SOVIET COUNTEROFFENSIVE

German hopes that heavy losses in the Battle of Kursk might have temporarily crippled the Soviet war machine quickly proved unfounded, as Russian forces swiftly pressed forward on many different fronts. From Kursk itself, they drove west to Smolensk, which fell in September, and south into Ukraine, recapturing Kyiv early in November. In the far north, the siege of Leningrad was lifted early in 1944, following another Russian offensive. By April of that year, Axis forces were in retreat on all fronts, and the Soviets had won back much of the land lost following Hitler's Operation Barbarossa (*see p.112*).

▽ **A Russian stamp** commemorating the 20th anniversary of the Battle of Kursk

1 August 1943
OPERATION TIDAL WAVE

In what turned out to be the costliest Allied air mission of the war, US Army Air Force bombers targeted oil refineries in Ploesti, Romania, as part of an ongoing campaign to reduce Axis access to fuels needed for the war effort. Of the 177 planes that took part, 53 were destroyed, with the loss of 660 crewmen. One plane crashed into a women's prison, killing a further 100 civilians.

◁ A Consolidated B-24 Liberator bomber flying over a burning oil refinery at Ploesti, Romania, 1943

1943

1 AUGUST

4 August 400 US B-17 Flying Fortress bombers attack Naples, targeting the Axis submarine base there

1–2 August Race riots break out in Harlem, New York, after a white police officer shoots an African-American soldier

6 August The US island-hopping campaign in the Pacific moves on to Vela Lavella, in the Western Province of the Solomon Islands

15 August 1943
US FORCES RECLAIM THE ALEUTIANS

After the successful but bloody campaign to retake Attu in the Aleutian Islands from its Japanese occupiers, a 35,000-strong joint US and Canadian invasion force landed on Kiska, the last of the islands still thought to be in Japanese hands. Unbeknown to the Allies, the final Japanese forces had been evacuated from the island two weeks earlier under cover of fog. Even so, the Allies suffered more than 300 casualties as a result of Japanese booby traps, frostbite, and friendly-fire incidents.

▷ US and Canadian forces landing on Kiska, in the Aleutian Islands, August 1943

Japan's action in the Aleutian Islands was the first significant foreign invasion of US territory since the War of 1812

17 August 1943

SICILY LIBERATED

Less than six weeks after the first Allied landings on Sicily, the last Axis units abandoned the island, leaving it in their opponents' hands. The Allies' success in Sicily had broader significance because it forced Hitler to divert badly needed resources from the Eastern Front, setting the scene for major Soviet advances there (*see p.191*).

◁ **A British Sherman Mk III tank** carrying jubilant Sicilian children in the village of Milo, near Catania, August 1943

17 August Portugal's dictator, Antonio Salazar, allows Allied forces to use air and naval bases in the Azores

17 August A force of 376 USAAF bombers strikes the Messerschmitt plants in Regensburg at a cost of 60 aircraft

20–21 August Polish resistance fighters launch Operation Belt, a coordinated assault on German border posts

1943

21 AUGUST

△ **Allied aerial reconnaissance photo** showing evidence of rocket research at Peenemünde

17 August 1943

OPERATION HYDRA

As the first step in its campaign to disable Germany's V-weapons programme, RAF Bomber Command launched a night raid on the rocket research site at Peenemünde. Forty bombers were lost and several hundred civilians and slave labourers killed, but development of the rockets was delayed by two months.

19 August 1943

THE QUEBEC AGREEMENT

Signed by Roosevelt and Churchill at a conference convened in Quebec City in Canada, this secret accord committed the USA and the UK to pooling resources in the development of nuclear weapons. Both countries agreed not to use them against other nations without mutual consent. The USA also maintained the right to limit British commercial exploitation of nuclear energy after the war.

▷ **Canada's and Britain's prime ministers, William Lyon Mackenzie King** and Winston Churchill (*top*), with President Franklin D. Roosevelt and Canada's governor-general, Sir Alexander Cambridge

22 August 1943

ADVANCE FROM KURSK

In the wake of their success at Kursk (*see p.190*), Soviet troops swept southwards to liberate Kharkiv, in Ukraine, which had already changed hands twice in the conflict. En route to Kharkiv, the Soviets also freed Orel and Belgorod. By the end of the offensive, the Germans had been forced to retreat behind Ukraine's river Dnieper.

△ A Soviet military SSh-40 helmet

3 September 1943

THE INVASION OF ITALY

British 8th Army troops crossed the Straits of Messina from Sicily into mainland Italy, landing at Reggio Calabria, on its southernmost tip. The secret armistice signed by the Italian government with the Allies that day meant the German forces would have to resist the invaders on their own.

△ Map of the invasion of Italy, September 1943

1943

22 AUGUST

28 August King Boris III of Bulgaria, who had taken his country into war on the Axis side, dies suddenly

29 August Martial law is proclaimed in Denmark following the government's refusal to accede to German demands for a crackdown on dissent

3 September The new Italian government signs a secret accord with the Allies to take Italy out of the war

4 September In New Guinea, Australian forces launch Operation Postern, aimed at capturing the port town of Lae

More than 60,000 Allied troops were killed in the campaign to liberate Italy

1943-45
THE LIBERATION OF ITALY

The Allies made slow and costly progress northwards through Italy. Axis forces set up a series of defensive lines designed to keep them at bay.

17 Jan 1944 Allied troops are held up for months by fighting at Monte Cassino, southeast of Rome.

4 June 1944 Declared an open city by the Italians and left undefended, Rome is entered by US forces under General Mark Clark.

August–December 1944 Allies breach the Gothic Line, the last major German defensive position, which stretches across Italy.

29 April 1945 A final Allied offensive sees the Germans driven north of the river Po and the signing of a formal instrument of surrender.

> "I said, 'I'm just going to get my head down and my tail up, and I'm going to go.' And I did."

MAJOR ARMIN PUCK, 36TH DIVISION, US ARMY, REMEMBERING THE LANDINGS AT SALERNO, SEPTEMBER 1943

9 September 1943
IRAN ENTERS THE WAR

Strategically important because of its oil resources, Iran had been invaded by Allied forces in 1941. Iran's neutral ruler, Reza Shah, had been replaced by his son, Mohammed Reza Shah, who was favourably disposed to the Allied cause. Now the country formally declared war on Germany. This qualified it for membership of the planned United Nations organization, which was to be set up when peace returned for countries committed to the Allied cause. In exchange, the Soviet, US, and British governments promised to respect Iran's independence and provide economic assistance during and after the war.

△ **US and British engineers** standing on an American locomotive in Iran, 1943 (hand-coloured image)

8 September General Eisenhower publicly announces the unconditional surrender of Italy

1943

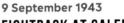

9 SEPTEMBER

7 September Polish resistance fighters assassinate Gestapo officer Franz Bürkl and seven of his colleagues in a Warsaw street shootout

8 September German naval forces launch Operation Zitronella, a surprise attack on the island of Spitsbergen, north of Norway

9 September British forces land almost unopposed at Taranto, on the heel of Italy

9 September 1943
FIGHTBACK AT SALERNO

In contrast to the relatively uncontested landings at Reggio Calabria, the US forces attempting to establish a beachhead at Salerno, 400 km (250 miles) further north, on the Mediterranean coast, faced stiff resistance from the Germans. Responding to intelligence reports suggesting this was to be the main invasion hub, four Wehrmacht battle groups, supported by fighter planes and bombers, fiercely contested the landings. They almost forced a retreat before Allied air and naval support and the threat of the British 8th Army advancing northward tipped the balance.

◁ **A US landing craft** heading for Salerno takes a direct hit

THE ALLIED BREAKTHROUGH

During 1944, the German Army was relentlessly forced backwards along the Eastern Front. In summer, the Soviet Red Army concentrated on the central sector, destroying a German army group during Operation Bagration, before turning southwards and clearing the Balkans. By the end of 1944, Soviet forces had expelled the invaders from Russia and were on the cusp of crossing the border into Germany itself.

In Eastern Europe and the Balkans, resistance movements tied down German occupation units. Yugoslavian partisans under Marshal Tito engaged German troops in open combat, and in August 1944, the Polish resistance wrestled for control of central Warsaw, fighting a bloody seven-week battle before eventually being defeated by the Germans.

The invasion of Normandy

The extraordinarily thorough preparation made by the Anglo-American forces for the invasion of Normandy in June 1944 was one of the war's great success stories. Two things were central to the Allied victory on D-Day and beyond: vastly superior intelligence, which helped confuse the Germans as to the site of the invasion; and air supremacy, which ensured that the Luftwaffe was held at bay while the ships of the invasion fleet were loaded with soldiers and armaments. Without these advantages, it is unlikely that the invasion would have succeeded.

With a growing sense of hope that their enemy was facing defeat, resistance movements in the countries occupied by the Germans gained traction during 1944. The Allied decision to invade Normandy helped increase local support for the French Resistance enormously.

To Germany's gates

The initial success of the Allied landings in Normandy on 6 June 1944 was, however, tempered by strong German resistance around the beachheads established by the British, Canadian, and US forces. The Germans managed to hold off the Allies for several weeks, until an American breakthrough at Avranches opened the floodgates to a general Allied advance that liberated France and Belgium. In September 1944, the offensive stalled as the overstretched Allies came up against improved defences along the German border region. Scraping together his remaining reserves, Hitler ordered a last-ditch attack in Belgium's Ardennes region for December 1944. After some initial German success, the Allies contained the offensive – better known as the Battle of the Bulge.

The Pacific strategy

In the Pacific, US strategists decided on two separate axes of attack. The first was spearheaded by the US Navy carrier forces and comprised an advance towards Japan via the Central Pacific islands. After suffering heavy casualties in securing Tarawa in November 1943, the US forces adopted new methods and tactics, as it became clear that the Japanese would have to be flushed out of their caves and bunkers using grenades, satchel charges, and flamethrowers. The second line of advance came in the southwest Pacific, where the US Army, supported by Australian forces, made steady progress in the Solomon Islands in preparation for an offensive that would drive the Japanese from the Philippines.

At sea, the Japanese suffered a significant defeat at the Battle of the Philippine Sea in June 1944, when the bulk of its naval aviation capacity was destroyed. This setback was swiftly followed by another – the Battle of Leyte Gulf – in October. This was a large-scale, complex engagement that allowed the Americans to land in the Philippines with little opposition and that all but destroyed what remained of the Japanese Imperial Navy.

In the wider Pacific theatre, US submarines and aircraft played important roles in disrupting the transportation of oil, coal, and other vital resources to Japan. By mid-1944, Japan's economy was being strangled to death. After US forces captured the Mariana Islands, bringing the Japanese homeland into the range of the US B-29 bombers by the end of 1944, Japan was bombed mercilessly.

10 September 1943
GERMANS OCCUPY ROME

After Mussolini was deposed in July, Italy's new government declared Rome a nominally demilitarized open city to spare it from damage. However, after the Allies proclaimed the terms of the armistice, revealing that Italy had in fact switched support from the Axis to the Allied cause, German troops moved to occupy the capital on 10 September. The day before, King Victor Emmanuel and his government had fled the city for Brindisi, in southern Italy, an area already liberated by Allied forces.

◁ **German officers questioning Italian soldiers** in Rome following the armistice with the Allies

1943

10 SEPTEMBER

12 September Hitler orders German troops in Corsica to transfer to Italy

14 September Axis forces in Crete launch reprisals against civilians around Viannos for their support for resistance fighters. Some 500 people are killed

13 September In Italy, German forces finally pull back after fighting around the US 5th Army's Salerno beachhead reaches a climax

▽ **Allied troops being dropped on Leros** to support paratroopers who have landed there

12 September 1943
MUSSOLINI RESCUED

In an airborne operation, German paratroopers and SS commandos rescued Italy's deposed leader, Benito Mussolini, from captivity in the Apennine Mountains. Hitler then pronounced him head of a puppet Italian state, later known as the Republic of Salò after the Lombardy town where it was headquartered.

△ **Mussolini leaving the hotel** where he had been held captive by the Italian government

17 September 1943
FREEING THE DODECANESE

Following Italy's switch of support to the Allies, British forces launched an attempt to secure control of islands in the Dodecanese group (in the Aegean Sea) that had previously been under Italian control. British troops supported by Greek special forces secured Kos, Samos, Leros, and smaller territories, but only temporarily. The Germans gained control of the islands within the next two months.

Around 3,000 Italian soldiers drowned when the ships taking them from Cephalonia to concentration camps were sunk by the Allies

△ **A propaganda poster** showing Major von Hirschfeld addressing Hitler Youth members

21 September 1943
THE CEPHALONIA KILLINGS

German forces sought to disarm the Italians, their former allies, who were occupying the island of Cephalonia, off Greece's west coast. Soldiers of the Italian Acqui Division initially resisted, but were forced to surrender when they ran out of ammunition. Wehrmacht soldiers under the command of Major Harald von Hirschfeld then started carrying out mass executions, killing 5,000 prisoners of war over the course of the following week.

18 September German forces withdraw from Sardinia following Italy's switch to the Allied cause

1943

25 SEPTEMBER

25 September On the Eastern Front, Russian troops retake Smolensk, captured by German forces two years earlier

20–22 September 1943
OPERATION SOURCE

Aided by intelligence provided by Norwegian resistance fighters, six Allied midget submarines were dispatched to attack three German warships stationed in fjords in northern Norway. One of the German vessels – the *Tirpitz* – was badly damaged and put out of action for six months. The success of the operation came at a price, however: all the submarines were lost, and six of the 24 crew members involved were captured and 10 killed. Their exploits were celebrated after the war in the 1955 film *Above Us the Waves*.

◁ **A crewman emerges** from an X-class midget submarine of the type used in Operation Source

26 September 1943
OPERATION JAYWICK

Travelling initially in a vessel disguised as an Asian fishing boat, Allied commandos took to collapsible canoes to attach limpet mines to Japanese shipping in Singapore harbour. Three ships were sunk and another three damaged, leading to a wave of reprisals against suspected saboteurs in the local population.

▽ **The radios** used in the Jaywick operation remain in working order to this day

▽ **American engineers** watching British troops crossing a bridge over the river Volturno

5 October 1943
BREAKING THE VOLTURNO LINE

Advancing from beachheads in southern Italy, Allied forces broke through the Volturno Line – the southernmost of a succession of German defensive positions that blocked their progress northward up the peninsula. It would take four weeks of fighting for them to reach the Barbara Line, about 30 km (20 miles) to the north.

1943

26 SEPTEMBER

27 September German forces take over the Greek island of Corfu from the Italian troops who had previously held it

4 October Free French forces liberate Corsica of the residual German presence, leaving 1,000 dead

4 October In Operation Leader, US airmen launch a surprise attack on German shipping off the northern coast of Norway, sinking five ships

27 September 1943
UPRISING IN NAPLES

Inspired by the Italian government's switch to the Allied side, townspeople and resistance fighters in Naples launched an unplanned popular uprising against the German forces still occupying the city. As the Wehrmacht soldiers prepared to move out, they faced spontaneous rioting that escalated into violence. The uprising came to be known as the "Four Days of Naples". The departing Germans responded by burning down the city's State Archives. Allied forces reached Naples on 1 October, entering the city without meeting resistance.

◁ **Joyful crowds** greet an American GI as Naples is liberated

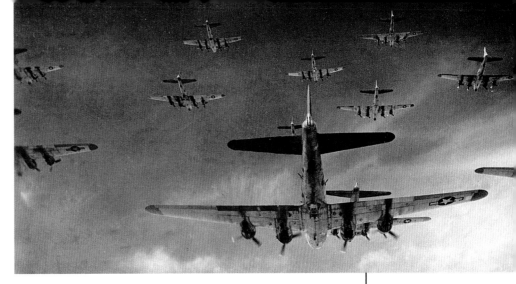

1892–1980
JOSIP BROZ TITO
A committed communist, Tito quickly established himself as leader of Yugolsavia's resistance fighters following the Axis invasion. After the war, he served as the country's prime minister and president.

14 October 1943
BLACK THURSDAY
Following an earlier raid that had sustained heavy losses, the USAAF took extra precautions for a second daytime sortie to Schweinfurt in Bavaria, targeted at ball-bearing factories considered vital for German war production. However, the measures proved inadequate: 77 planes were lost in the raid, and a further 121 damaged, out of a fleet of 291 B-17 bombers.

△ **B-17 Flying Fortresses** from the 398th Bombardment Group

6 October US and Japanese naval forces
clash off Vela Lavella, in the Solomon Islands, as the Japanese complete the evacuation of their remaining garrison on the island

13 October Italy's new Italian government, under Pietro Badoglio, officially declares war on Germany

1943

14 OCTOBER

9 October Yugoslav guerrillas led by Josip Broz Tito open an offensive against Axis forces in the Trieste region

14 October Prisoners at the Sobibor extermination camp in Poland rise up against their Nazi captors; some 300 of them escape

▽ **A priest leading prayers** for a B-17 Flying Fortress bomber crew at an airfield in southern England

1943–45
COMBINED BOMBER OFFENSIVE
Following plans drawn up in April 1943 by the chiefs of the US and British air forces, the Combined Bomber Offensive was launched in June. Its goals, set out in the Pointblank directive, included the specific targeting of Germany's fighter aircraft production (rather than its war industries in general). Britain's Bomber Command favoured nighttime sorties, while the USAAF concentrated on daylight raids. Although activities were to some extent coordinated, the British resisted US pressure for a single strategic commander. Losses suffered in the Black Thursday raid led the USAAF to temporarily pause missions deep into Germany until adequate fighter escorts were available.

▷ **A diorama** in Kassel's City Museum showing the devastating effects of the raid

21 October 1943
FREE INDIA PROCLAIMED

A longstanding proponent of Indian independence from the British Empire, Subhas Chandra Bose proclaimed the establishment of Azad Hind, the Provisional Government of Free India, with the support of Japan. Bose had also earlier taken charge of the Free Indian Army (or Indian National Army), which fought for the Axis under the command of the Japanese. Although independence was a hot topic in India, Bose's regime was recognized only by the Axis powers and their allies abroad.

▷ **A badge** with Azad Hind's leaping-tiger motif and "Free India" written in German

22 October 1943
THE KASSEL RAID

The Allies launched the deadliest of a succession of bombing raids on Kassel – home to German tank and warplane production plants. The raid destroyed much of the city centre; an estimated 6,000 people died in the raid and in the subsequent seven-day firestorm, which also left some 150,000 people homeless.

1943

19 October German Army Ordnance contracts the Mittelwerk factory in central Germany to produce 12,000 V-2 rockets

22/23 October In the Battle of Sept-Iles, boats escorting a German blockade-runner sink HMS *Charybdis* and damage HMS *Limbourne* off the French coast

15 OCTOBER

18 October The foreign ministers of the USA, the UK, and the Soviet Union meet in Moscow to discuss the future course of the war

21 October Learning of a planned German deportation of Jews from occupied Denmark, sympathetic Danes help more than 7,000 people to escape to Sweden

1897-1945
SUBHAS CHANDRA BOSE

Elected president of India's pro-independence Congress Party in 1938, Bose moved to Germany in 1941, later transferring to Japanese-held Southeast Asia, where he took command of the Indian National Army. He died in a plane crash in 1945.

1943-45
ISLAND HOPPING IN THE PACIFIC

In the first months after their entry into the war, Japanese planners sought to create a defensive island shield in the Pacific Ocean, stretching from the Marshall Islands in the east down to New Guinea and the Solomon Islands to the south. From mid-1943, Allied forces – having already succeeded in winning back Guadalcanal in the previous year – set about reclaiming lost territory by concentrating attacks on weaker links in the island chain, leapfrogging those that were heavily fortified.

▷ **US Marines wade ashore** at Cape Gloucester, New Britain, Papua New Guinea, 1943

25 October 1943
BREAKTHROUGH ON THE DNIEPER

Having retaken Kharkiv in August, Soviet troops pushed south, establishing a first bridgehead across the river Dnieper in September. On 25 October, they successfully retook the major river port of Dnipropetrovsk, which had been occupied by the Germans since August 1941. This action effectively secured the western bank of the Dnieper and cut off Axis-held Crimea from other German forces.

◁ **By a sign reading "To Kyiv!",** Soviet soldiers prepare rafts to cross the Dnieper

24 October In the Dodecanese campaign, HMS *Eclipse* is sunk by a mine off Leros, with the loss of 253 men

30 October Parties to the Moscow Conference agree to set up a European Advisory Commission to discuss the future of the continent after Nazi Germany's defeat

1943
31 OCTOBER

27 October Commandos of Britain's Special Air Services launch two separate sabotage raids – Operations Candytuft and Saxifrage – behind enemy lines in northern Italy

27–28 October 1943
THE ALLIES MOVE ON BOUGAINVILLE

In the Pacific campaign, the Allies made preparations for an assault on Bougainville, the largest of the Solomon Islands. Two diversionary amphibious landings were made to draw Japanese troops away from Bougainville: New Zealand troops landed on the Treasury Islands 50 km (30 miles) to the south, while US Marines raided Choiseul, 150 km (95 miles) further east. The feints were successful in laying the ground for an assault on Bougainville on 1 November.

◁ **LST-980 tank lander** unloading an LVT (Landing Vehicle, Tracked)

> More than 90 per cent of Denmark's Jews survived the Holocaust

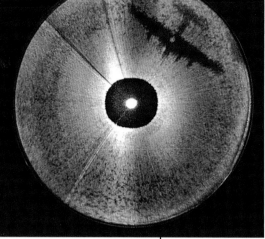

3 November 1943
ALLIED BOMBING INTENSIFIES

Poor weather over Europe, especially in the winter months, hampered Allied bombing raids on Germany until the development of a new ground-scanning radar system. Designated H2X and developed at the Massachusetts Institute of Technology, it was first used in combat in a US attack on Wilhelmshaven. Although not as accurate as visual bombing, it allowed raids in heavy cloud and marked the start of a fresh wave of so-called "Pathfinder" missions.

△ **An H2X radar** displaying the image of a B-17 Flying Fortress

6 November 1943
SOVIET FORCES RETAKE KYIV

After establishing bridgeheads across the Dnieper to the north and south of Kyiv, Soviet forces entered the city on 6 November. In the days that followed, they retained control of the city in spite of a German counterattack that was reinforced by a fresh panzer division. Meanwhile, other Soviet troops continued the drive westward.

△ **A Soviet stamp** from 1963 commemorating the liberation of Kyiv

9 November General de Gaulle becomes sole president of the French Committee of National Liberation, having previously shared the position with General Giraud

1943
1 NOVEMBER

3 November In Aktion Erntefest (Operation Harvest Festival), the SS shoot 43,000 Jews at three camps in Poland in reprisal for ghetto uprisings

1–2 November 1943
THE BOUGAINVILLE LANDINGS

To gain an advantage in the Pacific conflict, Allied planners recognized the need for an air base from which their aircraft could reach the principal Japanese station at Rabaul, New Guinea. The location they chose for their base was Bougainville, the largest of the Solomon Islands. On 1 November, they carried out amphibious landings at Empress Augusta Bay, on the island's relatively undefended west coast. Japanese commanders responded by sending a naval force from Rabaul, but this was driven off by the US Navy task force assigned to protect the beachhead.

◁ **US marines racing ashore** from a landing craft at Empress Augusta Bay

9 November 1943
UNRRA ESTABLISHED

In response to the civilian suffering caused by the war, 44 countries came together in Washington, DC, at the instigation of the USA, to sign the foundation document of the United Nations Relief and Rehabilitation Administration. UNRAA's aim was to provide aid, including food, fuel, shelter, and medical assistance, to areas liberated from Axis control. It operated from 1943 until 1948, by which time most of its functions had been taken over by the recently formed United Nations.

◁ **Polish and Russian orphans** being fed at an UNRRA-run camp

13 November Partisans assassinate the influential Italian Fascist Igino Ghisellini; 74 people were arrested in response, and 11 of them were executed

16 November In the decisive encounter of the Dodecanese campaign, British and Italian garrisons holding Leros surrender to an amphibious German invasion force

1943
16 NOVEMBER

14 November US bombers target the Tarawa Atoll, in the Gilbert Islands, launching the first US offensive in the Central Pacific

16 November US bombers attack the heavy-water power plant at Vemork, in Norway, but inflict only minimal damage

15 November 1943
ROMA AND SINTI TARGETED

Roma and Sinti people had been persecuted since the Nazis first came to power, but their situation worsened when SS leader Heinrich Himmler announced that, henceforth, they were to be put "on the same level as Jews and placed in concentration camps", unleashing a new genocide.

▷ **Axis paramilitary troops** rounding up Roma civilians in occupied Yugoslavia

Between 200,000 and 500,000 Roma and Sinti people were murdered by the Nazis and their collaborators

The British Expeditionary Force began moving into France three days after the outbreak of war. To keep the men occupied during the "Phoney War" (see p.59), games were dispatched to them, including these dartboards sent in November 1939.

1939-45
RECREATION

As the war drew on, military leaders recognized the need to keep their troops entertained, not only to boost morale but also to divert them away from activities that might endanger their health or mar relations with local communities. A priority was to provide places where soldiers could rest and relax, such as the German *Soldatenheime* ("Soldier's Hostels"), the US United Services Organizations' (USO) clubs, and the canteens operated by the British Navy, Army, and Air Force Institutes (NAAFI). These facilities were often close to front lines, allowing soldiers some relief from combat and a measure of comfort. Entertainment was also provided, most glamorously by the USO, which recruited Hollywood stars such as Laurel and Hardy, Bob Hope, and Marlene Dietrich. Not to be outdone, the British Entertainments National Service Association (ENSA) called on the likes of Noël Coward, Vera Lynn, and Laurence Olivier. Cinema screenings, dances, and sporting events, as well as musical and theatrical performances, were commonplace. Despite official efforts to provide such "wholesome" recreation, soldiers inevitably still pursued activities such as drinking, gambling, and patronizing local brothels.

KEY MOMENTS

1939-45 German *Soldatenheime*
There were more than 800 "Soldier's Hostels" in occupied Europe, such as the one in Paris (*right*), where soldiers and civilian personnel could socialize, read, and relax.

1939 ENSA established
ENSA was founded by two theatre actors and was part of the British NAAFI. It organized concerts by entertainers such as Vera Lynn (*right*), screenings, and variety shows for the British military around the world. The shows' variable quality led soldiers to joke that ENSA's acronym really stood for "Every Night Something Awful".

1941 The USO
A joint effort between six civilian charities, the USO enlisted performers to entertain the troops at home and overseas (by 1945, there were more than 7,000, performing 700 times a day). The USO ran more than 3,000 clubs, which were segregated. Shown here (*right*) is a club for Black service personnel.

20 November 1943
BLOODBATH IN TARAWA

In the next step of their island-hopping campaign in the Pacific, US military planners turned their attention to the Gilbert Islands, on the western edge of Japan's defensive shield. US forces made their first landing on Tarawa Atoll, unleashing one of the bloodiest battles in American military history. Over three days, the 4,500-strong Japanese garrison killed more than 1,000 Marines in fierce resistance that left almost all the defenders dead.

◁ **US Marines** preparing to advance from their beachhead (hand-coloured image)

1943

17 NOVEMBER

19 November Prisoners at the Nazi Janowska camp, in western Ukraine, attempt a mass escape when ordered to cover up evidence of mass killings

23 November At a summit meeting in Cairo with Roosevelt and Churchill, China's leader Chiang Kai-shek agrees to liberate Korea after Japan's defeat

△ The ruins of Berlin after Allied bombing

28 November 1943
THE TEHRAN SUMMIT

After the Cairo summit, Roosevelt and Churchill travelled to Tehran for a four-day summit with Stalin. It was the first of the "Big Three" meetings of the war. During discussions, the Allied leaders committed to opening a second front in Western Europe, setting the scene for the D-Day landings (*see p.228*), and also discussed relations with Türkiye and Iran.

18 November 1943
THE BATTLE OF BERLIN

A huge bombing raid on the German capital marked the start of a four-month RAF campaign designed to force Germany into submission. Over that time, Bomber Command lost more than 1,000 aircraft and 7,000 aircrew in the course of 16 raids that did immense damage to the city without achieving the desired result. An estimated 7,500 civilians were killed and half a million or more were left homeless.

▽ Stalin, Roosevelt, and Churchill in Tehran

1890–1969
DWIGHT D. EISENHOWER

After supervising the North African campaign and the invasion of Sicily, Eisenhower was appointed head of the Allied forces in Europe, in charge of preparations for D-Day and the reconquest of northwest Europe. He later served as US president.

15 December 1943
THE NEW BRITAIN LANDINGS

In a further development of Operation Cartwheel (*see p.189*) , US troops staged a landing at Arawe, on the southwest coast of New Britain, off New Guinea. They established a beachhead in preparation for the long-planned assault on the Japanese base at Rabaul, on the island's eastern tip. The Arawe landings served to divert enemy forces from Cape Gloucester, targeted for attack later that month.

▷ **Beach landing** at Arawe, 15 December 1943

2 December In a raid on the Italian port of Bari, German bombers sink 27 cargo ships and kill almost 2,000 military personnel and civilians

24 December Eisenhower is appointed commander of SHAEF (Supreme Headquarters, Allied Expeditionary Force), which will plan the Normandy landings

1943

26 DECEMBER

4 December Tito proclaims a democratic government-in-exile as head of the National Committee for the Liberation of Yugoslavia

13 December In reprisal for German deaths, Wehrmacht soldiers shoot dead the entire male population of the Greek town of Kalavryta

26 December 1943
THE BATTLE OF THE NORTH CAPE

In the last big-gun naval battle of the war, fought off Norway's northern tip, the British battleship HMS *Duke of York* and accompanying cruisers and destroyers sank the German battleship *Scharnhorst* while it was on an operation to attack Allied Arctic convoys. The destruction of the German vessel helped to free up the transfer of essential supplies to the Soviet Union.

▷ **The gun deck** of HMS *Duke of York*

△ Soldiers of Canada's 48th Highlanders preparing for an attack near Ortona

28 December 1943
CROSSING THE GUSTAV LINE
Continuing their fight northward through Italy, Allied troops reached the Gustav Line – the next of the German defensive positions drawn across the peninsula. After a week-long battle, Canadian troops finally forced a way into Ortona, at the eastern end of the line. The house-to-house fighting caused so many casualties that the battle became known as "'the Italian Stalingrad".

In July 1944, the Carpetbaggers dropped more than 4,680 containers, 2,909 packages, 1,378 bundles of leaflets, and 62 special operations agents

1943

27 DECEMBER

31 December On the Eastern Front, Soviet forces recapture Zhytomyr, site of the SS's Ukrainian headquarters during the Nazi occupation

5 January Soviet forces launch a fresh offensive against Germany's 8th Army around Kirovograd in central Ukraine

1 January 1944 In the ongoing Battle of Berlin, the RAF launches a 400-bomber raid, followed the next night by one of almost equal size

9 January In Burma, Indian forces take the port of Maungdaw, a critical point of entry for Allied supplies

4 January 1944
OPERATION CARPETBAGGER BEGINS
Using modified B-24 Liberators, US bomb crews based at Harrington Field in Northamptonshire, England, made the first of a series of flights to drop arms and ammunition to partisans and resistance fighters in occupied Europe. By the end of the war, 1,860 missions had been flown, with 25 planes lost and 208 airmen killed.

△ US troops on the island of Arawe

31 December 1943
CAPE GLOUCESTER FALLS
In New Britain, New Guinea, US forces followed up their successful attack on Arawe by focusing on their main target – the island's western tip. After staging earlier landings on both sides of Cape Gloucester, US Marines won control of two Japanese air bases.

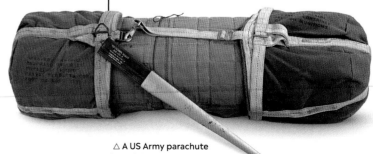

△ A US Army parachute container of the type dropped by the Carpetbaggers

△ **German soldiers** loading a rocket launcher to repel Soviet attacks

17 January 1944
THE FIGHT FOR MONTE CASSINO

On the western flank of the Gustav Line in Italy, Allied commanders unleashed the first of four assaults across the rivers Garigliano and Rapido. The area was dominated by the historic abbey atop Monte Cassino, which the Germans defended fiercely. The first push proved indecisive, leading the Allies to pause the offensive after 34 days.

14 January 1944
TARGET LENINGRAD

Three Soviet armies began a fresh offensive against the German forces surrounding Leningrad, with the aim of breaking the siege begun in September 1941. The timing of the offensive, in the depths of winter, meant that troops could move into their positions across the frozen river Neva.

△ **Red Cross staff** watching the early stages of the Battle of Monte Cassino

14 January To the south of Leningrad, Soviet forces launch a parallel offensive aimed at the town of Luga and railway lines nearby

19 January Operation Outward, a British sabotage operation using balloons, accidentally claims civilian lives by causing a train crash in Sweden

1944
19 JANUARY

12 January 1944
THE VICTORY SHIPS

In the US, the SS *United Victory* was launched in Portland, Oregon, making its maiden voyage the following March. This ship was the first of 530 Victory ships – a class of transport vessel that was slightly larger and faster than the earlier Liberty ships. Both types were invaluable in carrying personnel and supplies across the oceans to support campaigns in Europe and the Pacific region. The more powerful engines of the Victory ships gave them a top speed of 17 knots, 6 knots faster than their predecessors.

◁ **Victory ships under construction** in the yard of the California Shipbuilding Corporation

22–23 January 1944
THE ANZIO LANDINGS

In Operation Shingle, Allied forces staged a landing on the Italian coast, north of the Wehrmacht forces defending the Gustav Line and only 50 km (30 miles) south of Rome. They established a beachhead, but lost tactical advantage by entrenching their position against counterattacks instead of breaking out into the neighbouring hills. They thereby lost the opportunity to cut German supply lines to the troops fighting at Monte Cassino.

▽ **Captured German soldiers** are marched through Leningrad

△ **US soldiers making landfall** on the beach at Anzio (hand-coloured image)

27 January 1944
LENINGRAD RELIEVED

The push to relieve Leningrad succeeded when Soviet troops forced the German besiegers to withdraw south. Before quitting the city, Wehrmacht soldiers looted palaces and private homes, carrying valuable artworks back to Germany. By that time, the civilian death toll in the city had reached more than a million, and a similar number of military personnel had died in the fighting. Leningrad's liberation is still celebrated each year with a military parade on 27 January, the day that Stalin officially declared the siege to be over.

1944
20 JANUARY

20 January The RAF launches a 700-plane raid on Berlin, dropping 3,300 tons of bombs

23 January A German radio-controlled bomb sinks the British destroyer HMS *Janus* off Anzio

27 January The Red Army launches a fresh offensive in western Ukraine, targeted at the communications centres at Rovno and Lutsk

24 January 1944
CUTTING OFF THE KORSUN POCKET

In Russia, Soviet troops launched an operation to encircle 60,000 German troops trapped in an enclave centred on Korsun on the river Ros. Savage fighting ensued over the next three weeks, in the course of which some Wehrmacht soldiers managed to break out, but only at the cost of heavy losses of both men and weaponry.

▷ **General Zakharov (*left*),** chief of staff of the USSR's Second Ukrainian Front, discussing strategy with the front's commander, Marshal Ivan Konev, before the battle of Korsun

1939–45
NAZI PLUNDER

The looting of artworks happened on a massive scale in World War II at the hands of German, Japanese, and Soviet troops. However, Nazi plundering was carried out systematically, because Hitler cherished the idea (never realized) of creating a showpiece *Führermuseum* ("Leader's museum") in his home town of Linz. Works intended for the museum – many of them confiscated or stolen – were stored in salt-mine complexes as well as at Bavaria's celebrated Neuschwanstein Castle. At the end of hostilities, the Allies set up the Monuments, Fine Arts, and Archives (MFAA) programme – whose members were known as the Monuments Men, even though there were women among them – to find stolen works of art and return them to their rightful owners.

▽ **A US technical sergeant** examining an engraving by Albrecht Dürer retrieved from a salt mine in central Germany

30 January US Rangers advancing on Cisterna, 30 km (20 miles) inland from the Anzio beachhead, are driven back, with disastrous losses

30 January In the Andaman Islands, nominally under Free Indian control (*see p.202*), Japanese occupiers shoot 44 Indians suspected of spying

1944
31 JANUARY

△ **A French postage stamp** depicting de Gaulle at the Brazzaville Conference

31 January 1944
OPERATION FLINTLOCK BEGINS

In the next step of their island-hopping campaign in the Pacific, US forces began an assault on the Marshall Islands, 500 km (310 miles) to the north of the Gilbert chain. They landed on the atolls of Majuro, which fell quickly without any casualties, and Kwajalein, which was in US hands after just eight days. More than 7,000 Japanese troops were killed.

▽ **A Grumman Avenger** torpedo bomber over a US Navy task force heading for Kwajalein

30 January 1944
THE BRAZZAVILLE CONFERENCE

After France's African colonies transferred their allegiance from the Vichy regime to the Allied cause, Free French leaders met in Brazzaville, capital of French Equatorial Africa, to discuss the empire's future. The resulting Brazzaville Declaration promised citizens of the colonies equal rights with French nationals, social reforms, and an end to forced labour. In addition they were guaranteed the right to vote in French National Assembly elections once peace was restored.

5 February 1944
CAPTURING THE MARSHALL ISLANDS

Continuing their campaign in the Marshall Islands of the Central Pacific, the USA took Majuro on 1 February, then used the atoll as a staging point for further operations in the region. The 4th Marine Division took a string of small islands to the north of Kwajalein Island, while the 7th Infantry Division attacked Kwajalein itself. The Japanese were dug into a complex system of bunkers, but the island was secured on 5 February. By then 4,300 of the original 4,500 Japanese defenders had been killed.

▷ US troops clearing a Japanese position on Kwajalein (hand-coloured image)

1944

1 FEBRUARY

7 February The Germans launch an assault on "the Factory", the Allied stronghold at Aprilia, near Anzio

△ German soldier at a post on the Narva River, 1944

3 February 1944
SOVIET FORCES ENTER ESTONIA

The German 18th Army sought to impede the Red Army's progress into Estonia from its defensive positions at Lake Peipus and the river Narva. The Soviets succeeded in capturing Kingisepp, just east of the river, and then established several bridgeheads on the west bank. However, faced with counterattacks and supply difficulties, they were unable to resume the reoccupation of the Baltic republics for two months.

4 February 1944
THE JAPANESE COUNTERATTACK IN BURMA

After the failure of the British offensive in Arakan, Burma, the Japanese counterattacked in Operation Ha-Go. Their 55th Division slipped past the 7th Indian Division, stationed at the east of the British line, to attack it from the rear. Resupplied by air, the Indian troops stood firm in the "Admin Box" – a district centred on Sinzweya village. They blunted the Japanese attack and achieved one of the first genuine Allied successes in Burma (see p.217).

▽ Japanese and pro-Japanese Indian soldiers in Burma, 1944

1,220 men and 77 women were killed in the sinking of the troop carrier *Khedive Ismail*

△ **The ruined abbey** at Monte Cassino, 1944

15 February 1944
THE ALLIES ATTACK MONTE CASSINO

After the failure in January of their first assault on the German stronghold at Monte Cassino, the Allies launched a new assault, aimed at capturing the ridge that blocked their progress north. It was preceded by the controversial bombing of the abbey atop Monte Cassino, in which some 200 civilians but few German troops were killed. Parts of the 4th Indian Division pressed towards the abbey over two days, but a lack of close artillery support saw them repelled with heavy losses after bitter hand-to-hand fighting. Efforts to take Monte Cassino were then paused.

12 February The British troopship *Khedive Ismail* is sunk near the Maldives by Japanese submarine *I-27*

1944

16 FEBRUARY

10 February Allied forces link up in New Guinea as Australian troops advancing from Sio meet US forces at Yagomi, near Saidor

15 February The Polish government-in-exile rejects a Soviet proposal that the Curzon Line – a demarcation line suggested in 1919 – form the postwar Polish–Soviet border

1942–45
THE CAMPAIGN IN BURMA

By May 1942, the Japanese – aided by the forces of Azad Hind (*see p.202*) and the Burma Independence Army – had driven the Allies out of Burma. British counterattacks in 1942–43 were hampered by jungle conditions and disease. However, the Allies made headway in Arakan in the Battle of the Admin Box in February 1944, prompting the Japanese to renew their offensives. Field Marshal William Slim led the British and Indian forces to pivotal victories at Imphal and Kohima in June–July, after which the Allies pushed the Japanese back. The loss of Rangoon in May 1945 left the Japanese confined to an ever-smaller perimeter, but they went on fighting in Burma until September 1945.

▷ **The Burma Star medal** (replica) for subjects of the British Commonwealth who served in the Burma Campaign

1891–1970
WILLIAM SLIM

Slim's early war postings in East Africa and Syria were followed by command of the 14th Army in Burma from October 1943. His defeat of the Japanese at Imphal in 1944 secured his reputation, and Slim ended his career as governor-general of Australia.

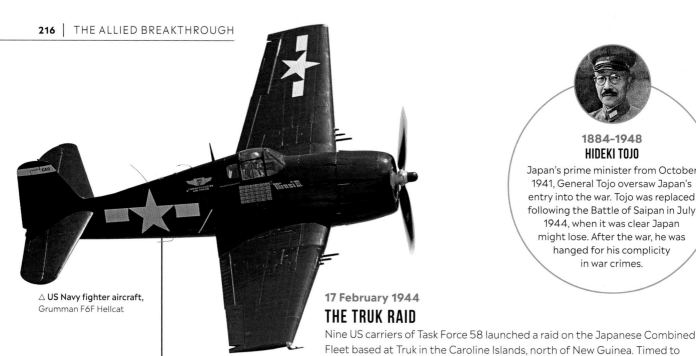

△ **US Navy fighter aircraft,**
Grumman F6F Hellcat

1884–1948
HIDEKI TOJO

Japan's prime minister from October 1941, General Tojo oversaw Japan's entry into the war. Tojo was replaced following the Battle of Saipan in July 1944, when it was clear Japan might lose. After the war, he was hanged for his complicity in war crimes.

17 February 1944
THE TRUK RAID

Nine US carriers of Task Force 58 launched a raid on the Japanese Combined Fleet based at Truk in the Caroline Islands, north of New Guinea. Timed to prevent the Japanese Navy from interfering with US landings on Eniwetok (*see below*), the attack came with little warning. The Japanese lost 270 planes and nearly 50 ships, including two cruisers and four destroyers, as Grumman F6F Hellcats peppered the atoll with high explosives.

1944

17 FEBRUARY

17 February The Red Army eliminates the Korsun-Cherkasy pocket west of the Dnieper in Ukraine; 55,000 Germans are killed

18–19 February In Italy, the Germans push on towards Anzio, but are driven back after heavy fighting

19 February The French Resistance attacks the Arsenal National, near Paris, crippling production of German light artillery

18 February 1944
PACIFIC ADVANCE

US forces landed on Eniwetok – a coral atoll of 40 small islands in the Marshall Islands group. Their primary aim was to neutralize the Japanese air base on Engebi Island. After a naval bombardment, two Marine battalions overran the base within an hour. The two other main islands of the atoll, Parry and Eniwetok, were heavily defended, with coastal sand dunes proving significant obstacles. It took five days for the Marines to overcome the Japanese. Only around 100 of the original 3,500 Japanese defenders survived the fighting.

▷ **US troops** with a captured Japanese flag on Eniwetok

20 February 1944
"BIG WEEK"

In Operation Argument, also known as the "Big Week", the US Army Air Force and RAF Bomber Command launched a series of raids targeting aircraft and ball-bearing factories in the German towns of Regensburg and Schweinfurt. Their aim was to destroy the Luftwaffe's ability to replace lost planes. The Allies dropped 15,200 tons of high explosives and shot down 517 German aircraft, but the impact on German war production was limited because the Luftwaffe had already dispersed production to other factories. The raids were ended after 25 February, as the Allies began preparing for the Normandy landings.

◁ **Ground crewmen** ready to load munitions onto a US P-51 Mustang fighter plane

21 February General Tojo becomes chief of the Imperial Japanese Army General Staff, taking direct control of the war's direction

22 February Greek resistance fighters derail a German troop train in the Tempe Valley, killing 400

24 February The Allies secure Arawe, in western New Britain, as part of Operation Cartwheel

1944

28 FEBRUARY

21 February 1944
SUCCESS AT ARAKAN

In Burma, at the conclusion of the Battle of the Admin Box, troops from the 5th Indian Division broke though Japanese lines, advanced through the Ngakyedauk Pass, and occupied the surrounding heights. This ended the Japanese siege of Sinzweya and their Arakan offensive, as the bulk of their forces retreated. Monsoon rains prevented the Allies capitalizing on this retreat – the first reversal of a major Japanese offensive in Burma.

▷ Indian troops in Burma, 1944

◁ **Soviet stamp** depicting General Fyodor Tolbukhin, a commander of the Kryvyi Rih operation

22 February 1944
THE RED ARMY ADVANCES IN DONBAS

The Soviet 3rd Ukrainian Front recaptured Kryvyi Rih in Ukraine's industrial Donbas region. The operations around Nikopol and Kryvyi Rih aimed to eliminate a salient occupied by the Germans to the east of the Dnieper. In blizzard conditions that made air support impossible, the Red Army threatened to cut off the German garrison of Kryvyi Rih, which pulled out just in time. Even so, more than 4,500 German troops were captured, and the Axis units that fell back to a new defensive line along the river Inhulets were severely depleted.

△ **Propaganda poster** for EAM, the Greek National Liberation Front, 1944

29 February 1944
CEASEFIRE IN GREECE

Tensions between Greece's resistance groups – the royalist EDES, republican EKKA, and communist ELAS-EAM – had been growing as each manoeuvred to secure dominance after Greece's eventual liberation. By mid-1942, this friction had escalated into a near civil war, as ELAS, supported by Soviet aid, destroyed the smaller EKKA group and confined the British-backed EDES to parts of Epirus. In February 1944, the British-brokered Plaka Agreement brought a halt to the fighting, but only temporarily.

> "What was I to do... I could not leave a sinking ship... in the greatest possible need of its captain."

ADMIRAL HORTHY ON HIS CONTINUED COOPERATION WITH THE GERMANS AFTER THE MARCH 1944 OCCUPATION OF HUNGARY

1944

29 FEBRUARY

29 February US forces land on Los Negros (Admiralty Islands), north of New Guinea

1 March In Estonia, Soviet forces break through German defensive lines south of Narva

4 March "Merrill's Marauders", the first US Army unit in combat in Burma, captures Walawbum

7 March The Japanese launch Operation U-Go, a major offensive in Burma, advancing towards Tiddim and then Imphal, but the Allies make gains in Arakan

9 March The Soviets drop incendiary bombs over Tallin, Estonia, destroying thousands of homes after saboteurs cut off the city's water supply

6 March 1944
THE FIRST MAJOR ALLIED DAYLIGHT RAID ON BERLIN

The US 8th Air Force launched the first large-scale daylight raid on the German capital. The attack, which targeted the city and the nearby Erkner ball-bearing factory, involved 730 B-17 and B-24 bombers and almost 800 accompanying fighters. The results of the raid were limited, but it succeeded in forcing the Luftwaffe to pull aircraft from northern France to defend Berlin.

▷ **View from USAAF bomber** dropping its load of bombs over Berlin

19 March 1944
GERMAN FORCES OCCUPY HUNGARY

Fearing that Hungary's regent, Admiral Horthy, might make peace with the Allies, Hitler summoned him to Germany and, in his absence, sent German troops into Hungary. Horthy chose to collaborate with the Nazis, vainly hoping to lessen the severity of the occupation. As a consequence, larger numbers of Hungarian troops were sent to the Eastern Front, and the Germans began deporting Hungary's 800,000 Jews to extermination camps.

◁ German soldiers at Budapest, 1944

15 March Allied bombers launch a major raid on Monte Cassino, virtually destroying Cassino town, while New Zealand and Indian troops attack the abbey

20 March US troops land on Emirau Island in the Bismarck Archipelago, intending to use it as an air base

1944

20 MARCH

15 March Konev's 2nd Ukrainian Front reaches the river Bug, having captured Uman on 10 March

17 March Finland rejects the USSR's terms for an armistice between the two countries

△ A Hungarian Panther tank on the Eastern Front, 1944

20 March 1944
VICTORY AT HUKAWNG

The US 5307th Composite Unit, known as Merrill's Marauders after its commander, General Frank Merrill, specialized in long-range jungle penetration in Burma. The force wrested control of the Hukawng Valley in the north from the Japanese 18th Division. It then moved south to Shaduzup and Inkangahtawng in a gruelling 1,200-km (746-mile) advance, during which almost one-sixth of their original 2,750 number became casualties through disease or exhaustion.

17 March 1944
SOVIET FORCES REACH THE DNIEPER

General Malinovsky's 3rd Ukrainian Front liberated the river Dnieper port of Kherson on 13 March, while to the north, General Konev's 2nd Ukrainian Front advanced to the river Dniester. Having retaken most of Ukraine, Soviet forces were now nearing the borders of Axis allies Romania and Hungary.

▷ General Frank Merrill, 1944

24 March 1944
BREAKOUT FROM STALAG LUFT III

In one of the war's most audacious actions, 76 men escaped from Stalag Luft III, a prison camp for Allied airmen near Sagan (now Zagan) in Poland. After painstakingly digging three long tunnels (nicknamed Tom, Dick, and Harry), the prisoners found that the only usable one (Harry) fell short of the nearby forest, slowing their escape. Almost all of the escapees were quickly recaptured, and 50 were executed. Only three made it to safety, two to Sweden and one to Spain. The breakout was later fictionalized in *The Great Escape* (1963).

◁ **German prison guards** sweeping the perimeter of Stalag Luft III with a searchlight

1944

21 MARCH

24 March Major General Orde Wingate (*see p.172*), commander of the Chindits in Burma, is killed in an air crash

24 March Flight Sergeant Nicholas Alkemade survives jumping from a blazing RAF Lancaster without a parachute in a raid over Berlin

26 March The communist-backed National Liberation Front (EAM) establishes a provisional government in northern Greece

△ **Relatives of victims** of the Ardeatine Cave massacre praying at the site, 1944

29 March 1944
THE BATTLE OF IMPHAL

The Japanese believed that the Allies were planning to attack Burma from their base at Imphal, northeast India, and so launched an assault on British India in early March. The Allies withdrew to the plain around Imphal while the Japanese advanced, cutting the supply road from Dimapur to Imphal and besieging the towns of Imphal and Kohima (*see opposite*). The defenders were reinforced, and they prevailed as Japanese supply lines faltered.

24 March 1944
THE ARDEATINE CAVES MASSACRE

Following a bomb attack in Rome on Nazi police by Italian partisans, German field marshal Albert Kesselring ordered a brutal reprisal. The SS gathered 335 men, including captured resistance members, civilians, and Jewish prisoners. They were taken to the Ardeatine Caves outside Rome and shot. Kesselring later issued a decree holding the Italian population responsible for acts of resistance. Though later convicted of war crimes, Kesselring was pardoned and freed in 1952.

▷ **A British officer** interrogating a Japanese prisoner during the Battle of Imphal

▷ Poster showing Indian Nationalist Subhas Chandra Bose mourning Japan's failure to take Kohima

8 April 1944
THE CRIMEAN OFFENSIVE

The Soviet 4th Ukrainian Front launched a major offensive in Crimea to clear out the German 17th Army garrison. More than 400,000 Red Army troops swept across the Perekop Peninsula, taking Simferopol and Kerch within four days and reducing the Germans and their Romanian allies to a perimeter around Sevastopol, where they held out until May.

6 April 1944
THE SIEGE OF KOHIMA

As part of their attack on India, the Japanese besieged Kohima in the Naga Hills, a town that overlooked the Dimapur to Imphal supply road. The small garrison and a brigade of the 7th Indian Division defended the stronghold until the siege was lifted on 19 April, after which Japanese ambitions in India were scaled back.

▷ Germans POWs taken in fighting near Sevastopol, 1944

29 March The Soviet 1st Ukrainian Front reaches the foothills of the Carpathians, an entry point to the Balkans

11 April An RAF raid destroys the Central Population Registry building in The Hague that contains Gestapo records

1944

11 APRIL

3–5 April The Allies target Romania with heavy bombing raids on Bucharest and oil installations at Ploesti

10 April Soviet forces take Odesa as the German 6th Army retreats to the Dniester to avoid encirclement

Flight Sergeant Alkemade fell 5,500 m (18,000 ft) without a parachute and survived

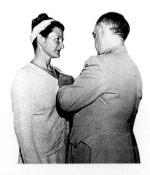

1942–45
GREAT ESCAPES

The war saw acts of courage, ingenuity, and endurance as prisoners, both individually and in groups, attempted to escape to freedom.

November 1942 Virginia Hall, a US SOE agent, flees across the Pyrenees to Spain to avoid arrest by the Gestapo. In two days, she walks more than 80 km (50 miles) on her artificial leg.

5 August 1944 1,100 Japanese POWs charge the gate and fences at Cowra camp near Sydney, Australia, on hearing the signal of a bugle blast; 230 die in the escape.

Spring 1945 British POWS at the high-security Colditz prison construct a glider in an attic above the chapel for use in an escape attempt. US troops liberate the camp before the glider can be used.

18 April 1944

THE SOVIETS BESIEGE SEVASTOPOL

With Fyodor Tolbukhin's 4th Ukrainian Front striking south through the neck of the Crimean Peninsula and the Soviet Independent Coastal Army advancing westwards from Kerch, the German 17th Army, under General Erwin Jaenecke, fell back rapidly. By 18 April, its 235,000 men were besieged in Sevastopol. Hitler ordered Jaenecke to defend the city to the last, but knowing he faced a disaster on the scale of Stalingrad, Jaenecke began evacuating his army by sea.

▷ **A Soviet serviceman** loading an anti-aircraft gun during the attack on Sevastopol

1944

12 APRIL

16 April Adolf Eichmann begins the concentration of 800,000 Hungarian Jews in ghettos prior to their deportation to death camps

17 April The Soviet 1st Ukrainian Front captures Tarnopol in the Carpathians, despite Hitler's order that it be defended to the last man

19 April The US House of Representatives votes to renew the Lend-Lease legislation (*see p.94*)

19 April Allied troops from Dimapur link up with Kohima's defenders to break the siege; the Japanese withdraw on 31 May, having suffered more than 6,000 casualties

18 April 1944

THE BABY BLITZ

In the final major attack of the "Baby Blitz" – a German strategic bombing campaign against Britain's cities – 125 German aircraft raided London. The Baby Blitz, which began on 21 January, inflicted relatively little damage compared to the Blitz of 1941. Its impact was blunted by reduced Luftwaffe numbers and improved British air defences. Even so, nearly 1,500 British civilians were killed. More than 500 German planes were destroyed, further limiting the Luftwaffe's operational capacity.

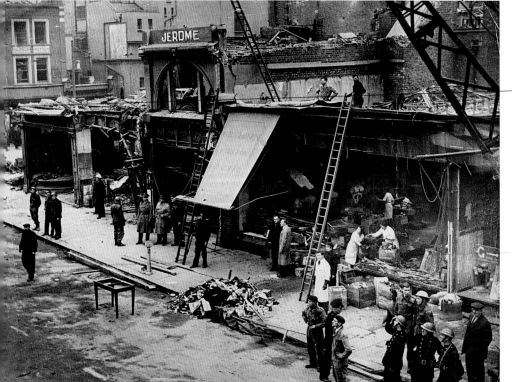

◁ **Wrecked buildings in South London** in the aftermath of a Baby Blitz bombing raid, 1944

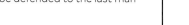

22 April 1944
US LANDINGS IN NEW GUINEA

With a mission to capture the airfields in the area and pin down the Japanese 18th Army at Wewak, 52,000 US troops were landed at Hollandia and Aitape in northern New Guinea. The Japanese were unprepared, and both landing points were lightly defended, so the Allies were able to take the airfields within four days, opening the way for an advance into western New Guinea unhindered by the substantial Japanese force still at Wewak.

◁ **US soldiers advancing along a beach** littered with the remains of Japanese supply dumps during the attack on Hollandia

> ## "The wounded German beast must be pursued and finished off in its lair."

JOSEPH STALIN'S ORDER OF THE DAY, 1 MAY 1944

22 April In China, the Japanese capture Wenzhou and Jujian to prevent their use as Allied air and naval bases

1 May Stalin marks the liberation of German-occupied Soviet territory in his Order of the Day speech

1944

5 MAY

5 May British, Australian, and South African planes dive-bomb and destroy the Pescara Dam in eastern Italy

△ **A German Kriegsmarine E-boat badge**

27 April 1944
ATTACK AT SLAPTON SANDS

At Slapton Sands in Devon, England, an exercise to simulate the planned landings in Normandy ended in disaster. Under cover of darkness, nine German E-boats had entered the training area; the German vessels attacked a convoy of landing craft delivering US troops to the beach, killing more than 700. Afterwards, the Allies almost called off the D-Day landings as they were worried that the Germans knew their plans.

◁ **General Heinrich Kreipe,** captured by Allied agents in Crete, April 1944

30 April 1944
GERMAN GENERAL KIDNAPPED

In an action by British SOE agents and Cretan partisans, General Heinrich Kreipe, the German commander in Crete, was seized while being driven from his residence near Knossos. After evading dozens of roadblocks, the Allied agents and their captive were evacuated by sea to Alexandria. The Germans executed 50 Cretan villagers in reprisal for the kidnapping.

In June 1944, following the D-Day landings, German POWs began arriving in Britain from Normandy. The number of German POWs in the UK peaked at more than 400,000, distributed in more than 1,000 camps across the country.

1939-45
PRISONERS OF WAR

Prisoners of war (POWs) have historically been vulnerable to bad treatment, torture, and even execution by their captors. In 1929, the revised Geneva Convention committed its signatories to more humane standards. POWs were to be given safety, medical care, and decent living conditions, which were to be inspected by the International Red Cross. The Red Cross was also able to distribute food parcels and letters to POWs. Captured men (other than officers) could be made to work, often in farming. Escape attempts were not that common, especially among German and Italian POWs. Many POWs even formed close relations with local communities. For example, 24,000 German POWs opted to remain in the UK at the end of the war. However, not all prisoners were treated well. Japan did not ratify the Geneva Convention, and the USSR refused to sign. Both treated POWs harshly, as exemplified by incidents such as the Bataan Death March (April 1942), in which the Japanese forced 75,000 Filipino and American POWs to march more than 100 km (60 miles) over rough terrain to their prison camps; nearly a quarter died en route. Conditions in Soviet and Japanese POW camps were often appalling, with disease and malnutrition rife. Likewise, Germany treated Soviet POWs horrifically, and more than half of them died in captivity, compared to just 4 per cent of Western Allied POWs.

KEY MOMENTS

1941-45 Soviet POWS
Germany captured 5.7 million Soviet military personnel (shown *right* being inspected by Himmler), subjecting them to reduced rations, forced labour, and summary execution. By 1945, over 3.3 million Soviet POWs had died from disease and starvation or been killed.

1940-43 The Burma Railway
Around 190,000 British and Commonwealth and 27,000 American troops were taken prisoner by the Japanese, who treated them brutally and worked many to death, most notably in the building of the Thailand–Burma "Death Railway" (*right*), during which 16,000 Allied POWs died.

1944 Time on their hands
POWs took any opportunity to fill their monotonous days. Theatrical performances were common (*right*), as were sporting contests, and lessons in arts and crafts. At one camp in Cornwall, UK, German POWs even made toys to give to war orphans.

11 May 1944
OPERATION DIADEM

The US 5th and British 8th Armies launched an operation to punch through the Gustav Line – a key German defensive line across the Italian Peninsula – and so open up the Liri Valley and the route northward. The Germans, expecting an amphibious attack, held their reserves far back, which allowed the 8th Army to establish bridgeheads over the river Rapido and break into the defences in the Liri Valley. General Sir Harold Alexander, commander of the Allied forces in Italy, ordered the US commander, General Mark Clark, to cut off the German 10th Army's retreat north. Clark instead chose to march towards Rome, allowing most of the German forces to escape.

▷ **British soldiers** at the eastern end of the Gustav Line, 1944

1944

6 MAY

6 May The Japanese Mitsubishi A7M – the replacement for the Zero fighter – has its first flight, but few are produced

8 May General Eisenhower selects 5 June as the date for D-Day – the Allied invasion of France

9 May Soviet forces recapture Sevastopol in Crimea after a final three-day offensive

10 May Chinese Nationalist forces launch an offensive against the Japanese across the river Salween in northern Burma

1892–1970
WLADYSLAW ANDERS

Held as a political prisoner by the USSR in 1939, Anders was freed in 1941 and allowed to take command of a Polish force. He led the Polish Army in the Middle East and Italy, playing a vital role at Monte Cassino.

18 May 1944
MONTE CASSINO CAPTURED

As part of Operation Diadem, the Allies renewed their assault on Monte Cassino, where the Germans held the high ground, on 11 May. In the final assault, Polish forces under General Wladyslaw Anders made their way to the summit under heavy German artillery fire. By the morning of 18 May, the Germans had withdrawn, and the Polish forces claimed victory by raising the Polish flag above the abbey's shattered ruins.

△ **Postcard commemorating** the Polish victory at Monte Cassino in 1944

2,400 pieces of Allied artillery bombarded Monte Cassino in preparation for the final assaults on 18 May 1941

28 May 1944
TANK BATTLE IN THE PACIFIC

When landing on Biak, an island northwest of New Guinea, the US 41st Division encountered little resistance. However, two days later, a Japanese counterattack erupted into one of the first tank battles in the southwest Pacific. General MacArthur proclaimed victory on 28 May, but the island's three airfields were not secured until August.

△ **American tanks** on Biak Island, New Guinea, 1944

▷ Field Marshal Shunroku Hata, architect of the Ichi-Go victory

26 May 1944
OPERATION ICHI-GO

The Japanese launched the second phase of Operation Ichi-Go, a series of interlinked offensives aimed at opening a corridor between Beijing and French Indochina. The Japanese advanced southward with more than 600,000 troops, forcing back the resisting Chinese Nationalist forces.

23 May The Allied VI Corps finally breaks out of the Anzio bridgehead, splitting apart the German 10th and 14th Armies

26 May The Germans repel the US 5th Army's attacks on the Hitler Line north of Valmontone in Italy

1944

4 JUNE

25 May Josip Tito, leader of Yugoslavia's communist partisans, narrowly escapes capture when a German airborne force attacks his secret base in Bosnia

▷ **Allied soldiers** in front of the Vittorio Emmanuele II monument in Rome, June 1944

4 June 1944
THE ALLIES ENTER ROME

The US 5th Army entered the Italian capital without encountering resistance. Rome was the first European capital taken by the Allies. Its occupation represented an important victory, but a controversial one. The Italians had declared Rome an open city in August 1943, and there was no strategic reason to occupy the city at that time. Moreover, General Clark's decision to call off the pursuit of the German 10th Army allowed it to establish defences to the north.

5 June 1944
OPERATION FORTITUDE

The Allies' elaborate deception operation to obscure their plans for the Normandy landings reached its finale. In Kent, the fictitious 1st US Army Group – complete with decoy tanks and barracks – was apparently preparing for an attack on the Pas-de-Calais, while airborne troops prepared to distract the Germans in northern France.

△ **British troops** marching through Bayeux

△ A rubber decoy tank

7 June 1944
ALLIED FORCES REACH BAYEUX

British troops advancing from Gold Beach, Normandy, reached Bayeux at around 9am. The Germans had already evacuated, avoiding the need for artillery or air raids on the town. It was the first major town in France to be liberated and became an important transport and logistics hub for the advance deeper into Normandy.

1944

5–6 June The RAF drops dummy parachutists over Caen and the Manche and Seine-Maritime regions, drawing attention away from Normandy's beaches

7 June British forces attack Port-en-Bessin, Normandy, needed as the terminal of the Allied PLUTO undersea fuel pipeline

5 JUNE

6 June 1944
OPERATION OVERLORD BEGINS

The Allied plan to open a new front and destroy the German war machine was named Operation Overlord. Mass seaborne landings were planned for Normandy (rather than the Pas-de-Calais, which was closer to the German heartland) because the Allies expected resistance there to be lighter following their campaign of deception. The date of the invasion – D-Day – was delayed by one day because of poor weather. On 6 June, troops were inserted behind German lines by glider and parachute before 155,000 American, British, Canadian, and Free French soldiers were landed on Normandy's beaches. The landings were supported by extensive bombing campaigns and French Resistance sabotage operations.

▷ **The US Army 1st Infantry Division** disembarking from a landing craft during the Normandy landings, 6 June 1944 (hand-coloured image)

6 June 1944
THE D-DAY LANDINGS

Airborne troops were dropped behind enemy lines while 2,500 Allied landing craft delivered 155,000 Allied troops to five beaches in Normandy. At Utah beach, the US 4th Infantry Division established a beachhead with little difficulty, but at Omaha, the US 1st Division was penned in by high cliffs and suffered nearly 5,000 casualties. The British at Gold faced stiff resistance once off the beach, but soon linked up with the 3rd Canadian Division, which came ashore at Juno. From Sword, commandos attached to the British 3rd Division quickly met up with airborne troops dropped northeast of Caen.

A foothold in France
Fierce fighting and congestion on the beaches prevented the Allies reaching their objectives on 6 June. Yet, by the end of the day, they had established a firm foothold from which to begin their advance into France.

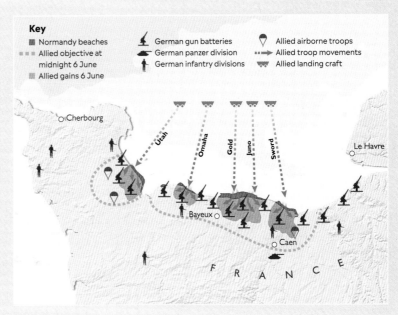

Key
- ■ Normandy beaches
- ▤ Allied objective at midnight 6 June
- ▤ Allied gains 6 June
- German gun batteries
- German panzer division
- German infantry divisions
- Allied airborne troops
- Allied troop movements
- Allied landing craft

Cherbourg · Utah · Omaha · Gold · Juno · Sword · Le Havre · Bayeux · Caen · FRANCE

---

8 June SOE operative Violette Szabo is parachuted into France, but is captured two days later

9 June The Red Army begins a major offensive against Finland on the Karelian Isthmus

10 June In the Oradour-sur-Glane massacre, an SS detachment murders 642 inhabitants of a village near Limoges, burning many to death

1944

12 JUNE

△ **American paratroopers** being dropped near Ste-Mère-Eglise on the morning of D-Day (hand-coloured image)

7 June 1944
US FORCES CAPTURE STE-MERE-EGLISE

At around 1:30am on 6 June, paratroopers of the US 505th Parachute Infantry Regiment attacked the small village of Sainte-Mère-Eglise. The US forces cleared the village and repelled a German counterattack before being relieved on 7 June by troops advancing by land from Utah beach.

12 June 1944 US
US TROOPS SECURE CARENTAN

The troops of the US 101st Airborne Division were badly scattered following their airdrop on D-Day, but were still able to capture the town of Carentan. The 2nd Armored Division then helped fight off a German counterattack and consolidate the position, which linked the beachheads at Utah and Omaha and provided a springboard for advances into Normandy.

▽ **US paratroopers** patrolling Carentan in a captured German vehicle (hand-coloured image)

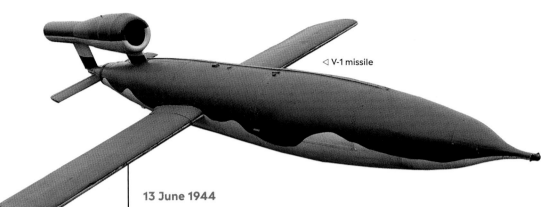

◁ V-1 missile

13 June 1944
GERMANY UNLEASHES THE V-1

V-1s, which became known as "doodlebugs", were catapult-launched German missiles carrying around a ton of high explosive. They were launched against England from sites in northern France. In the first V-1 attack, on 13 June, ten were fired as a range-finding exercise. Over the following days, the number increased substantially. V-1 attacks continued until the Allies overran the launch sites in late 1944; by then, they had caused more than 6,000 fatalities.

1885–1945
GEORGE PATTON

A hard-hitting leader, Patton led the US 7th Army in the Sicily landings in July 1943, but accusations of violent conduct caused his recall. He later led the US 3rd Army through Normandy, and finally into Austria.

13 June 1944 An experimental V-2 rocket crashes at Bäckebo, Sweden: the British government buys some of the wreckage for inspection

15 June In reprisals for resistance activities, German troops attack the town of Saint-Donat, raping and leaving for dead more than 50 French women and girls

1944

13 JUNE

△ **Queen Alexandra's Imperial Nursing Service** personnel carry a wounded soldier at Bayeux, June 1944

13 June 1944
BRITISH NURSES ARRIVE IN NORMANDY

British nurses of Queen Alexandra's Imperial Military Nursing Service (QAIMNS) became the first female military personnel to reach Normandy when they arrived to set up the 600-bed No. 79 General Hospital near Bayeux. By the end of the war, there were 12,000 nurses serving in the QAIMNS, on fronts from Burma to Germany.

15 June 1944
THE SAIPAN LANDINGS

More than 20,000 US troops landed on Saipan in the Mariana Islands of the western Pacific. They were supported by a naval bombardment from more than 70 warships. The first wave of Marines overcame a hail of Japanese defensive fire and a maze of barbed wire to establish a beachhead. Reinforcements from the US 27th Division drove back the 31,000 defenders under Lieutenant General Yoshitsugu Saito. However, the conquest of the island took 24 days to complete. Saipan became a strategic base for B-29 bombers, as it was within range of the Japanese home islands.

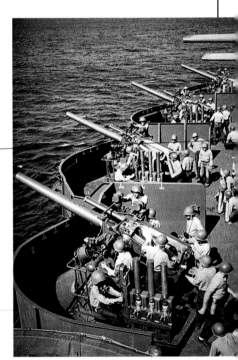

▷ **A 127mm gun battery** aboard the USS *New Mexico* off Saipan, 15 June 1944 (hand-coloured image)

15 June 1944
SUPERFORTRESSES BOMB JAPAN

The US strategic air offensive against the Japanese home islands got under way when 75 B-29 Superfortress bombers took off from forward bases in Chengdu, China, to attack the iron and steel works at Yawata, in the north of Kyushu Island. Only 48 of the B-29s dropped their payloads, and damage to Yawata's industrial area was very slight, but the poor performance of Japan's defensive anti-aircraft units and the realization that the Allies could strike at Japan's cities damaged Japanese morale.

◁ B-29 **Superfortress** aircraft dropping their bombs

16 June In Karelia, Finnish troops begin to retreat to the VKT (Viipuri-Kuparsaari-Taipale) line

18 June In France, the American capture of Barneville isolates German troops in the Cotentin Peninsula and Cherbourg

20 June The Russian offensive against the Finns on the Karelian Isthmus culminates in the capture of Viipuri

1944

20 JUNE

19–20 June 1944
THE BATTLE OF THE PHILIPPINE SEA

The war's largest carrier battle took place between US Admiral Spruance's 5th Fleet and Japanese Vice Admiral Ozawa's 1st Mobile Fleet. In what became known as the "Great Marianas Turkey Shoot", nearly 1,000 US aircraft easily detected and shot down four waves of 373 Japanese planes. Meanwhile, US submarines torpedoed Ozawa's flagship, *Taiho*, and another carrier. Spruance pursued the retreating Japanese ships, destroying a further carrier, but then pulled back, losing the chance to definitively smash Ozawa's fleet.

▷ **The Japanese aircraft carrier** *Zuikaku* (*centre*) and the destroyers *Akizuki* and *Wakatsuki* under attack by US aircraft during the Battle of the Philippine Sea

Germany launched 6,725 rockets at Britain during its V-1 campaign

23 June 1944

OPERATION BAGRATION

Named after a Russian general of the Napoleonic era, Bagration was a vast Soviet offensive designed to crush the Germans in the east. More than 1.5 million troops poured into Belorussia. The 1st Baltic Front attacked north of Vitebsk, and the 3rd Belorussian Front to the south, enveloping 40,000 Germans. Vitebsk soon fell and the Red Army tore a hole in Germany's Army Group Centre that allowed the liberation of the rest of Belorussia.

△ **Canadian soldiers** advancing through the ruins of Caen, 1944

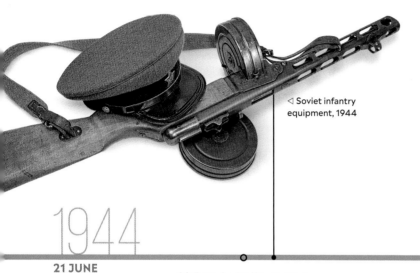

◁ **Soviet infantry equipment**, 1944

26 June 1944

THE BATTLE AT CAEN

General Montgomery launched Operation Epsom to take Caen, a key objective in Normandy. Advancing 10 km (6 miles) across fields around the city, his 60,000 troops secured some high ground, but failed to capture the strategic Hill 112. In the face of German counterattacks, Montgomery called off the operation. The Allies returned to the battle for Caen in July.

26 June Mogaung, Burma, falls to the Chindits after five days of fighting, but high casualties and sickness leave the unit barely effective

1944

21 JUNE

22 June In India, British reinforcements help lift the Japanese siege of Imphal after eight weeks

28 June The Soviet 3rd Belorussian Front begins crossing the river Berezina

June–August 1944

THE BATTLE OF NORMANDY

The Allies sought to capture key inland towns such as Caen and Falaise after securing the Normandy beaches. Allied air superiority prevented the Germans from mounting concerted counterattacks, but the difficulty of moving through the *bocage* – mixed terrain punctuated by dense hedgerows – and German resistance slowed the progress of troops on the ground. It was two months, rather than the anticipated few days, before Caen fell to the Allies. With the British drawing much of the German fire, the US 1st Army took Avranches in Operation Cobra, and soon threatened to encircle the Germans in Normandy.

▷ **US airmen** painting slogans on their bombs before a raid over Caen and Calais, June 1944

29 June 1944
CHERBOURG FALLS

US forces followed up their landing at Utah beach with an advance westward that isolated the German garrison in Cherbourg by 18 June. Lieutenant General von Schlieben, the garrison's commander, had 21,000 troops, many of them badly trained conscripts, but hoped to hold out behind the fortress walls. He repulsed an assault by the US VII Corps on 22 June, but after concerted naval bombardment and the gradual capture of key defences, he surrendered on 29 June.

◁ **US troops marching German prisoners** through Cherbourg, June 1944 (hand-coloured image)

30 June Allied forces secure Biak Island off New Guinea, but Japanese remnants resist until August

5 July Günther von Kluge replaces Field Marshal von Rundstedt as German supreme commander in the West

6 July Admiral Nagumo commits suicide as US forces clear the island of Saipan. Nagumo's co-commander, General Saito, kills himself four days later

1944

6 JULY

"You and your existence! We can die honourably, like soldiers."

GERMAN COMMANDER GENERAL MARCKS, SECONDS BEFORE BEING FATALLY WOUNDED BY AN ALLIED FIGHTER-BOMBER, NORMANDY

3 July 1944
MINSK CAPTURED

As Operation Bagration swept through Belorussia, Hitler declared Minsk a fortress city, to be held at all costs. He reinforced its defence with the 5th Panzer Division, but in vain; by 3 July, the Soviet 5th Guards Tank Army had pushed into the city centre. The advancing Soviets then encircled 100,000 men of the German 4th and 9th Armies to the west, killing 40,000 of them before liquidating the pocket.

◁ **Symbol of the Red Army Guards** from a Soviet memorial complex

1923–2011
TUL BADAHUR PUN

A Nepalese Gurkha, Pun was awarded Britain's Victoria Cross for gallantry for his part in the Battle of Mogaung. On 23 June 1944, after his comrades were injured during a charge, Pun continued alone, single-handedly taking an enemy position.

9 July 1944
THE END AT SAIPAN

The battle of Saipan ended after the Japanese commander, General Saito, ordered a suicidal assault by his remaining troops on 7 July. They almost overran the US 105th Infantry Regiment, but the Americans fought back fiercely. Of Saipan's original 29,000-strong Japanese garrison, almost none survived.

◁ **The funeral of General Saito,** who died by ritual suicide after the failure of the final Japanese attack

3,000 Japanese troops took part in the final attack at Saipan

1944

7 JULY

10 July A Soviet offensive in the Baltic States begins with an attack northwest of Vitebsk

16 July In Italy, the British 8th Army breaks through at Arezzo, reaching the river Arno; on 24 July, US forces capture Pisa

18 July Japan's General Tojo resigns and is replaced by General Koiso, with Admiral Yonai as his deputy

17 July Rommel suffers serious injuries after his car is attacked by a British fighter-bomber in northern France

△ A crashed Japanese plane near Aitape

13 July 1944
THE CAPTURE OF VILNIUS

As part of Operation Bagration, the Soviet 3rd Belorussian Front led by General Chernyakhovsky encircled Vilnius, in Lithuania. The Red Army's rapid advance thwarted the Polish Home Army's attempt to seize the city. A counterattack by the 6th Panzer Army allowed 3,000 Germans to escape, but could not prevent the Soviets taking the city on 13 July.

10 July 1944
NEW GUINEA OFFENSIVE

The Japanese 18th Army, based around Wewak, on the north coast of the island of New Guinea, launched a counteroffensive west over the river Driniumor towards Aitape. Led by General Adachi, they reached as far as Afua. In the face of an upcoming US counterattack, Adachi ordered a withdrawal on 4 August, having suffered more than 8,000 casualties.

▽ Captured German soldiers being marched through Vilnius, 13 July 1944

20 July 1944
THE PLOT TO KILL HITLER

Hitler narrowly escaped assassination at his headquarters near Rastenburg. The plot was led by Count von Stauffenberg, the head of the German Home Army and part of a group of dissident Wehrmacht officers who wanted to replace Hitler. Von Stauffenberg set a briefcase bomb close to where Hitler was sitting in a conference room. However, the bomb was moved away, and Hitler was only slightly wounded when it exploded. Von Stauffenberg's planned coup was rapidly suppressed, and he and his fellow conspirators were executed.

▷ **Hermann Göring and Nazi dignitaries** in the conference room after the attempted assassination (hand-coloured image)

18 July In Normandy, Canadian forces begin Operation Atlantic around the river Orne, and the British commence Operation Goodwood against Caen

22 July Moscow announces the formation of a pro-Soviet Polish Committee for National Liberation in Chelm, Poland

27 July The Soviet Ukrainian Front takes Lviv in Ukraine, and Brest-Litovsk the next day

1944
27 JULY

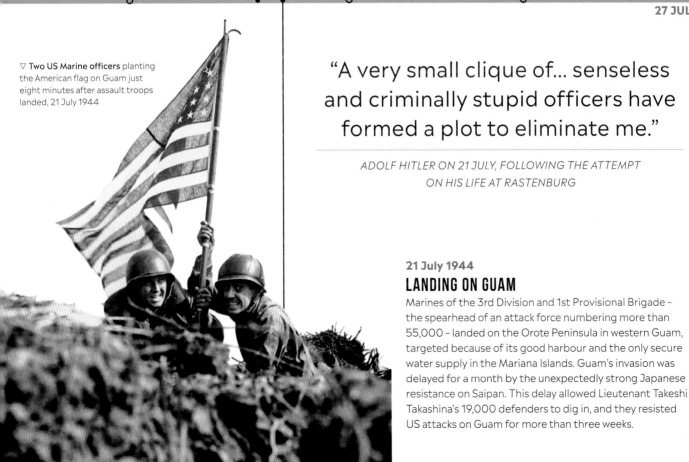

▽ **Two US Marine officers** planting the American flag on Guam just eight minutes after assault troops landed, 21 July 1944

"A very small clique of... senseless and criminally stupid officers have formed a plot to eliminate me."

ADOLF HITLER ON 21 JULY, FOLLOWING THE ATTEMPT ON HIS LIFE AT RASTENBURG

21 July 1944
LANDING ON GUAM

Marines of the 3rd Division and 1st Provisional Brigade – the spearhead of an attack force numbering more than 55,000 – landed on the Orote Peninsula in western Guam, targeted because of its good harbour and the only secure water supply in the Mariana Islands. Guam's invasion was delayed for a month by the unexpectedly strong Japanese resistance on Saipan. This delay allowed Lieutenant Takeshi Takashina's 19,000 defenders to dig in, and they resisted US attacks on Guam for more than three weeks.

1939-45
ANIMALS IN THE WAR

Total warfare such as that experienced in World War II profoundly affects animal as well as human populations. When Britain entered the conflict in 1939, a government-sponsored pamphlet suggested that pet owners should consider having their animal companions euthanized. Worried about food shortages, many people followed the advice; one estimate suggests that 750,000 pets were killed in this way.

Other animals played an unwitting part in the conflict. Accounts of whales being mistaken for submarines led the Australian Navy to issue a report on how to differentiate between the two. Allied soldiers in the Burma campaign told of Japanese troops forced into mangrove swamps being devoured by saltwater crocodiles, although recent research suggests most more likely drowned.

While the Red Army had a unit that trained dogs to act as living bombs, most animals in active service played a less destructive role. Horses and mules were used as pack animals, while camels and even elephants were put to work in desert and jungle locations. The US Army encouraged pet owners to donate their dogs to help with guard and patrol duties. And dogs, cats, goats, pigs, and even mice boosted morale as mascots for military units.

KEY MOMENTS

1939-45 Mascots
Dogs like this USAAF pilot's pet (*left*) have served as military mascots since at least the 18th century. Among the more unusual mascots was Wojtek, a Syrian brown bear that accompanied Polish II Corps soldiers to Italy.

1941-45 Elephants in Asia
Elephants saw service as baggage animals in the Burma campaign, where they were used to haul heavy loads in the difficult jungle terrain. One such elephant, captured by Chinese troops in 1943, survived the war and lived on in a Taiwan zoo until 2003.

1941-45 Soviet anti-tank dogs
The Red Army put dogs – mostly German shepherds – to lethal use. They were trained to run under tanks, where the bomb they had strapped to them would detonate. The experiment had little success: in the noise of battle, many dogs chose to run back to their trainers, sometimes killing them.

A terrier from an animal-rescue shelter sniffs through rubble for possible survivors following a bombing raid in November 1942. In all, seven British search-and-rescue dogs were rewarded for their efforts with the Dickin Medal, given for animal bravery.

1 August 1944

THE POLISH UPRISING BEGINS

As Soviet troops approached Warsaw, the Polish Home Army (the Armia Krajowa, or AK) began an insurrection against the capital's German occupiers. Some 50,000 poorly equipped AK fighters seized the Old Town and much of the centre. They were pushed out in bitter street fighting by 2 September. Pockets held on until 2 October, by which time 15,000 insurgents and 250,000 civilians had died. Meanwhile, the Red Army waited outside Warsaw, allowing the Poles to be massacred.

▷ **A Polish Home Army propaganda poster** urges "Poles to arms!"

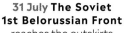

The last Japanese holdout on Guam surrendered in 1974

1944

28 JULY

28 July As part of Operation Cobra, the 4th Armored Division of the US 1st Army takes Coutances in Normandy

31 July In the Normandy breakout, the US 1st Army captures Avranches and is joined by the 3rd Army under George Patton, which later takes Angers and Nantes

31 July The Soviet 1st Belorussian Front reaches the outskirts of Warsaw

1 August The 3rd Belorussian Front captures Kaunas, capital of Lithuania

1895–1966
TADEUSZ BOR-KOMOROWSKI

Commander of the AK, Komorowski ordered the Warsaw Uprising in August 1944. He was captured by the Germans and imprisoned in Colditz Castle. After the war, he served as prime minister of the Polish government-in-exile in London.

1942–45
THE SEABEES

US Naval Construction Battalions (NCBs, or "Seabees") were formed in 1942 to address the US Navy's need for personnel trained in construction. More than 325,000 were recruited by the war's end, including 12,500 African Americans. They built a variety of military structures, such as harbours, pontoons, bridges, and advance bases, and served as stevedores for the rapid unloading of ships. Although 80 per cent served in the Pacific (including more than 50,000 at one time in Okinawa), they were also deployed to North Africa, Italy, and the Rhine, often working under fire on the front line.

△ **Crest of the US Seabees.** Their motto was: "We build, we fight"."

7 August 1944
GERMAN STRONGHOLDS SURROUNDED

Moving westward into Brittany, US troops encircled Brest, aiming to capture its harbour. The 36,000 German defenders under General Ramcke refused to surrender and held out in intense fighting until 19 September, by which time Brest's destroyed port was useless. US forces also surrounded Lorient and Saint-Nazaire, which surrendered only in May 1945.

▷ **An American artillery unit** firing an 8-inch gun into Brest, France

▷ **1st US Airborne Division** paratroops over the Provençal Alps in southern France

15 August 1944
THE ALLIES INVADE SOUTHERN FRANCE

In Operation Dragoon, three divisions of the US VI Corps, supported by French commandos, landed near Cannes, aiming to capture Marseille and thrust north towards Lyon. German resistance was weak, because much of General Blaskowitz's Army Group G had been redeployed to Normandy. The Allies advanced rapidly on Marseille and Toulon.

3 August Stilwell's Chindits finally capture Myitkyina in Burma, opening up the road to Ledo

10 August US forces secure Guam, but thousands of Japanese soldiers remain at large

1944

20 AUGUST

6 August In Normandy, the Germans launch a counterattack from Mortain to cut off the American advance southwards from Caen

19 August French Resistance fighters stage an uprising in Paris, holding out until Free French forces arrive five days later

> "The Germans were trying to run and had no place to run. They were probably too tired even to surrender."

US OFFICER ON THE SITUATION AT FALAISE, 20 AUGUST 1944

19 August 1944
THE BATTLE OF THE FALAISE POCKET

Allied troops met at Chambois, east of Falaise, sealing 50,000 German troops of Army Group B inside a pocket. Under assault by US forces from the south and Canadians and British from the north, 10,000 German soldiers were killed and 50,000 were captured, destroying Germany's last major fighting force in Normandy.

▷ **The meeting between American and Canadian troops** to mark the closing of the Falaise pocket (hand-coloured image)

21 August 1944
THE DUMBARTON OAKS CONFERENCE

Delegates from the USA, the USSR, the UK, and China met near Washington, DC, to establish a framework for postwar global security. The participating nations agreed a 12-chapter set of principles for the establishment of a United Nations organization and an International Court of Justice. The USA resisted Soviet demands that all 16 of its republics have separate UN membership.

△ **Romanian coin** with portrait of King Michael, 1944

△ **Delegates enjoying** an outdoor lunch at Dumbarton Oaks, Washington, DC

23–25 August 1944
ROMANIA LEAVES THE AXIS

King Michael of Romania ordered the arrest of military dictator General Antonescu and declared Romania's withdrawal from the war. The Germans attempted to retain control, but the Romanian Royal Guard resisted. The German 8th Army retreated into Hungary, allowing Soviet forces to enter Bucharest on 31 August.

23 August In Normandy, US forces capture Evreux; in the south, they take Marseille and reach Grenoble

25 August The Soviet 3rd Baltic Front captures Tartu, Estonia, and fights off German attempts to retake it

1944
21 AUGUST

23 August A German V-1 kills 211 people in London, the worst death toll from a single such bomb

26 August Bulgaria's government announces its withdrawal from the war and the disarmament of its German garrison

24–25 August 1944
PARIS LIBERATED

General von Choltitz, commander of the German garrison in Paris, agreed a ceasefire with resistance fighters from the French Forces of the Interior on 23 August. General Patton permitted parts of Philippe Leclerc's Free French 2nd Armoured Division to push into central Paris, where they occupied the Hôtel de Ville ("city hall") on 24 August. The next day, von Choltitz surrendered and General de Gaulle entered Paris to the cheers of huge crowds.

▷ **A parade celebrating** the liberation of Paris, August 1944

August–September 1944
FRANCE AND BELGIUM REGAINED

The long-awaited Allied breakout from Normandy on 30 July was followed by rapid advances as the German front lines collapsed to the south and the east. Amid disagreements between Eisenhower, who favoured an advance along a broad front from Antwerp to the Swiss border, and Montgomery, who championed a narrow front, the Allies crossed into Belgium on 2 September and into the Netherlands on 4 September. They reached the German border a week later. In France, only small pockets of resistance on the coast remained by mid-September.

Allied advances
While the Allies fanned out eastward and northward across northern France and Belgium, an invasion force swept northward from the south.

Key
- ■ Allied gains by 13 Aug
- ■ Allied gains by 26 Aug
- ■ Allied gains by 14 Sept
- ■ Axis territory 14 Sept
- → Allied advance from Normandy 13 Aug–14 Sept
- → Allied invasion of southern France and advance 15 Aug–14 Sept

26–29 August German forces retreat across the river Seine; they are followed by Allied troops who ensure that they cannot regroup

29 August Allied troops take Pinbaw, on the Myitkyina–Katha railway, as they move south through northern Burma

28 August The German garrison in Marseille surrenders, and the Allies clear Toulon

29 August A Slovak national uprising occurs when German troops move to occupy Slovakia

1944
30 AUGUST

26 August 1944
THE GERMANS LEAVE GREECE

German garrisons began to withdraw from mainland Greece after the collapse of the Axis position in Romania. They left Athens on 12 October and had completed the evacuation by the beginning of November, provoking a scramble among resistance groups to fill the power vacuum.

"Only the dead stopped fighting."

FRENCH GENERAL DE LATTRE DE TASSIGNY, ON THE GERMAN RESISTANCE AT TOULON

30 August 1944
FRENCH TOWNS FALL

In a single day, the Canadians took Rouen, the British Beauvais, and the Americans Reims. The accelerating pace of the Allied advance began to create logistics problems, as none of the Channel ports was yet in sufficiently good repair to accept supplies in volume.

▷ **Destroyed bridge** and the ruins of Rouen Cathedral

3 September 1944

THE LIBERATION OF BRUSSELS

The British Guards Armoured Division entered the Belgian capital at 8pm after advancing 360 km (220 miles) across France and Belgium in just four days. The German garrison had fled Brussels that morning. On 8 September, the Belgian government returned to Brussels after nearly four years in exile.

▷ **Inhabitants of Brussels** celebrating the end of four years of German occupation with a wreath symbolizing the death of Nazism

▷ **Stamp commemorating** the liberation of Bucharest

31 August 1944

THE RED ARMY TAKES BUCHAREST

The Red Army advanced rapidly through Romania after the coup of 23 August. The German forces occupying the country soon crumbled and Romanian units began attacking their former allies. On 31 August, the 2nd Ukrainian Front advanced nearly 60 km (40 miles) in a single day to capture Bucharest.

31 August The Allied advance across France continues: the Free French capture Bordeaux; the British take Amiens and cross the Somme

2 September The US 5th Army captures Pisa and, near Rimini, the British 8th Army breaks through the Gothic Line – the Germans' last major line of defence in Italy

1944

31 AUGUST

1 September Allied progress in France sees Canadian forces reach Dieppe, the British take Arras, and the Americans capture Verdun

2 September Retreating across Romania, German forces reach the border with northern Bulgaria

Finland had to pay the USSR US$300 million as part of their 1944 armistice

1944–45
V-WEAPONS

The Germans launched the first V-1 bombs against southern England in June 1944, and the first V-2 rockets in September.

28 August 1944 90 of 94 V-1 launches are destroyed by anti-aircraft guns, fighters, and barrage balloons.

12 October 1944 The Germans begin V-2 attacks on the Belgian port of Antwerp. Around 107 rockets hit central Antwerp by March 1945.

25 November 1944 The worst casualties of the V-2 campaign occur when a rocket hits a Woolworth store in London, killing 168 people.

3–4 April 1945 The Allies bomb the Mittelwerk V-2 weapons factory, killing more than 1,000 forced labourers from Mittelbau-Dora camp.

11 September 1944
THE ALLIES ENTER GERMANY

A patrol from the US 5th Armored Division crossed the river Our, which forms the border between Luxembourg and Germany near Stolzembourg. This early penetration into the enemy's homeland was of symbolic importance; however, the Allies made no real progress into Germany until mid-October because they were diverted to clearing the Scheldt estuary and securing Antwerp and its port.

▷ **US Army Signal Corps** personnel at the German border, October 1944

4 September Allied forces capture Antwerp, in Belgium, after brief skirmishes

7 September The Japanese take Lingling (now Yongzhou), the gateway to Guangxi province, home to the main US air bases in China

8 September Advancing though the Balkans, the Red Army enters Bulgaria, which then declares war on Germany

1944

11 SEPTEMBER

5 September A ceasefire ends fighting between Finland and the USSR. They sign an armistice on 19 September

△ **The aftermath of the V-2 explosion** in Chiswick, London, September 1944

11 September 1944
THE ALLIES MEET IN QUEBEC

Allied leaders gathered in the Canadian city for the Second Quebec Conference, code-named Ocatgon, and a series of other meetings. There, they agreed a timetable for the reconquest of Burma and the dispatch of British troops to Greece, and developed a postwar policy for Germany.

▽ **Allied leaders** at the Second Quebec Conference, September 1944

8 September 1944
V-2 ROCKET ATTACKS ON LONDON BEGIN

A V-2 rocket launched from a site near The Hague, in the Netherlands, was the first to hit London, killing three people in Chiswick, in the west of the city. After a brief pause while the Germans moved their rocket batteries further east, the attacks resumed in October. The V-2 was harder to intercept than the V-1 and by March 1945, more than 1,100 V-2s had been fired at England, causing over 8,000 civilian casualties.

12 September 1944
ROMANIAN ARMISTICE

Romania – by now largely occupied by the Red Army – signed an armistice with the Allies in Moscow. It placed itself in the hands of a commission made up of the USSR, the USA, and the UK, and committed to providing 12 divisions to fight the Axis. The Romanians were forced to cede Bessarabia and Northern Bukovina to the USSR.

△ An anti-German sign in Romania, 1944

"We can hold it [Arnhem Bridge] for four [days]. But I think we might be going a bridge too far."

GENERAL BROWNING, COMMANDER, 1ST AIRBORNE DIVISION, SEPTEMBER 1944

15 September 1944
THE 1ST POLISH ARMY ENTERS WARSAW

Elements of the pro-Soviet 1st Polish Army crossed the river Vistula from the Warsaw suburb of Praga and made contact with the Polish Home Army, whose forces were leading the Warsaw Uprising. However, the Red Army did not reinforce them, and the bridgehead was evacuated after four days. Without Soviet support on the ground, the uprising was doomed to fail.

13 September The Red Army drops arms to the Poles in Warsaw, but released without parachutes, most are damaged on landing

15 September US forces land on Morotai, a Pacific island needed as a support base for the planned retaking of the Philippines

1944

12 SEPTEMBER

14 September Maastricht is the first Dutch city to be liberated when it is recaptured by the US 1st Army and the Dutch resistance

15 September 1944
THE BRAZILIAN EXPEDITIONARY FORCE IN ITALY

The soldiers of Brazil's expeditionary force (the Força Expedicionária Brasileira), who called themselves *Cobras Fumantes* ("smoking snakes"), fought their first combat engagement in Italy, supporting the US 5th Army in the capture of Massarosa. This was followed by hard fighting for the 25,000 Brazilian soldiers as they breached the Gothic Line and advanced through northern Italy. They reached the French border by May 1945, having suffered almost 1,000 fatalities along the way.

▷ **The 1st Division** of the Brazilian Expeditionary Force on parade in Naples, 1944

17-25 September 1944
THE BATTLE OF ARNHEM

The Allies launched Operation Market Garden, an ambitious, and ultimately disastrous, attempt to seize bridges over the Rhine at Arnhem, in the Netherlands, to accelerate their advance into Germany. Allied paratroopers were dropped behind enemy lines and quickly seized several river crossings, while ground forces advanced from the south. However, German counterattacks left the British forces in Arnhem isolated. On 25 September, the Allies managed to evacuate 2,400 men from Arnhem, but some 1,500 others had died and 6,500 had been captured.

◁ **A unit of the British 1st Airborne Division** in a glider on the way to Arnhem, September 1944 (hand-coloured image)

19 September The German garrison at Brest, in northwest France, surrenders after a six-week siege

22 September The Channel port of Boulogne surrenders to the 3rd Canadian Division after a five-day-long assault

24 September British troops begin landing on the Greek islands and mainland after the German forces withdraw

1944

24 SEPTEMBER

21 September Canadian troops of the 8th Army capture the Adriatic port of Rimini on the Gothic Line

24 September The Red Army crosses the Transylvanian Alps and reaches Hungary's border

21 September 1944
SAN MARINO DECLARES WAR

San Marino's government declared war on the Axis after troops from the 4th Indian Infantry Division expelled German forces, which had occupied the country on 13 September. The tiny state of San Marino in Central Italy had remained neutral throughout the war, although its government was broadly aligned with Italy and Germany's right-wing regimes. However, as the Allies advanced northward through Italy, German soldiers had pre-emptively occupied San Marino, bringing the country into the war.

1897-1985
E. L. M. BURNS

"Tommy" Burns led the I Canadian Corps to success at Rimini, Italy, in September 1944, but criticism of his leadership saw him removed from the front line. Burns became a respected negotiator in the UN's peacekeeping efforts after the war.

▷ San Marino's national flag

25 September 1944
GERMANY'S MILITIA

Adolf Hitler ordered the creation of a national militia – the Volkssturm ("People's Storm") – to help protect Germany from the advancing Allies. Its members were men aged between 16 and 60 who were not otherwise serving in the military. Supervised by the Nazi Party rather than the military, the Volkssturm had limited training and lacked weapons. However, the men's morale was high, and many fought to the bitter end, with 60,000 helping defend Berlin in 1945.

◁ **Wilhelm Schepmann** (*right*), chief of staff of the Volkssturm training programme

1944

25 SEPTEMBER

25 September The Allies abandon Operation Market Garden, withdrawing the British 1st Airborne Division from Arnhem

4 October British forces land in the Peloponnese and begin driving the Germans out of the peninsula and into mainland Greece

2 October The remnants of the Polish Home Army surrender to the Germans, ending the Warsaw Uprising. Around 200,000 Poles have been killed

7 October The US 1st Army penetrates the Siegfried Line north of Aachen, but German counterattacks slow further progress into Germany

6 October 1944
THE BATTLE OF THE HÜRTGEN FOREST

The US 1st Army began an offensive to capture the Hürtgen Forest, near Aachen, Germany's westernmost city. The Allies intended to pin German Army Group B in place, but the campaign quickly turned into a costly disaster. Thick vegetation, deep gorges, mud, and snow made progress near impossible and provided cover for the Germans' anti-tank units. The Americans suffered over 30,000 casualties without securing the forest. The battle ended only when the Germans diverted their forces to the Ardennes in December (*see p.254*).

▷ **German bunker** in the Hürtgen Forest

1936–44
THE SIEGFRIED LINE

The Siegfried Line (or West Wall) was a defensive bulwark stretching more than 600 km (370 miles) from Kleve, on the Dutch border, to northern Switzerland. It was constructed between 1936 and 1939 by more than 100,000 forced labourers. Not needed since the German occupation of France and the Low Countries in 1940, the Siegfried Line was put back into service when the Allies began to advance from Normandy in summer 1944. The Allies took six months to penetrate the vast network of wire, tank-traps, and bunkers.

▷ **A line of** *Höckerhindernisse* (a type of anti-tank barrier) placed along a section of the Siegfried Line

> There were approximately 22,000 bunkers along the Siegfried Line

9 October Churchill and Stalin meet in Moscow to discuss postwar arrangements for Eastern Europe, particularly the Polish-Soviet border

11 October German units trapped at Aachen refuse to surrender. US forces begin a massive artillery bombardment of the city

12 October The US 3rd Fleet launches attacks on the Japanese 2nd Air Fleet in preparation for landings at Leyte Gulf

1944

12 OCTOBER

△ **Russian soldiers in action** near Riga, 1944

10 October 1944
THE BATTLE OF RIGA

In its campaign against the German North Army in the Baltic states, the Red Army drew within artillery range of the Latvian capital, Riga. The Germans retreated through the city into the Courland Peninsula, leaving only a token force to defend their rear. The Soviets had captured Riga almost unopposed by 13 October.

12 October 1944
ATHENS IS LIBERATED

Under pressure from advancing British soldiers and Greek resistance fighters, the commander of the occupying German forces in Greece ordered the evacuation of Athens. The last German troops departed the city on 12 October, and a committee of Greek resistance fighters took control. Over the next two days, British paratroopers seized the nearby Megara airfield and the Royal Navy occupied Piraeus.

▷ **British Army soldiers** in Athens, October 1944

23–26 October 1944
THE BATTLE OF LEYTE GULF

The Japanese responded to the US landings on the Philippine island of Leyte (*see below opposite*) by sending the Imperial Fleet to destroy the US invaders. What ensued was the largest naval battle of the war, involving 282 warships and hundreds of planes. In the first clashes, US submarines and aircraft sank three Japanese cruisers and a battleship, and engagements at Samar, the Surigao Strait, and Cape Engano resulted in further losses. The Imperial Fleet was shattered by the loss of some 30 ships, including four carriers. The battle turned the war in the Pacific in the Allies' favour, giving them near complete control of the ocean.

▷ **American warships** using smokescreens to hinder Japanese air attacks during the Battle of Leyte Gulf

1944

14 October The RAF's 2,000-bomber raid on Duisburg, in western Germany, kills 2,450 people

20 October The Red Army advances from Romania into Hungary, capturing its second-largest city, Debrecen

21 October The US 1st Army captures Aachen after a week of hand-to-hand fighting in the city

13 OCTOBER

14 October Erwin Rommel dies by suicide after being implicated in the July 1944 plot to kill Hitler

15 October 1944
THE GERMANS TAKE CONTROL IN HUNGARY

In Operation Panzerfaust, SS operatives overthrew Hungary's regent, Admiral Horthy, after he announced that he was seeking an armistice with the Allies. The Germans installed Ferenc Szálasi, leader of the fascist Arrow Cross Party, in his place. Szálasi unleashed a pogrom against Hungary's remaining Jewish population in which thousands were killed.

△ The liberation of Belgrade, October 1944

△ **The Shoes Monument** commemorating the victims of Nazi oppression in Budapest

20 October 1944
BELGRADE IS LIBERATED

Attacking from north and south, the Red Army's 3rd Ukrainian Front and Tito's National Army of Liberation liberated Yugoslavia's capital in a joint campaign. It was a huge victory for Tito that increased his political standing in the country and gave him a valuable edge over his rivals. Meanwhile, the remnants of the German forces in Yugoslavia were forced to make a perilous retreat through the mountains of Bosnia.

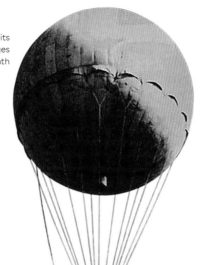

▷ **A Japanese Fu-Go balloon,** with its payload of explosive charges suspended underneath

1880–1964
DOUGLAS MACARTHUR

A veteran general, MacArthur was recalled to active duty in 1941 to lead the US Army in the Far East. He was forced out of the Philippines in 1942, but returned in 1944 to fulfill what he felt to be his moral duty to expel the Japanese from the islands.

1 November 1944
BALLOON BOMBING

The Japanese began their Fu-Go offensive against the USA, releasing 700 hydrogen-filled balloons. Each was loaded with four high-explosive bombs and an anti-personnel device. The balloons were supposed to drift 8,000 km (5,000 miles) across the Atlantic to the USA. However, fewer than 5 per cent of the 9,300 balloons launched made it to America. The only fatalities occurred when six civilians were killed by a balloon exploding in Fremont National Forest in Oregon.

"I have returned."

GENERAL MACARTHUR AFTER LANDING IN THE PHILIPPINES, 20 OCTOBER 1944

25 October Russian forces land near Kirkenes in Norway, but suspend their advance as Norwegian partisans begin to take back control from the Germans

28 October Bulgaria and the Allies sign an armistice in Moscow. Bulgaria agrees to pay reparations and evacuate its forces from Greece and Yugoslavia

1 November British commandos begin securing Walcheren, a Dutch island in the Scheldt controlling access to the port of Antwerp

1944
1 NOVEMBER

October–December 1944
RETURN TO THE PHILIPPINES

By October, the Allies had island-hopping across the Pacific from the Marshall Islands to the Marianas and were ready to reconquer the Philippines. The campaign began with bombing raids on the Japanese airfields. Then, on 20 October, a 700-strong fleet of ships landed 160,000 men at Leyte, in the central Philippines. With them was General MacArthur, fulfilling his 1942 promise to return to the islands. The brutal battle to secure Leyte took until December and cost 3,500 US lives.

▷ **General MacArthur** (*centre*) wading ashore at Leyte (hand-coloured image)

△ **A poster** depicting Belgium as a woman breaking free from her shackles, 1940s

2–4 November 1944
BELGIUM FREED

The last pockets of Axis resistance in northeast Belgium – the German garrisons at Zeebrugge, Westkappelle, Knocke, and Heyst – surrendered, Almost all of Belgium had, by now, been liberated, leaving the Allies free to take their offensive into the Netherlands and towards the Rhine.

> "In this year of liberation, which has seen so many millions freed... it is fitting that we give thanks with special fervour."
>
> *PRESIDENT FRANKLIN. D. ROOSEVELT, THANKSGIVING PROCLAMATION, 1 NOVEMBER 1944*

1944

2 NOVEMBER

2 November Allied forces advance in northeast Burma, recapturing Mawlu, on the Myitkyina–Mandalay railway

3 November Canadian troops cross over to the island of Walcheren, in the Netherlands, as the Allies continue to clear the Scheldt estuary of Axis forces

6 November In the Balkans, Yugoslavian partisans enter Monastir (annexed by Bulgaria in June 1941) and gain control of the Bulgaria–Greece frontier

9 November The British 8th Army captures Forlì, in Italy, as the Allies make progress beyond the Gothic Line towards Bologna and Ravenna

7 November 1944
ROOSEVELT REELECTED

Franklin D. Roosevelt won an unprecedented fourth term in office as US president against his Republican opponent, Thomas E. Dewey. Popular for his successful conduct of the war, Roosevelt won the election comfortably, with a margin of 7.5 per cent. His victory meant that there would be continuity in the USA's military strategy. However, Roosevelt's health was deteriorating and he died just three months later. His vice president, Harry S. Truman, was left to lead the USA in the final stages of the war and to help devise the postwar peace settlement.

▷ **The American Labor Party** showing its support for Roosevelt with a large placard outside a branch of the International Ladies Garment Workers Union

△ Loading a Lancaster bomber with a 5,400 kg (12,000 lb) "earthquake" bomb of the type that sank the *Tirpitz*

12 November 1944
THE TIRPITZ IS SUNK

The 43,000-ton German battleship *Tirpitz*, dubbed "the beast" by Churchill, was a long-standing target for the Allies. In the last of a series of raids on the ship, 30 Lancaster bombers caught the *Tirpitz* near Tromsø, in Norway. It had been left unprotected by air cover and was an easy target. The *Tirpitz* suffered several direct hits and sank within 10 minutes of the operation's start.

16 November 1944
THE RED BALL EXPRESS ENDS

The Red Ball Express was a convoy system that carried 12,500 tons of supplies daily to the Allied forces in France from August 1944. The drivers of its 6,000 trucks – the majority of whom were African Americans – braved mud, mechanical breakdowns, and enemy air attacks on the route from Cherbourg to the Allies' advance logistics base at Chartres. The Red Ball Express became redundant when the northern French railway system became operational again.

▷ A Transportation Corps badge worn by Red Ball Express drivers

9 November In Burma, Chinese troops cross the river Irrawaddy and occupy Shegwu

20 November French tanks breach the German line at the Belfort Gap, between the Vosges and the Jura mountains

1944

21 NOVEMBER

10 November Wang Jingwei, president of the pro-Japanese puppet government of Central China, dies

▽ Albanian partisans parading through Tirana, November 1944

17 November 1944
TIRANA LIBERATED

Communist partisans led by Enver Hoxha liberated Albania's capital from the Germans, who had occupied the city since Italy withdrew from the war in 1943. The British had, by then, removed their support from Hoxha's non-communist nationalist opponents, leaving him free to install a communist regime in Albania.

△ General Omar Bradley

16 November 1944
THE AACHEN OFFENSIVE

The US 12th Army Group, commanded by Omar Bradley, launched Operation Queen to the east of Aachen. The Americans hoped to capture the dams along the river Roer to prevent the Germans from blowing them up and so flooding the area. However, progess was slower than hoped, especially through the Hürtgen Forest. The Americans reached the dams in mid-December, just as the Germans unleashed a counteroffensive.

24 November 1944
B-29S RAID TOKYO

The USAAF was able to make its first air raid on Tokyo since 1942 after the capture of the Mariana Islands in June 1944 brought Tokyo well within reach of the new B-29 Superfortress bomber. More than 100 B-29s attacked the Musashino aviation works; 24 hit their target, but high winds blew many of the bombs off course.

"We shall not hesitate to use the considerable British Army now in Greece... to see that law and order are maintained."

WINSTON CHURCHILL, 5 DECEMBER 1944

△ US Boeing B-29A **Superfortress** strategic bomber, 1944

1944

22 NOVEMBER

25 November American soldiers advance through the Hürtgen Forest and move towards the river Roer

26 November 1944 US forces breach the Maginot Line, having reached Strasbourg on the French–German border on 23 November

29 November The Red Army and Yugoslav partisans advance on Budapest, in Hungary, crossing the Danube and capturing Mohács and Pécs

1 December 1944
PATTON AT THE GERMAN BORDER

After capturing Metz, in northeast France, Patton's US 3rd Army pursued the German 1st Army towards the river Saar. By 1 December, the Americans had taken Sarre-Union, on the river's east bank. This gave them a base for an attack on the Siegfried Line protecting Germany's border.

△ General Harold Alexander, 1944

24 November 1944
GENERAL ALEXANDER IS PROMOTED

General Harold Alexander was appointed supreme Allied commander in the Mediterranean and made a field marshal after having served with distinction during the North African and Italian campaigns. He continued in the role until the end of the war and accepted the German surrender in Italy on 29 April 1945.

▷ US 3rd Army soldiers looking out over the river Saar

3 December 1944
CONFLICT IN GREECE

By early December 1944, relations between Greece's communist ELAS and nationalist EDES resistance fighters had broken down. When the Greek prime minister ordered the groups to integrate into a single nationalist army, ELAS called a general strike. This escalated into an uprising after government troops opened fire on a demonstration in Athens, killing 28 protesters. The British sent reinforcements from Italy to help end the insurrection, but it still took more than a month to dislodge the communist fighters from Athens.

◁ **Communist partisans are arrested** by British troops in Athens during the December 1944 disturbances

4 December In Italy, Canadian forces capture Ravenna, but stiff German resistance stalls further northward advances

15 December The Chinese capture Bhamo, in Burma, after advancing south from Myitkyina

1944

15 DECEMBER

2 December The British take Kalewa, in northwest Burma, as part of an offensive to reopen the Burma Road supply route to China

5 December 1944
THE BUDAPEST OFFENSIVE

Soviet forces attacked the German 6th and 8th Armies from the northeast of Budapest, and managed to outflank the city from the north. Over the next weeks, sufficient Soviet troops arrived at Budapest to attack the city from north and south. They encircled it by 24 December, trapping around 80,000 German and Hungarian defenders and 800,000 civilians in the city for 50 days.

▽ **Tank-borne infantry** of the 2nd Ukrainian Front attack on the approaches to Budapest, December 1944

16 December 1944
THE ARDENNES OFFENSIVE

The Germans launched a surprise counteroffensive in the forested Ardennes of southeast Belgium, sending 20 divisions against a sector of the Allied front line held by the US Army. German infiltrators dressed in US uniforms spread confusion, and the Allied commanders did not realize for hours that a major operation was underway. German panzers broke through the Allied line and advanced towards the bridges over the river Meuse, which guarded the route to their ultimate destination – Antwerp. They had almost reached the Meuse when American forces stopped their advance.

◁ **German paratroopers** on a "King Tiger" tank during the Ardennes Offensive, December 1944

1944

16 DECEMBER

16 December Advancing in northern Italy, the British take Faenza, as New Zealand forces reach the river Senio

17 December Waffen-SS troops capture and murder more than 80 US and Belgian prisoners of war at Malmédy, Belgium, during the Battle of the Bulge

18 December US B-29 bombers raid the Mitsubishi aircraft works at Nagoya, in central Japan, but inflict little damage

20 December In the Ardennes Offensive, German panzers reach Stavelot, east Belgium; US counterattacks stop them advancing further north

16 December–7 February 1945
THE BATTLE OF THE BULGE

Under orders from Hitler, Germany's generals devised a plan to make a lightning strike through the Ardennes to Antwerp that would cut the Allied front in two. On 16 December, German panzers surged forward along a 130-km (80-mile) front from Monschau to Echternach. In the centre, they reached Celles by 24 December. This was as far west as they went before the Allies contained their advance. US counterattacks helped funnel the Germans into a narrow salient, nicknamed "the Bulge". The Allies began pushing the Germans back as their offensive stalled amid supply issues and a lack of reserves. The battle was one of the bloodiest fought by the US Army during World War II.

The Allied counteroffensive
By late December, the Allied forces were on the offensive. In January, they attacked in a pincer movement from north and south, pinching out the salient in early February.

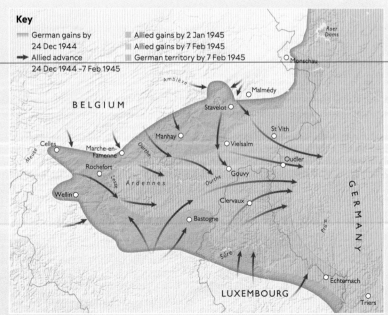

Key

- German gains by 24 Dec 1944
- → Allied advance 24 Dec 1944 –7 Feb 1945
- Allied gains by 2 Jan 1945
- Allied gains by 7 Feb 1945
- German territory by 7 Feb 1945

26 December 1944
BASTOGNE RELIEVED

The US forces besieged in Bastogne were outnumbered and running low on food and ammunition, but they refused to abandon the town. On 26 December, the bad weather that had grounded the USAAF lifted, and US planes began pounding the German supply lines. Relief forces from the US 3rd Army's 4th Armored Division reached the town and broke the siege. The siege of Bastogne was a turning point in the Battle of the Bulge. It wasted German resources, held up the German advance towards the Meuse, and gave the Allies time to regroup.

△ **US infantrymen firing** at German troops surrounding Bastogne during the Battle of the Bulge, December 1944 (hand-coloured image)

The Germans lost 550 tanks in the Battle of the Bulge

21 December The Allies cut the north–south Myitkyina–Rangoon railway as they advance southeast towards Mandalay, in central Burma

26 December Soviet tank units cut the Budapest–Vienna road, encircling Budapest and trapping the German forces inside the city

31 December In the Battle of the Bulge, the Allies launch a counteroffensive near Bastogne

1944
31 DECEMBER

25 December The German advance in the Ardennes is halted at Celles, 5 km (3 miles) east of the Meuse

△ **Two US infantrymen** in Bastogne, December 1944 (hand-coloured image)

21 December 1944
BASTOGNE BESIEGED

As their advance from the Ardennes stalled in the north, the Germans focused on capturing the strategically important town of Bastogne further south. Bastogne was at the centre of a network of roads; its capture would allow the Germans to disrupt the Allied supply lines. However, the Germans could not break through the US defences and were forced to besiege the town.

26 December 1944
THE LEYTE CAMPAIGN ENDS

In the last phase of the campaign to secure the Philippine island of Leyte, General MacArthur landed US forces near Ormoc on the island's west coast. They advanced north to join US forces moving south, and split the Japanese defenders in two by 21 December. Five days later, the Americans took the last Japanese-controlled port on Leyte, Palompon, ending the Leyte campaign.

▽ **A US soldier showing** Filipino children on Leyte a captured Japanese samurai sword, 1944

Shoes from the prisoners of Auschwitz concentration camp. Upon arriving at concentration camps, people were systematically dehumanized by being stripped of all their possessions, which were confiscated by the Nazis and used for their war effort. This heap of shoes from Auschwitz hints at the sheer scale of the tragedy.

1933-45
THE HOLOCAUST

The foundations for the Holocaust – the murder of European Jews by the Nazi regime – were laid in the early 1930s, when German Jews were stripped of their civil and human rights. After March 1938, thousands of German and Austrian Jews were imprisoned in concentration camps, where many were worked to death in forced labour.

Once war broke out in 1939, millions more Jews came under Nazi control in occupied areas. They were forced into unhygienic and overcrowded ghettos, and in Eastern Europe, around 500,000 Jews were killed by SS death squads called Einsatzgruppen ("task forces"). In 1941, Hitler authorized the "Final Solution" – the systematic, physical annihilation of the European Jews – and the first "extermination camp" was opened at Chelmno, in Poland. The ghettos were cleared as their inhabitants were sent to concentration camps or directly to extermination camps. After the Allies liberated the first camps in 1944, thousands died on brutal death marches as the Nazis relocated the inmates of the remaining camps to sites in Germany.

Ultimately, more than 6 million Jews died in the Holocaust; only 300,000 survived. However, they were not the only victims of Nazi persecution: hundreds of thousands of Roma and Sinti people, gay people, and people with disabilities, among others, were also murdered by the Nazis.

KEY MOMENTS

1933 Building the system
In 1933, the Nazis established Dachau concentration camp, 16 km (10 miles) from Munich. It was the first of 30 main camps built in Germany and occupied Europe, which were all commanded by a branch of the SS called the Totenkopfverbände ("death's head units") from 1934.

1942 The killing centres
From 1941, "gas vans" whose exhaust fumes were diverted to a sealed compartment were used to kill Jews and others considered "undesirable". In 1942, mass killings began in gas chambers, first using carbon monoxide, then Zyklon B, a cyanide-based poison.

1944-45 The camps liberated
From July 1944 to May 1945, Allied forces liberated the concentration camps as they advanced into Germany, revealing to the world the scale of the Nazis' atrocities. The survivors almost all suffered from disease, malnutrition, and psychological trauma.

THE AXIS DESTROYED

As World War II entered its final phase, German and Japanese commanders realized that they faced inevitable defeat. However, neither Hitler nor the Japanese military government was prepared to accept the humiliation of unconditional surrender – the only terms the Allies were prepared to offer. Thus, war continued even though its outcome was no longer in doubt. The last year of the conflict was a striking testament to the control that the Axis dictatorships exercised over their peoples, forcing them to fight to the last.

By this time, Allied domination of the air and at sea was almost total. In Europe, whole air fleets from Britain and the United States roamed over Germany virtually at will, while acute shortages of aircraft, pilots, and fuel made German opposition minimal. By early 1945, Allied air strategists were running out of valid targets on which to drop their bombs.

Despite the destruction meted out from the air, the German Army continued its defence of the fatherland. Although Allied air commanders had once boasted that they could win the war on their own, victory was achieved only by ground troops fighting their way forward to gain physical possession of enemy territory.

In the west, Anglo-American forces finally broke through the formidable Rhine barrier in March 1945, advancing deep into the German heartland, at which point organized resistance began to collapse. In Italy,

Allied troops steadily pushed the Germans back towards the Alps; and at the end of April, local German commanders prepared to surrender their forces.

The Red Army advance

On the Eastern Front, the Germans fought on with an almost crazed determination, so great was their fear of Soviet retribution. Complicating matters was the westward migration of millions of German civilians, fleeing from East Prussia, Silesia, and the Baltic. A last-gasp German offensive in Hungary was snuffed out by Soviet forces in March, while the bulk of the Red Army drove towards Berlin.

On 25 April, Soviet and American troops met at Torgau on the river Elbe, and a few days later, Soviet tanks smashed their way through central Berlin. Hitler escaped Allied retribution, dying by his own hand, but following Germany's unconditional surrender on 7 May, German civilians and soldiers alike had to come to terms with their new status as a defeated people.

Onward to Japan

Victory in Europe allowed the Allies to redirect their overwhelming resources towards Japan, already struggling to survive relentless pressure from air and sea. During 1945, British, Indian, and other Commonwealth forces exploited their earlier victories against the Japanese and retook Burma. The Soviet declaration of war against Japan in August was followed by rapid advances of Red Army tank columns through Manchuria. In China, the Japanese Army was isolated from other Japanese forces, unable to help in the defence of the homeland.

In the Pacific, the US seizure of Iwo Jima and Okinawa put Japan within reach of an amphibious invasion. However, the determined defence of these islands was such that American planners became deeply concerned at the losses they might incur in an attack on Japan – the most pessimistic suggested a figure close to 1 million US casualties.

Atomic weapons

These misgivings played their part in the decision to use atomic weapons against Japan, although other means – a blockade of the country, a conventional bombing campaign, and the Soviet conquest of Manchuria – would almost certainly have forced a capitulation without resort to nuclear weapons.

In early August, US B-29 bombers dropped atomic bombs on Hiroshima and Nagasaki. On 14 August, after intense debate, the Japanese government thought the unthinkable and agreed to surrender unconditionally. Allied naval units entered Japanese ports, and the Japanese delegation signed the instrument of surrender aboard the USS *Missouri* in Tokyo Bay on 2 September 1945. The war was over.

1 January 1945
GERMANY'S FINAL OFFENSIVE BEGINS

The Germans launched Operation Nordwind ("North Wind"), aiming to break through the US lines in Alsace-Lorraine and retake Strasbourg. They were soon caught in brutal fighting in the eastern Vosges that exhausted both sides. The Germans halted the offensive on 25 January, when US reinforcements began to arrive from the Ardennes.

▽ **US infantry soldiers** on their way to cut off the Saint Vith–Houffalize road in Belgium

△ **A stamp commemorating** the liberation of Strasbourg and Metz, 1945

16 January 1945
US FORCES LINK UP IN THE ARDENNES

The US 1st Army advanced from the north and the 3rd Army from the south to begin reducing the German salient in the Ardennes. The two forces met on the road out of Houffalize, northeast of Bastogne, on 16 January. Within a week, only St Vith to the north remained of the salient known as "the Bulge".

1945

1 JANUARY

1 January In Operation Bodenplatte, 800 German fighters attack Allied airfields in Belgium and the Netherlands; it is the last major German air offensive of the war

7 January The German Navy begins to evacuate the remnants of Army Group North from Courland, in Latvia

12 January The Soviets launch the Vistula–Oder Offensive, the final push into Germany

9 January 1845
US FORCES LAND IN LINGAYEN GULF

To secure the capital of the Philippines – the city of Manila on the island of Luzon – General MacArthur ordered landings at Lingayen, 175 km (110 miles) to the north. This exposed the US fleet to days of intense attack by kamikaze planes as it travelled northward up Luzon's western coast. Some 68,000 US troops landed at Lingayen on the first day – more than were landed in France on D-Day. They went largely unopposed, as the Japanese commander General Yamashita abandoned the beaches to defend Luzon from inland positions.

◁ **US warships** entering Lingayen Gulf, 1945

2 million men and 6,460 tanks took part in the Vistula-Oder Offensive

12 January–18 February 1945

TO THE GATES OF BERLIN

Soviet progress in Eastern and Central Europe had been limited since summer 1944, but in early 1945, the Soviet commanders launched the Vistula-Oder Offensive. While maintaining existing pressure on Hungary and East Prussia, the Red Army launched a massive attack, by Zhukov's 1st Belorussian Front and Konev's 1st Ukrainian Front, through the centre. By mid-February, the Soviet forces had punched through from the Vistula to the Oder, capturing Breslau, Warsaw, and Krakow, and were around 70 km (40 miles) from Berlin.

▷ **Soviet tanker badge,** awarded to Soviet tank crewmen during World War II

18 January Marshal Konev's 1st Ukrainian Front captures Krakow in southern Poland

22 January The Allies reopen the Ledo Road, the land route from Burma to India and China

20 January Hungary's Provisional National Government signs an armistice with the Allies and declares war on Germany

23 January In the Philippines, the US XIV Corps reaches Clark Field, the main air base on Luzon

1945

23 JANUARY

17 January 1945

SOVIET FORCES CAPTURE WARSAW

Marshal Zhukov finally launched an attack on Warsaw, having paused to the east of the capital in September 1944. Most of the German garrison escaped the double envelopment he planned, so Zhukov entered the city unopposed. He found it in ruins, with five in six buildings utterly destroyed.

◁ **The Old Town** of Warsaw in ruins, 1945

27 January 1945
AUSCHWITZ LIBERATED

Soviet forces of the 60th Army liberated the concentration camps at Auschwitz-Birkenau near Krakow in southern Poland. More than 1.1 million prisoners – mainly Jewish, but also Romany people, homosexuals, and Polish resistance fighters – had been murdered there during the course of the war. As the Soviets approached, most of the survivors were evacuated westwards on "death marches". Only around 7,000 prisoners, many too ill to be moved, were still in the camps when the Red Army arrived.

◁ **Children at Auschwitz** on the day of liberation, January 1945

1945

24 JANUARY

27 January Chinese forces clear the Japanese from the Ledo Road, which joins the Burma Road to link India and China

29 January In Poland, Zhukov surrounds the large German garrison in Poznan, but limited supplies curtail his progress

29 January Units of the US 3rd Army cross the river Our around Oberhausen, breaching the German frontier

26 January Rokossovsky's 2nd Belorussian Front breaks through at Danzig, isolating German forces in East Prussia

1896–1968
KONSTANTIN ROKOSSOVSKY

Rehabilitated after a purge of the Soviet leadership, Rokossovsky served at the Battle of Stalingrad in 1943 and fought through Ukraine to Warsaw, ending as commander of the 2nd Belorussian Front. After the war, Stalin made him Poland's defence minister.

▽ Civilians near Königsberg on their way to the west, after East Prussia is taken by the Red Army

27 January 1945
GERMANS EVACUATED AS THE RED ARMY ADVANCES

The Soviet army captured Klaipeda (Memel) in Lithuania, isolating many German civilians and troops in a pocket in Courland. German naval commander Admiral Karl Dönitz ordered Operation Hannibal, evacuating more than 800,000 civilians and 350,000 military personnel to German-controlled ports in the southern Baltic. The operation also evacuated people from East Prussia and Pomerania as the Red Army advanced.

△ **The Yalta Conference** with Churchill, Roosevelt, and Stalin (*front row*)

4 February 1945

THE YALTA CONFERENCE

As the defeat of Germany approached, "the Big Three" – Roosevelt, Churchill, and Stalin – met at Yalta on the Black Sea to discuss postwar arrangements. They determined that Germany would be divided into occupation zones and must pay reparations, and they agreed on the establishment of the United Nations. Poland was to lose territory in the east, but gain it in the north and west from Germany.

▷ **A shoulder flash** of the 21st Army Group

9 February 1945

BRITISH ARMY FORCES REACH THE RHINE

British and Canadian troops of the 21st Army Group reached the Rhine east of Nijmegen as part of Operation Veritable, a plan to clear the Germans from between the Ruhr and Rhine rivers. The Germans released water from the Ruhr dams, postponing Operation Grenade, a similar planned advance by American forces, for two weeks.

30 January Adolf Hitler makes his last radio broadcast, saying "no nation can do more!"

4 February Konev's tanks begin crossing the river Oder near Breslau (Wroclaw), which is taken on 6 February

13 February The Red Army takes Budapest after a siege lasting seven weeks

1945

13 FEBRUARY

25,000 civilians were killed in the Allied firebombing of Dresden on 13–14 February 1945

13–15 February 1945

THE ALLIES BOMB DRESDEN

1,300 British and American bombers raided Dresden, close to the leading edge of the Soviet advance. They dropped around 3,400 tons of bombs on the German city, creating a giant firestorm that destroyed 6.5 sq km (2.5 sq miles) of buildings and killed 25,000 civilians, many of whom were trapped in domestic cellars and died from smoke inhalation or burns.

▷ **Bomb and fire damage** at Pragerstrasse in Dresden

The Six Triple Eight was awarded the Congressional Gold Medal in 2021 for its service during the war

19 February–26 March 1945
AN ISLAND FORTRESS

The USA expected to take the small Pacific island of Iwo Jima quickly. However, the Japanese were led by General Tadamichi Kuribayashi, whose "Courageous Battle Vows" ruled out surrender. Turning the island into a fortress, the Japanese attacked from inland caves and tunnels, resisting the Allied onslaught for five weeks. Some 6,800 US Marines died and 19,200 were wounded, while almost 18,500 Japanese died. The fierce fighting at Iwo Jima convinced the USA that Japan would never surrender, bringing the use of the atomic bomb one step closer.

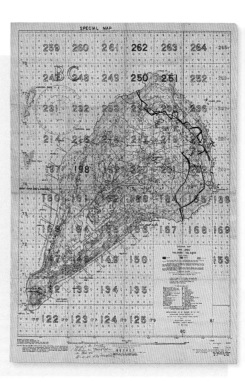

▷ **A US map from early 1945** showing the Japanese gun emplacements and defensive installations (in red) on Iwo Jima

1945

14 February **The US mistakenly bombs Prague,** possibly owing to a navigation error; the air raid kills hundreds of civilians

17 February **Gabrielle Weidner,** a Dutch resistance fighter who helped rescue at least 1,080 people, dies

18 February **Germany's Operation Solstice fails** to re-establish a cohesive defensive line as the Soviets advance towards Berlin

14 FEBRUARY

14 February 1945
THE "SIX TRIPLE EIGHT" ARRIVES IN BRITAIN

The US 6888th Central Postal Delivery Battalion, nicknamed the "Six Triple Eight", arrived in Britain. Given six months to clear a two-year backlog of 17 million pieces of mail, they finished in three months. They were then sent to France. Part of the Women's Army Corps, they were the only all-female, predominantly Black unit to serve overseas in WWII. They worked in poor conditions and faced prejudice, segregation, and sexism. The unit provided essential support in linking service people with loved ones at home; its motto was "No Mail, Low Morale".

◁ **Captain Abbie N. Campbell inspecting** a contingent of African-American women assigned to overseas service in the Six Triple Eight

"Were it not for the Navajos, the Marines would never have taken Iwo Jima."

MAJOR HOWARD CONNOR, US 5TH MARINE DIVISION SIGNAL OFFICER

▽ "Raising the Flag on Iwo Jima" by Associated Press photographer Joe Rosenthal

23 February 1945
US FORCES CAPTURE MOUNT SURIBACHI ON IWO JIMA

After savage fighting, US Marines captured Mount Suribachi on the island's southwest tip and raised a US flag at the summit – the subject of one of the most enduring images of the conflict (*left*). Further progress was difficult, as the Japanese were dug into defensive complexes, such as the notorious "Meat Grinder", which was finally taken on 2 March.

22 February The Allies defeat Japanese forces at the Battle of Ramree Island in Burma; many Japanese combatants are purported to have been killed by crocodiles

27 February US Marines on Iwo Jima secure the Motoyama airfields to support Allied fighter planes and bombers raiding Japan

1945
7 MARCH

19 February 1945
THE BATTLE OF IWO JIMA BEGINS

The USA mounted an amphibious invasion of Iwo Jima, landing 30,000 US Marines on the southeast beaches as part of its Pacific campaign against Japan. Halfway between Tokyo and the Mariana Islands, the island was a strategic base for the Allies. Led by General Tadamichi Kuribayashi, the Japanese soldiers were well prepared for the attack and inflicted significant casualties on the Americans.

7 March The Allies win the Siegfried Line campaign as Eisenhower's "broad front" forces reach the west bank of the Rhine

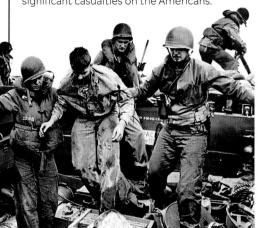

△ A soldier of the American Marine Infantry, wounded while landing on Iwo Jima

▽ Women and children picking their way through the wreckage of North Manila

3 March 1945
MANILA AND BATAAN FALL

Ending almost three years of Japanese occupation in the Philippines, the month-long battles of Manila and Bataan resulted in more than 100,000 civilian deaths. Manila was the scene of the worst urban fighting in the Pacific theatre, and was completely devastated. Its capture was a key victory for General MacArthur and secured Manila Bay for use as a harbour by the Allies.

△ **Tokyo children being evacuated** after Allies dropped leaflets warning people to leave

9-10 March 1945
THE USAAF FIREBOMBS TOKYO

In a change of tactics from the precision targeting of Japanese military sites, US warplanes dropped 2,000 tons of firebombs and napalm on Tokyo in just 48 hours. Almost 27 sq km (10 sq miles) was incinerated and at least 100,000 people killed, with tens of thousands injured and even more displaced. It was the most deadly bombing raid in history.

1891-1945
TADAMICHI KURIBAYASHI

Born into a samurai family, General Kuribayashi attended Harvard University and the US Army War College. He commanded the Imperial Japanese forces on Iwo Jima and died in battle there.

"At 5,000 ft, you could smell the flesh burning... I couldn't eat anything for two or three days."

B-29 PILOT CHESTER MARSHALL RECALLING THE BOMBING OF TOKYO

15 March Operation Spring Awakening fails. Aimed at stopping the Soviet advance towards Vienna, it is Hitler's last major offensive of the war

16-17 March In Japan, the centre of Osaka is reduced to ashes by an intense US firebombing raid

1945

8 MARCH

14 March The US Navy begins attacking Japanese ships carrying fuel between Hokkaido and Honshu islands

▽ **US forces firing** at Japanese cave positions on Iwo Jima

20 March 1945
THE BATTLE OF MANDALAY ENDS

In Burma, British and Indian troops won the concurrent large-scale battles of Mandalay and Meiktila (a Japanese supply point for central and northern Burma). Led by William Slim, the Allies outnumbered, outgunned, and had air superiority over their Japanese enemies. Most of the Japanese forces were destroyed, and the Allies cleared the road to Rangoon in the south, opening the way for the recapture of Burma.

△ **Allied troops** advancing on Mandalay, 1945

11 March 1945
LAST STAND AT "BLOODY GORGE"

Battles had raged for weeks in the northern part of Iwo Jima, where General Kuribayashi had concentrated his forces in underground bunkers and gun positions linked by miles of tunnels. On 11 March, he and his remaining 1,500 men made a desperate last stand in the rugged ravines and caves of "Bloody Gorge", also known as "Death Valley".

24 March 1945

OPERATION VARSITY

The largest one-day airborne operation in history, and the last of WWII, Operation Varsity involved several thousand Allied aircraft. More than 16,000 British, American, and Canadian paratroopers were landed east of the river Rhine in northern Germany. Quickly connecting with the ground forces of Operation Plunder, they successfully secured the area around the Rhine. Overwhelmed by the speed and size of the operation, the German defenders put up little resistance.

◁ **Allied paratroopers** landing during a practice jump over an airfield in Sissonne, France, 14 March 1945

26 March US Marines capture Iwo Jima after 300 Japanese soldiers are gunned down in a final attack, ending the five-week battle – one of the bloodiest of the Pacific theatre

1945

27 MARCH

27 March Argentina abandons its neutral stance and declares war on Japan and Germany

22 March 1945

THE WESTERN ALLIES CROSS THE RHINE

After driving back the German counteroffensive in the Ardennes, Allied forces advanced towards the Rhine – the main barrier in their final assault on Germany. Elements of the 1st US Army had captured a bridge that German defenders had failed to blow up at Remagen on 7 March, but around 22 March, crossing began in earnest. British and Canadian forces under Field Marshal Montgomery began a series of crossings in northern Germany, while General Patton's 3rd US Army crossed at Oppenheim to the south. They established bridgeheads before pressing eastward.

◁ **Churchill, Montgomery,** and a party of US commanders and soldiers landing on the German-held east bank of the Rhine, March 1945 (hand-coloured image)

30 March 1945

SOVIET FORCES CAPTURE DANZIG

Thousands of residents tried to flee Danzig, on the Baltic coast, as the Red Army destroyed this last German stronghold in the region, which Hitler had taken in 1939. According to Soviet claims, 39,000 German soldiers died and 10,000 were captured in the battle for the city. Danzig eventually became part of Poland and was renamed Gdansk. Polish settlers mostly replaced the expelled ethnic Germans.

◁ **Soviet troops** in the centre of Danzig, March 1945

More than 3,800 kamikaze pilots died in World War II

1945

28 MARCH

28 March Eisenhower tells Stalin that he will leave the final battle in Berlin to the Soviet forces

31 March A Soviet operation to secure industrial and natural resources in Upper Silesia ends after two weeks

31 March The French 1st Army crosses the Rhine near Germersheim and goes on to clear southwestern Germany

1 April US forces encircle the Ruhr Valley, which Hitler commands must be defended to the last man, and overrun it within three weeks

1 April–22 June 1945

THE BATTLE OF OKINAWA

The final campaign of the Pacific war centred on Okinawa, a Japanese island that the Allies had indentified as a base for their invasion of Japan's home islands. On 1 April, 260 warships, the largest Allied fleet in the Pacific theatre, swarmed around the island. More than 60,000 soldiers and US Marines stormed ashore. A three-month-long battle followed, involving 500,000 combatants from five Allied nations, who fought savagely in the air, on land, and at sea. Japanese forces counterattacked from inland strongholds, and as many as 150,000 Japanese civilians and 110,000 defenders died in the battle. After the fall of Okinawa, Japan's leaders realized that the war was lost.

▷ **Allied military ambulances** on Guam awaiting casualties from Okinawa

6 April 1945
KAMIKAZE ATTACKS ON OKINAWA

As part of Operation Ten-Go, 355 Japanese kamikaze planes and more than 300 fighter escorts attacked the Allied fleet invading Okinawa. It was to be the first of 10 large-scale attacks given the name *kikusuis* ("floating chrysanthemums"). Some planes hit their targets, causing catastrophic damage. The next day, US torpedo bombers intercepted the Japanese naval force led by the *Yamato*, the world's largest battleship, and destroyed it.

◁ **Fire aboard the aircraft carrier USS** *Bunker Hill* after a kamikaze attack, 1945 (hand-coloured image)

2 April Louis Mountbatten, the Allied commander in Southeast Asia, decides to mount "Operation Dracula" – an assault on Rangoon

9 April The final offensive in Italy begins as Allied forces attack from Ravenna towards Ferrara through the Argenta Gap

1945

9 APRIL

8 April 1945
JAPAN ADOPTS A PLAN TO DEFEND ITS HOME ISLANDS

Knowing that invasion was imminent, Japan began planning Ketsu-Go ("Operation Decisive"), its national defence strategy. This focused on destroying US amphibious forces and maximizing casualties to undermine American morale. The Japanese hoped to force a negotiated peace that might prevent the postwar occupation of Japan.

◁ **A Japanese officer** training civilians to use spears to combat a US invasion

9 April 1945
THE RED ARMY CAPTURES KÖNIGSBERG

Soviet forces had encircled the German fortress city of Königsberg in January 1945. By April, when the Soviets began their final assault, the city was far to the east of the front line. After four days of artillery bombardment, the Soviets penetrated the city's outer defences at multiple points and began to close in on the centre. The garrison surrendered on 9 April, after much of the city was destroyed.

▷ **Soviet troops** fighting in the suburbs of Königsberg

The Allies found more than 13,000 unburied bodies and around 60,000 surviving inmates at Bergen-Belsen

▽ Prisoners of the Bergen-Belsen concentration camp collecting bread rations after their liberation by British forces in April 1945

15 April 1945
ALLIED TROOPS LIBERATE BERGEN-BELSEN

British and Canadian troops of the 11th Armoured Division liberated the Bergen-Belsen concentration camp near Celles, in northern Germany. They were horrified at what they found there: piles of unburied bodies and thousands of sick and starving survivors living in inhumane conditions. The British Red Cross was sent to help the survivors, many of whom were housed in a displaced persons' camp set up nearby. Bergen-Belsen's buildings were burned to the ground to stop the spread of diseases such as typhus and typhoid.

12 April Canadian forces liberate Westerbork transit camp in the Netherlands

16 April The Japanese stronghold on Cebu, in the Philippines, falls to US forces in the Battle of Visayas

1945

10 APRIL

△ **President Roosevelt** (*right*) with Vice President Truman, 1945

13 April The Soviets secure Vienna and turn their attention towards the northwest and Czechoslovakia

16 April 1945
THE SOVIET BERLIN OFFENSIVE BEGINS

Stalin did not trust the USA not to advance on Berlin and so accelerated his own plans to take the city, pitting his generals against each other in a race for the capital. With 2.5 million troops, 6,000 tanks, and more than 40,000 artillery pieces amassed along the Oder and Neisse rivers, the Soviets began their final assault on 16 April. Within one day, they had taken the Seelow Heights, east of Berlin, and broken the 4th Panzer Army to the south.

12 April 1945
PRESIDENT ROOSEVELT DIES

The death of Roosevelt from a cerebral haemorrhage after a period of ill health was met with shock around the world. Churchill later likened the news to having "been struck a physical blow". President since 1933, Roosevelt had served four terms in office and guided the USA through the Great Depression and a global conflict. His successor, Harry S. Truman, was faced with the challenge of leading America through the last months of WWII, and the later trials of the Cold War and the Korean War.

▽ **Soviet artillery** at the Seelow Heights, April 1945

18 April 1945
THE RUHR POCKET DISINTEGRATES

After crossing the Rhine, the US 1st and 9th Armies had encircled the Ruhr – the industrial heartland of Germany – trapping Field Marshal Walter Model's Army Group B. The Germans resisted or delayed the US advances from north and south, but the Americans had split the pocket in two by 14 April. Facing defeat, Model wanted to withdraw his forces, but Hitler refused. To avoid surrendering his command, Model dissolved Army Group B and took his own life. More than 300,000 German troops surrendered to the US forces – the largest single German surrender in Western Europe.

▷ **Thousands of German POWs** taken by US troops in the Ruhr, 1945

17 April A final Allied aerial attack on Dresden severs the city's southeastern rail links

19 April British troops reach the river Elbe near Lauenburg, northwest of Berlin

20 April US forces capture Nuremberg after taking Dresden on the previous day

1945

20 APRIL

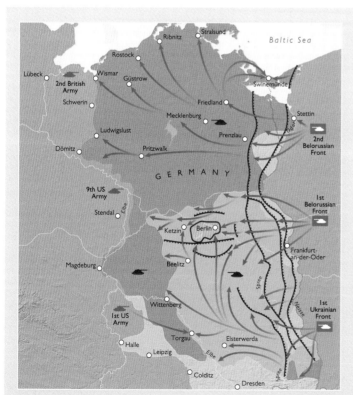

16–28 April 1945
CLOSING IN ON BERLIN

Caught between the Allied armies advancing from the west and the Red Army's 200 divisions in the east were around one million German soldiers and 1,500 tanks. On 25 April, the two main Soviet forces met at Ketzin, northwest of Berlin, while a Soviet spearhead joined the 1st US Army at Torgau, in the southwest. In the north, a third Soviet army fanned out towards the Baltic coast, preventing German reinforcements from coming to Berlin's aid. With 2.5 million Soviet soldiers poised to strike from three sides, the Battle of Berlin would be the last major battle in the European theatre.

Key

→ Allied movements 16–25 April
◣ British and US forces
▭ Soviet forces
◣ German forces
〰 German defensive lines
▱ German territory, 28 April

Allied territorial gains
▪ 15 April
▫ 18 April
▪ 25 April
▫ 28 April

A city surrounded

Konstantin Rokossovsky's 2nd Belorussian Front swept westwards north of Berlin, isolating the German forces there. Meanwhile, the 1st Belorussian Front and 1st Ukranian Front moved towards Berlin from the east and southeast, while the US and British forces held their positions west of Berlin, leaving the Soviets to capture the city.

21 April 1945
BOLOGNA LIBERATED

After bombarding the city from 9 April, Allied forces finally liberated Bologna, a strategic communications hub for the Germans. First to enter the city were the Polish Army's II Corps – part of the largest army-in-exile to fight in the war. With his defences broken, General von Vietinghoff issued orders for Army Group C to withraw towards the river Po.

△ **Polish soldiers** with local women and children in Bologna, April 1945

24 April–1 May 1945
THE BATTLE OF HALBE

Southeast of Berlin, the German 9th Army tried to break out from Halbe, where it had been encircled, along with thousands of civilians and refugees. The trapped soldiers had orders to join the 12th Army in its attempt to relieve Berlin, but they were held in place by fierce Soviet air attacks. Some 25,000 did escape the pocket and surrendered to the Americans; the rest chose to defy Hitler's orders and defend their position.

23 April Hitler declares he will remain in Berlin to take personal command of the city's defence to the end

△ **Commemorative bell sculpture** at Halbe's war cemetery

1945

21 APRIL

21 April 1945 US infantry capture Kakazu Ridge on Okinawa; both sides suffer heavy losses

25 April 1945
BERLIN ENCIRCLED

With elements of the 1st Ukrainian Front meeting soldiers from the 1st US Army at Torgau and the 1st Belorussian Front at Ketzin, Berlin was finally encircled. As the Soviet noose around the city tightened, fighting began in the suburbs. Hitler had assumed personal command of Berlin, but mistrust and disagreements resulted in a confused defence plan. About 100,000 German defenders remained in the city; most were older people or members of the Hitler Youth. Meanwhile, the potential relief forces of the 9th and 12th Armies were facing their own battles against the Red Army to the south of the city.

▷ **American troops** with a female Soviet sergeant in the German town of Torgau (hand-coloured image)

28 April 1945
HIMMLER STRIPPED OF OFFICE

As leader of the SS and minister of the interior, Heinrich Himmler was the second most powerful man in wartime Germany. After the failure of the plot to assassinate Hitler in July 1944, Himmler had considered negotiating peace with the Western Allies, but held off. In April 1945, he asked the Swedish Red Cross to carry a proposal to General Eisenhower, offering Germany's surrender on the Western Front. On hearing this news, Hitler stripped Himmler of all his offices and ordered his arrest.

▷ **Heinrich Himmler** making a radio broadcast, 1939

25 April Italian partisans and the Brazilian Expeditionary Force liberate Parma

27 April The Lapland War between Finland and Nazi Germany ends; the last German troops finally leave Finland

1945

28 APRIL

28 April Mussolini and his mistress, Clara Petacci, are executed by Italian partisans as they attempt to flee to Switzerland

25 April 1945
THE SAN FRANCISCO CONFERENCE

The two-month-long United Nations Conference on International Organization (UNCIO) was held in San Francisco, USA. Delegates representing 50 Allied nations worked on the Dumbarton Oaks proposals (*see p.240*), the Yalta Agreement (*see p.263*), and various amendments to develop the United Nations Charter and the statute of the new International Court of Justice. They aimed to build a peaceful postwar world.

◁ **"United for Peace",** poster for the San Francisco Conference, 1945

850 delegates from 50 countries attended the San Francisco Conference, together with 6,000 advisers, staff, press, and observers

29 April–2 May 1945
THE FINAL DAYS IN BERLIN

With Germany's armies trapped outside the city, Berlin's defence was in the hands of General Weidling and about 100,000 members of the Volkssturm (*see p.246*), Hitler Youth, and SS. They resisted fiercely but could not stop the Red Army from storming the heart of the Nazi regime and taking the Reichstag building on 30 April. Hitler's death on the same day threw the Nazis into disarray, but the battle continued. The Soviet forces closed in on the Reich Chancellery and the bunker that sheltered the Nazi leaders.

The Soviets take Berlin

After fighting its way through the city streets, the Red Army captured the Reich Chancellery on 2 May. Weidling was running low on ammunition and, unable to continue the battle, he surrendered the city to the Soviet forces.

Key

- ▨▨▨ Railway
- ▪ Key targets
- ◣ Soviet forces
- ◆ Remnants of German forces
- ⟶ Soviet attacks 29 April–2 May 1945
- ▨ Hitler's bunker

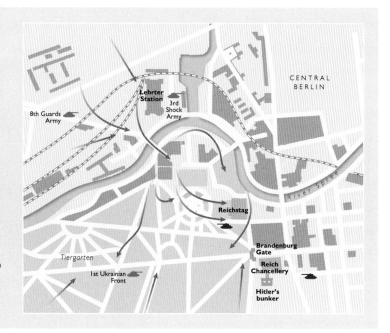

CENTRAL BERLIN

Lehrter Station
8th Guards Army
3rd Shock Army
River Spree
Reichstag
Tiergarten
Brandenburg Gate
Reich Chancellery
1st Ukrainian Front
Hitler's bunker

1945

29 APRIL

29 April **The remaining German** and Italian Fascist forces in Italy formally surrender to the Allies at Caserta, in southern Italy

1 May **Hundreds of civilians** in Demmin, Germany, take their own lives after the Red Army ransacks the town. It is one of several mass suicides driven by despair and fear of the advancing Soviets

2 May **British troops and Yugoslavian partisans** secure Trieste, in Italy. Yugoslavia later lays claim to the town and its vital port

△ **The entrance** to the *Führerbunker* in the Reich Chancellery's garden

1897–1945
JOSEPH GOEBBELS

Reich minister of propaganda from 1933 to 1945, Goebbels expertly manipulated public opinion to garner support for the Nazis' ideology and their racist and antisemitic policies. One of Hitler's most devoted acolytes, he killed himself after Hitler died.

30 April 1945
HITLER DIES BY SUICIDE

Finally conceding defeat, Hitler authorized the remaining troops in Berlin to break out of the city. He and his wife, Eva Braun, then killed themselves in the *Führerbunker*. Upon Hitler's death, Karl Dönitz became head of state and Joseph Goebbels chancellor. The next day, Goebbels and his wife, Magda, took their own lives after poisoning their six children.

3 May 1945
THE ALLIES RECAPTURE RANGOON

After retaking Mandalay in March, the Allies' next major target in their campaign to regain Burma was Rangoon. The city was vital to the Japanese, as it served as a landing port for supplies and reinforcements in Burma. On 1 May, the Allies launched Operation Dracula, an amphibious assault on Rangoon. By 3 May, they had retaken the port. The Japanese were forced to abandon key equipment and a strategically important location they had held since May 1942.

△ **British and Indian soldiers** creeping past a statue of the Buddha in Burma during Operation Dracula, 1945

5–9 May 1945
THE PRAGUE UPRISING

As the Red Army approached German-occupied Prague, the Czech resistance called for a general uprising. More than 30,000 civilians and resistance fighters took to the streets, and part of the pro-Nazi Russian Liberation Army (the POA) defected to help the Czechs. There were atrocities on both sides and fighting continued until the Soviets liberated the city on 9 May (see p.277).

△ **Sleeve patch** of the POA

4 May As the Nazi regime collapses, German forces in northwest Germany, Denmark, and the Netherlands surrender

1945

5 MAY

2 May 1945
THE FALL OF BERLIN

The two-week-long battle for Berlin ended when the Red Army captured the Reich Chancellery early in the morning of 2 May. At 6am, General Weidling surrendered with his staff and soon after ordered the city's remaining defenders to surrender. Some SS units continued fighting, but Soviet soldiers quickly destroyed their bases. The Red Army took violent revenge on Berlin and its citizens. Many thousands of women were raped, and looting and murder were rife in the days following the city's fall. With Hitler dead and Berlin in Allied hands, World War II in Europe was all but over.

◁ **A Red Army solider** raising the Soviet flag over the Reichstag, Berlin, May 1945

6 May 1945

THE SIEGE OF BRESLAU ENDS

On 13 February 1945, Soviet troops encircled Breslau (now Wroclaw in Poland), one of the fortress cities that Hitler wanted defended at all costs. After months of intense urban fighting, the German garrison capitulated. The siege was one of the last major battles on the Eastern Front. An estimated 6,000 Germans and 13,000 Soviets died, and thousands of civilians were killed or injured in the fighting.

1893–1946
HERMANN GÖRING
One of the most powerful figures in the Nazi Party, Göring was a key architect of the Nazi police state in Germany and created the Gestapo, the brutal enforcers of Nazi policy. He died by suicide after being convicted of war crimes and crimes against humanity.

◁ **German POWs** captured by Soviet soldiers in Breslau, 1945

1945

6 MAY

6 May German propagandist "Axis Sally" delivers her last broadcast to Allied troops

8 May The German surrender enters into force at 11:01pm, although fighting rumbles on in Czechoslovakia, Austria, and northern Yugoslavia

7 May Hermann Göring surrenders to US forces southeast of Salzburg, Austria

9 May Stutthof camp, near the city of Danzig, is the last concentration camp liberated by the Allies. More than 60,000 people have died there

7 May 1945

GERMANY SURRENDERS

Germany formally signed an unconditional surrender at the Reims headquarters of the commander of the Allied forces in Europe, General Dwight D. Eisenhower. During negotiations, Generaloberst Alfred Jodl focused on saving Germany's soldiers from capture by the Soviets. Eisenhower agreed to allow German forces retreating from the east to pass through the Allied lines until the surrender came into force on 8 May. After that, they would have to accept their fate.

◁ **Generaloberst Alfred Jodl** (*centre*) signing the German Instrument of Surrender, Reims, 7 May 1945

△ **Illustration marking** the liberation of Czechoslovakia, 1945

11 May 1945
SURRENDER IN CZECHOSLOVAKIA

The Red Army's last major operation in World War II was the Prague Strategic Offensive, which began on 6 May. By 9 May, the Soviets had liberated Prague. On 11 May, the remaining 1 million German troops concentrated in southeastern Germany and Czechoslovakia surrendered.

15 May 1945
THE JAPANESE COUP IN FRENCH INDOCHINA ENDS

By March 1945, the Japanese were worried that the French colonial administration in Indochina would support an Allied invasion, so they launched a coup to overthrow the French. By the coup's end in May, the Japanese had established three new states in Indochina: the Empire of Vietnam and the kingdoms of Kampuchea and Luang Phrabang. They hoped that these nominally independent states would support Japan and help forestall an Allied invasion.

◁ A French anti-Japanese poster

14 May The remaining German soldiers in Yugoslavia surrender to Tito's forces, who take 150,000 POWs

1945

15 MAY

11 May Truman orders the end of Lend-Lease, but Churchill and Stalin convince him to continue providing aid until Japan is defeated

8 May 1945
VE DAY

The Allies declared the day after Germany officially surrendered to be Victory in Europe (VE) Day. A holiday marked by celebrations across Europe and North America, it was also a day of mourning for the countless dead and sadness for relatives missing in action or still serving abroad. Both Truman and Churchill warned that many difficulties still lay ahead, especially as the war in the Pacific was not yet over. Stalin had insisted on a separate surrender ceremony in Berlin on 8 May; accordingly, victory celebrations in the USSR took place on 9 May.

▷ **A crowd celebrating** the end of the war in Europe in London, May 1945.

1945

THE PROBLEM OF GERMANY

Among the Allies, the prevailing view in 1945 was that Germany should be punished after the war. In the USA, the Morgenthau Plan called for Germany to be demilitarized, deindustrialized, and decentralized. However, some argued that the plan was too harsh and would lead to longer-term economic and social problems. The Allies eventually agreed to demilitarize Germany but also to stabilize its economy and place it on a more democratic path. However, Germany's division into occupied zones (see p.284) complicated its postwar reconstruction.

▷ **People queuing** for water in the devastated German city of Magdeburg, April 1945

1945

16 MAY

23 May British soldiers arrest the Reich president, Karl Dönitz, and his government at Flensburg, northern Germany

30 May The Czechs expel 20,000 ethnic Germans from Brno. About one-tenth of them die from exhaustion on the walk from Czechoslovakia to Austria

25 May The US Joint Chiefs of Staff issue the directive for the invasion of Japan, to begin on 1 November

3 June Japan approaches the USSR about negotiating peace with the Allies on their behalf, but Japanese leaders are divided on how to end the war

29 May 1945

US TROOPS TAKE SHURI CASTLE

US forces finally broke through the Japanese defensive lines and captured Shuri Castle on Okinawa after weeks of close-combat fighting. It was a major breakthrough in the Battle of Okinawa. The castle guarded the route to the southern half of the island, and its capture enabled the Allies to complete their conquest of Okinawa. They achieved this on 21 June, when the Japanese holding out in the Kiyan Peninsula capitulated.

▽ **A US Marine planting the American flag** on one of the ramparts of Shuri Castle

Of the 1 million Australians who served during World War II, 3,000 or more were Aboriginal or Torres Strait Islander peoples

7 June 1945
THE BATTLE OF WEST HUNAN ENDS

In April, the Japanese invaded west Hunan in southern China. They initially made good progress towards their primary goal of capturing the US air base at Zhijiang. However, the Chinese and Americans counterattacked on 3 June. They outflanked the Japanese, forcing them back to their starting position by 7 June. The battle was the last major offensive of the Second Sino-Japanese War and contributed to Japan's ultimate defeat.

▽ **Australian troops** landing at Labuan, north Borneo, 10 June 1945

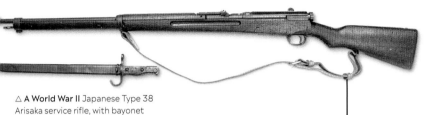

△ **A World War II** Japanese Type 38 Arisaka service rifle, with bayonet

10 June 1945
AUSTRALIAN TROOPS LAND IN NORTH BORNEO

In Operation Oboe, the ongoing campaign to capture Borneo from the Japanese, 30,000 Australian troops stormed ashore in the north of the island. They secured Brunei Bay for the British Pacific Fleet and gained control of vital oil and rubber facilities. The last major Allied campaign in the Southwest Pacific, the operation had begun on 1 May, when the Allies retook Tarakan Island.

6 June Japan passes a resolution to fight to the end, to uphold *kokutai* (meaning, the essence of the country), and to resist the Allies' demand for unconditional surrender

6 June Brazil declares war on Japan, affirming its solidarity with other Allied nations in the Americas

14 June US and Filipino forces capture the Bessang Pass in northern Luzon, opening the way to the last Japanese stronghold on the island

1945
14 JUNE

5 June 1945
THE BERLIN DECLARATION

In Berlin, the American, British, and French supreme commanders – Eisenhower, Montgomery, and de Lattre de Tassigny – met for the first time with the Soviet Union's General Zhukov. They signed the Berlin Declaration, proclaiming the end of the Third Reich. They also set up the Allied Control Council, which would govern occupied Germany and Austria and be responsible for their postwar reconstruction.

◁ **Georgy Zhukov** (*with red sash*) and other Red Army leaders with Bernard Montgomery (*centre*) in Berlin, June 1945 (hand-coloured image)

The radioactive plume from the bomb dropped on Nagasaki on 9 August 1945 is pictured from the town of Koyagi-jima, around 10 km (6 miles) from the city. The photograph was taken around 15 minutes after the bomb detonated.

1934–45
THE ATOMIC BOMB

In 1938, after decades of study into the nature of radioactivity, scientists in Berlin were the first to identify the process of nuclear fission – that is, how an atom (of uranium in this case) could be split to release huge amounts of energy. Their discovery awakened the possibility of making nuclear weapons capable of unprecedented destruction.

In 1939, Albert Einstein wrote to President Roosevelt urging the USA to develop nuclear weapons before Germany did. A committee was set up to conduct preliminary research; by 1942 it had developed into a large enterprise called the Manhattan Project, headed by General Leslie Groves. The British–Canadian nuclear project, code-named Tube Alloys, was merged with the Manhattan Project in 1943. Germany and Japan had their own nuclear bomb programmes.

The Allied efforts culminated on 16 July 1945 with a successful test detonation of one of three prototype bombs at the Trinity Site in New Mexico. President Truman decided to unleash the remaining two bombs on Japan; the first, "Little Boy", was dropped on Hiroshima on 6 August, while "Fat Man" detonated over Nagasaki three days later. The scale of destruction was instrumental in causing Japan to surrender on 15 August, and it also ushered in a new and dangerous nuclear age.

KEY MOMENTS

1943 Oppenheimer appointed director
A brilliant polymath, J. Robert Oppenheimer obtained his doctorate in physics in 1927 before embarking on a stellar academic career. In 1942 he was recruited for the Manhattan Project, and became director of its laboratory in Los Alamos, New Mexico, the following year.

1944 The Manhattan Project peaks
From 1939, the Manhattan Project grew quickly to produce weapons, including "Fat Man" (*replica pictured right*). By 1944, it had 130,000 staff at sites across the USA and Canada; by the end of the war, it had spent more than US$2.2 billion.

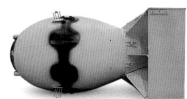

1945 Hiroshima bombed
The bombing of Hiroshima was carried out by a Boeing B-29 Superfortress, a long-range bomber, commanded by Colonel Paul W. Tibbets, who named the aeroplane *Enola Gay* after his mother. Taking off from the Mariana Islands, the Enola Gay successfully dropped its payload, killing more than 100,000 people.

1913–2005
LUIS MANGALUS TARUC

The son of poor Filipino peasants, Taruc co-founded the communist Hukbalahap movement in central Luzon. He led this powerful guerrilla force against the Japanese and continued to fight for farmers' rights and socialist land reforms after World War II.

▷ **Japanese nurses and soldiers** surrendering to US forces on Cebu Island, the Philippines, 1945

30 June 1945
THE BATTLE OF VISAYAS ENDS

Part of the broader campaign to clear the Japanese from the Philippines, the operation to secure the Visayas region (in the central Philippines) began in March, when US troops landed on Panay. Within two weeks they had secured the island with the help of Filipino guerillas. The Allies were equally swift to take Cebu, Bohol, and southeastern Negros. The success of the operation meant that Japanese resistance in the Philippines was limited to small pockets on Mindanao and Luzon by the end of June.

1945

19 June Japanese troops begin to surrender voluntarily on Iwo Jima and Okinawa – a sign that Japanese morale is ebbing

22 June Japan's Emperor Hirohito tells the Japanese government that it is necessary to pursue peace

15 JUNE

22 June Allied forces secure Okinawa, ending the bloodiest battle in the Pacific theatre: 20,000 of the 21,000 Japanese soldiers on the island have died in the fighting

UNITED NATIONS CONFERENCE

▷ **Detail of an envelope** commemorating the UN Conference, 1945

THE FIGHTING FILIPINOS

WE WILL ALWAYS FIGHT FOR *FREEDOM*!

1942–45
GUERRILLA FIGHTERS IN THE PHILIPPINES

Filipino guerrillas, such as Luis Taruc, played a significant role in the Allied campaign to drive the Japanese from the Philippines. Up to 1.3 million Filipinos may have supported an extensive network of more than 1,000 guerrilla units. Some of these units worked with the US forces in the islands; others remained independent. As well as fighting on the front line, the guerillas engaged in irregular warfare, espionage, sabotage, and prison raids. Enduring exhaustion, disease, and malnourishment, tens of thousands of Filipino guerrillas lost their lives in the war.

◁ **Propaganda poster** showing a Filipino freedom fighter

26 June 1945
THE UNITED NATIONS CHARTER

At the end of the San Francisco Conference (*see p.273*), the delegates unanimously accepted the text of the United Nations' founding document. All but one of the UN's 51 founding members signed the Charter that day; Poland signed it in October. The Charter established the purpose and principles of the UN, committing its members to securing peace.

△ **The mushroom cloud** following the explosion of the Trinity plutonium bomb, 16 July 1945

16 July 1945

THE TRINITY NUCLEAR BOMB TEST

The world's first nuclear explosion, the "Trinity" plutonium bomb test, took place in the New Mexico desert in America as part of the top-secret Manhattan Project (*see p.281*). The bomb released around 20 kilotons of power, generating enough heat to melt the desert sand over a wide area. The test's success meant the USA could begin preparing similar bombs for use against Japan.

About half of Okinawa's prewar population of 300,000 died in the battle for the island

3-19 July With most of Burma in Allied hands, Japanese forces try to tie down Allied forces north of Rangoon to allow the Japanese 28th Army to escape across the river Sittang

5 July General MacArthur announces that the Allies have secured the Philippines

17 July The Allied leaders meet in Potsdam to discuss Germany, Europe's postwar boundaries, and the war against Japan

20 July US forces besiege the remaining Japanese in Luzon and Mindanao in mopping-up operations

1945

20 JULY

◁ **Australian soldiers** pounding Japanese positions during the Battle of Balikpapan, July 1945

1-21 July 1945

THE BATTLE OF BALIKPAPAN

The final stage of Operation Oboe (*see p.279*) was the Battle of Balikpapan. This was the Australian Army's last major ground operation of World War II and its largest amphibious operation. Around 100 Allied ships landed 33,000 Australian personnel on Borneo's east coast. They outnumbered the 10,000-strong Japanese force and secured Balikpapan, the airfields, and oil facilities in three weeks. The Borneo campaign was controversial: the Japanese on Borneo were already cut off from Japan, so some strategists thought it unnecessary to waste resources recapturing the island.

30 July 1945

JAPAN SINKS THE USS INDIANAPOLIS

A Japanese torpedo hit the US Navy heavy cruiser *Indianapolis* as it made its way from Tinian, in the northern Mariana Islands, to Leyte Gulf. The ship had recently delivered a secret cargo from San Francisco to the US air base at Tinian – later revealed to be parts of the atomic bomb destined for Hiroshima. The *Indianapolis* went down with 300 of its crew. Around 600 of the 900 crew members who survived the initial sinking later died from shark attacks, dehydration, and salt poisoning.

▽ The USS *Indianapolis* on 10 July 1945, just before it delivered atomic bomb components to Tinian

1945

21 JULY

26 July The Allies issue the Potsdam Declaration, calling on Japan to surrender unconditionally or face "prompt and utter destruction"

3 August Organized Japanese resistance in Burma ends; the Allies turn their focus to regaining control of Malaya and Singapore

"Just how many did we kill? My God, what have we done?"

CAPTAIN ROBERT A. LEWIS, CO-PILOT ON THE ENOLA GAY, FOLLOWING THE BOMBING OF HIROSHIMA

1–2 August 1945

THE POTSDAM AGREEMENT

At the end of the Potsdam Conference, the US, the USSR, and the UK signed the agreement that shaped postwar Europe. Germany was to be divided into four occupation zones – the Soviet, American, British, and French – and demilitarized; it would also pay reparations. Poland's boundaries were redrawn, and its territory expanded. The Allies agreed to prosecute war criminals, paving the way for the Nuremberg trials (*see p.294*). Looking beyond Europe, the USSR reaffirmed the promise it had made at Yalta, in February, to launch an invasion of Japanese-held areas.

▷ Churchill, Truman, and Stalin at the Potsdam Conference, July–August 1945

6 August 1945
NUCLEAR WAR

At 2:45am, US B-29 bomber *Enola Gay* departed the island of Tinian, south of Japan. At 8:15am, it dropped the "Little Boy" atomic bomb over the Japanese city of Hiroshima. The bomb released energy equivalent to around 15 kilotons of TNT. At least 120,000 people were killed or fatally wounded by the blast, which reduced around 13 sq km (5 sq miles) of the city centre to ashes. The devastation was shocking, but the USA believed the A-bomb attacks to be the best way to convince Japan to surrender.

◁ **Hiroshima, devastated** by the atomic bomb, August 1945

8 August The USSR declares war on Japan; it invades the Japanese puppet state of Manchukuo, in northeast China, the next day

14 August Hard-line army officers in Japan attempt to seize control of the government and reject the Allies' peace terms; Hirohito intervenes to end the coup

1945

15 AUGUST

10 August Emperor Hirohito signals his willingness to surrender to the Allies in a radio transmission made in Morse Code in English

▽ **Atomic bomb,** Nagasaki, 1945

9 August 1945
NAGASAKI BOMBED

Three days after bombing Hiroshima, the USAAF detonated a second atomic bomb, "Fat Man", over the Japanese city of Nagasaki. The bomb was originally intended for Kokura, but poor weather meant the B-29 carrying it was diverted. The blast killed at least 35,000 people and injured another 60,000; it destroyed 5 sq km (2 sq miles) of the city.

▽ **A Japanese prisoner of war** in Guam after hearing Hirohito announce Japan's surrender

14 August 1945
JAPAN SURRENDERS

Emperor Hirohito finally ordered Japan's unconditional surrender. The next day, he addressed the nation for the first time, to announce Japan's surrender in the so-called "Jewel Voice Broadcast". Also on 15 August, the Allies celebrated Victory over Japan (VJ) Day. Japan's defeat ended more than eight years of conflict in Asia.

17 August 1945

INDONESIA DECLARES INDEPENDENCE

Nationalist leaders Sukarno and Mohammad Hatta declared Indonesia's independence after its liberation from Japan, becoming president and vice president respectively. The Dutch attempted to reassert their authority over their former colony, sparking a four-year war that ended with them accepting Indonesia's independence.

△ **Monument** to Sukarno and Hatta in Surabaya, Indonesia

> "Today the guns are silent. A great tragedy has ended... We must go forward to preserve in peace what we won in war."

GENERAL MACARTHUR, ANNOUNCING PEACE TO THE WORLD, 2 SEPT 1945

1945

16 AUGUST

17 August General MacArthur issues General Order No. 1 instructing Japanese forces to surrender to a specified Allied power

25 August Vietnam's emperor, Bao Dai, abdicates and hands power to Ho Chi Minh and the Viet Minh

19 August Ho Chi Minh, communist leader of the Viet Minh, stages the August Revolution in Vietnam, calling for a national uprising against the French and Japanese

27 August The Japanese forces in the Dutch East Indies surrender; the remaining Japanese units across the Asia-Pacific theatre soon follow

19 August 1945

US AND JAPANESE DELEGATIONS MEET IN MANILA

A Japanese delegation arrived at General MacArthur's headquarters in Manila to make arrangements for the Allied occupation of Japan. This had been among the Potsdam Declaration's terms for Japan's surrender. The initial occupation plan included the safe and immediate repatriation of about 36,000 Allied POWs and civilians detained in 140 camps in Japan. MacArthur's staff worked intensely to draft the Japanese Instrument of Surrender and organize the signing ceremony so that all hostilities could be brought to an end as quickly as possible.

▷ **Japanese emissaries boarding a plane** to Manila, for their meeting with MacArthur, 19 August 1945

2 September 1945
JAPAN FORMALLY SURRENDERS

The Instrument of Surrender was signed aboard the US battleship *Missouri* in Tokyo Bay, officially ending World War II. Japan's foreign minister, Mamoru Shigemitsu, and General Yoshijiro Umezu signed for Japan in front of representatives from the Allied powers. General MacArthur accepted the surrender for the USA, Republic of China, UK, and USSR, and "in the interests of the other United Nations".

◁ **Shigemitsu, Umezu,** and the Japanese delegation on the USS *Missouri* in Tokyo Bay

28 August US forces arrive in Japan to lay the operational groundwork for the Allied occupation of the country

30 August The Allied Control Council in Berlin issues its first proclamation, informing the Germans of its authority and powers

1945

2 SEPTEMBER

◁ **Ho Chi Minh,** first president of the Democratic Republic of Vietnam (hand-coloured image)

29 August Communist and KMT forces clash at Xinhua as their wartime truce crumbles and civil war in China restarts (*see p.295*)

1945–52
JAPAN REFORMED

The American occupiers of Japan directed a series of social, political, and economic reforms designed to weaken Japan's power structures and ensure it could never again wage war. They disbanded the military, broke up the national police force and large business conglomerates, and improved the rights of women and other marginalized groups. In 1947, the USA changed its approach, shifting to strengthening and stabilizing Japan as a potential ally in the developing Cold War (*see p.303*) with the USSR.

▷ **A Japanese police officer** and a US Army MP directing traffic in Tokyo, 1945

2 September 1945
VIETNAM DECLARES INDEPENDENCE

Ho Chi Minh proclaimed Vietnam's independence and the creation of the Democratic Republic of Vietnam to a crowd of more than 400,000 people at Ba Dinh Square in Hanoi. More than two million Vietnamese people had died of famine, partly caused by French mismanagement, in 1944–45. The country was ready for peace and self-rule. The French, however, were unwilling to give up their former colony, and they dragged the country back into war in 1946.

Lyudmila Pavlichenko, a student at Kyiv University, enlisted in the Red Army in 1941 as a sniper. At the sieges of Odesa and Sevastopol, she recorded 309 kills and was promoted to lieutenant, earning the nickname "Lady Death". After being wounded in 1942, she spent the rest of the war working as an instructor.

1941-45
RED ARMY WOMEN

No nation committed as many soldiers to World War II as the USSR. More than 30 million people served in its armed forces, of whom 8–11 million lost their lives. Some 800,000 women were enlisted, and unlike in other combatant nations, many served in combat units. This was partly because the USSR wished to show that it had created an equal society, but also to meet a desperate need for reinforcements after huge Soviet losses in the aftermath of Operation Barbarossa (*see p.112*). Even though some in the Red Army leadership were reluctant to send women to the front line, women went on to serve in a range of combat positions, including as snipers, machine gun operators, tank crew, and pilots.

In common with women in other countries, female recruits also worked in auxiliary roles, as nurses, military police, doctors, and so on. The Soviet partisans also included many women, who often volunteered for the dangerous job of crossing enemy lines to disrupt the Axis occupation. One of the most famed was Zoya Kosmodemyanskaya, who was summarily executed by German troops in 1941 after being caught committing acts of sabotage; she was declared a Hero of the Soviet Union, the first woman to achieve this accolade.

KEY MOMENTS

1941-44 Partisan menace
After Axis forces overran the western Soviet Union in 1941, civilians formed resistance groups to carry on the fight behind enemy lines. Posters denounced fascism as "the most evil enemy of women".

1941 Women snipers to the front
After heavy losses in Operation Barbarossa, more than 2,000 women were recruited as Red Army snipers; only a quarter of them survived. One of the many casualties was Nina Petrova, who had more than 100 kills to her name. She died fighting in Poland in 1945, at the age of 51.

1941-45 Aviation combat pioneers
Marina Raskova, a prewar aviator, persuaded Stalin to allow women to enlist for combat in the Soviet Air Force. In 1941, three women's aviation regiments , flying Polikarpov Po-2 aircraft (*right*), were formed. Pilots Lydia Litvyak and Yekaterina Budanova became the only female flying aces of the war.

A NEW WORLD ORDER

After the surrender of Japan, the USA had total authority over the defeated country, but despite civilian fears, the Americans proved reasonable masters. Under the direction of General Douglas MacArthur, a democratically based constitutional monarchy was established, which helped Japan to move on from its militarist, feudal past and develop into a modern, highly industrialized nation.

In China, the end of hostilities with Japan led to the expansion of civil war between the Chinese Communists, led by Mao Zedong, and the Nationalists, or Kuomintang (KMT), under the control of Chiang Kai-shek. The larger KMT forces were defeated by the Communists, who were more organized and ruthless, and the KMT retreated to Taiwan. Mao proclaimed the People's Republic of China in October 1949.

Another consequence of war was that the Western colonial empires in Asia collapsed. The exhaustion of the imperial powers – primarily Britain, France, and the Netherlands – was paralleled by popular movements demanding national self-determination, which proved impossible to deny. Within a matter of a decade or so, Western overlordship of Asia was gone for good.

Postwar divisions

In Europe, the political situation was more complicated. The continent was divided between the Western powers, represented by the USA, Britain, and France, and the

USSR (which developed its own atomic weapons in 1949) and its communist allies. In the opening moves of a new conflict that came to be known as the "Cold War", Europe was divided in two, partitioned by an ideological "Iron Curtain" between east and west, with the USSR building a defensive line to prevent any crossing of the new border – in either direction.

In Western Europe, the old parliamentary democracies were re-established after the war ended. With American help in the form of the Marshall Plan, economic reconstruction was soon under way. This policy was extended to the western half of Germany, which – as the Federal Republic of Germany – became a remarkable success on economic, political, and social levels. In Eastern Europe, however, the heavy hand of Soviet control kept East Germany, Poland, the Baltic states, Czechoslovakia, Hungary, Romania, and Bulgaria in a form of limbo that lasted until the collapse of Soviet Communist rule in 1989.

Whatever the political system adopted in Europe, there was no disguising the fact that European dominance in world affairs had faded as a result of the world war. Real power was now divided between the USA and the Soviet Union, and much of the world would be an ally of either one or the other. This bipolar world became the new normal, with the two superpowers fighting to maintain control and influence on a global scale.

This inherently unstable situation developed into full-scale war in Korea in 1950, as the communist government in the north of the country – supported by the USSR and China – attempted to overcome the Western-supported southern Korea. The resulting war ended in a stalemate, with Korea divided into a communist North and a liberal-capitalist South.

Reducing conflict

There were, however, some reasons for optimism, with the introduction of transnational organizations. The most important was the United Nations, created in October 1945 as a successor to the old League of Nations, but with far more members and with greater powers to maintain peace.

As part of the UN, umbrella organizations came into being, including UNICEF (United Nations Children's Fund), UNESCO (United Nations Educational, Scientific and Cultural Organization), and the WHO (World Health Organization). Other transnational institutions followed, including the International Monetary Fund (IMF) and the World Bank. Although not universally popular, these organizations did much to create an increasingly prosperous and relatively stable world order. Despite the proliferation of nuclear weapons, the Cold War, and a succession of smaller-scale wars, there has been no direct conflict between the world's major powers since 1945.

8 September 1945
KOREA DIVIDED

At Potsdam (*see p.283*), the Allies had agreed to temporarily divide Korea into two zones after the end of the war in Asia. These zones were demarcated by the 38th parallel. In the north, the Japanese would surrender to the Soviets; in the south, to the Americans. The arrangement was designed to limit Soviet influence in Southeast Asia. On 8 September, US troops arrived in southern Korea. By then, the Soviets had already begun to seal off the 38th parallel. The division in Korea solidified over the next years, and north and south had different regimes. In 1950, a US attempt to reunite the country ended in war (*see p.306*).

▷ **A Japanese soldier** unbuckling his sidearm as he surrenders to American soldiers in Korea, 1945

1945

3 SEPTEMBER

5 September The British Military Administration takes control of Malaya and Singapore; civilian government is restored on 1 April 1946

11 September The Council of Foreign Ministers meets in London to discuss Allied peace treaties with Italy, Bulgaria, Hungary, Romania, and Finland

9 September Japanese forces surrender to the Kuomintang at Nanjing, China, ending the Second Sino-Japanese War

△ **Britain's Union Jack flag** being hoisted to mark the liberation of Penang, September 1945

3 September 1945
THE BRITISH RETAKE PENANG

The Allies liberated their first city in Malaya when British Royal Marines took George Town, Penang. The city was an important base between Rangoon and Singapore. The next day, infantry from the Indian Army arrived to reoccupy Singapore. The Japanese forces in Southeast Asia formally surrendered in the city on 12 September.

20 September 1945
LEND-LEASE ENDS

The USA provided military and other vital supplies and services worth US$49.1 billion to nearly 40 countries through the Lend-Lease scheme during World War II. This war aid significantly contributed to the Allied victory. The UK and the USSR were the largest recipients. The UK repaid its US$4.25 billion debt in 50 instalments, the last of which was paid in 2006. The Soviet Union repaid only 25 per cent of its debt.

▷ **British propaganda poster** showing an Allied convoy carrying supplies to the USSR

WAR SUPPLIES FOR RUSSIA . . . A convoy of British and American lorri streams along the Persian route to Russia.

10 November 1945

THE BATTLE OF SURABAYA

Surabaya was the site of the largest battle in Indonesia's independence war. For three weeks, the Indonesians fiercely resisted British forces advancing through the city. Between 6,000 and 15,000 Indonesians died in the battle. Although unsuccessful, their defence of the city became a symbol of Indonesian resilience, sacrifice, and independence.

△ **A bronze frieze** depicting Indonesia's struggle for independence

24 October 1945

THE UNITED NATIONS IS ESTABLISHED

Marking the formal foundation of the United Nations, the United Nations Charter came into effect. The organization proclaimed its commitment to maintaining global peace and security through its peacekeeping and human rights work. However, some now view the UN as an instrument created by World War II's victors to legitimize the world order they established.

◁ Flag of the United Nations

10 October In the Double Tenth Agreement, Mao Zedong recognizes Chiang Kai-shek's Nationalist government as legitimate, but the Chinese civil war continues

25 October China's Nationalist government takes control of Taiwan and the Penghu Islands, which China had ceded to Japan in 1895

25 October Robert Oppenheimer, creator of the atomic bomb, voices his regret in a meeting with President Truman, saying he feels he has "blood on his hands"

13 November The USA and UK agree to an inquiry into the issue of Palestine and Europe's displaced Jews

1945

13 NOVEMBER

1945

JAPAN'S WAR ORPHANS

On Japan's surrender, some 1.5 million Japanese military personnel and civilians were stranded in Manchuria, in northeast China. Civilians in particular faced chaos and violence as they tried to return to Japan, and around 4,000 children were separated from their parents and left behind in China. Many of these war orphans were saved by local people and raised as Chinese civilians. Those that returned to Japan joined more than 120,000 children in the country who had lost their parents or been abandoned. With space in orphanages for only 12,000 children, the government left the majority to live on the streets and fend for themselves. These children faced tremendous hardship and stigma. Many were abused, jailed, or sold for labour.

▷ **Young Japanese war orphans** from Manchuria arrive in Tokyo

20 November 1945

THE NUREMBERG TRIALS BEGIN

From November 1945 to October 1946, the Allies staged the International Military Tribunal, known as the Nuremberg Trials. Twenty-four individuals, including Hermann Göring and Rudolf Hess, and seven organizations (including the SS, SA, and Gestapo) were indicted for war crimes. By the end, the tribunal had tried 22 leading Nazis. It sentenced 12 to death by hanging, imprisoned seven, and acquitted three. Göring killed himself on 15 October, the night before his scheduled execution. Further trials followed from December 1946, including the Doctors' Trial and the Judges' Trial.

◁ **Hermann Göring** being cross-examined at the International Military Tribunal, Nuremberg, Germany, 1946

16–26 December The USA, UK, and USSR agree to jointly (with China) govern Korea for five years, but Korea rejects this Allied trusteeship and demands independence

5 March 1946 Winston Churchill's "Iron Curtain" speech (*see p.303*) marks the increasing division between Eastern and Western Europe

1945

14 NOVEMBER

30 November 1945

JAPANESE REPATRIATIONS

On 30 November, Japan dissolved its war and navy ministries, replacing them with two new ministries of demobilization. These were to continue the work of repatriating around 7 million Japanese nationals scattered across Asia and the Western Pacific and returning more than 1.1 million displaced Koreans, Chinese, Taiwanese, and Southeast Asians in Japan to their homes. Progress was slow until the USA released more ships to help in March 1946. By the end of 1946, more than 5 million Japanese people had been returned, but more than 1 million Japanese were still being held in the USSR and China.

▷ A **Japanese child** repatriated by the Americans

△ Filipino Veterans Congressional Gold Medal

18 February 1946

FILIPINOS DENIED VETERAN BENEFITS

The 1944 GI Bill provided US veterans with a generous package of benefits to help them adjust to civilian life. However, in February 1946, the Rescission Act took these benefits away from Filipino veterans (then US citizens) by redefining their war service as "non-active". The act denied Filipino veterans the support they needed and devalued their contribution to the war. In 2017, the US government finally honoured Filipino veterans with a Congressional Gold Medal, but this could not make up for their earlier unfair treatment.

1945-49

THE CHINESE CIVIL WAR

After Japan's defeat, the uneasy truce between the Chinese Nationalist Party (the KMT) and Chinese Communist Party (the CCP) collapsed and the civil war flared up again. In 1947-48, the Communists made inroads into central China and secured vital support among the rural peasantry. After winning control of Manchuria and the northeast, they captured Beijing and other cities, including the Nationalist capital, Nanjing, in early 1949. The war ended with a Communist victory. The KMT government retreated to Taiwan and continued to claim to be China's legitimate government.

▷ **Propaganda poster** of the Chinese Communist leader, Mao Zedong

毛泽东思想是当代马克思列宁主义的顶峰
MAO ZE DONG SI XIANG SHI DANG DAI MA KE SI LIE NING ZHU YI DE DING FENG

April-June A Communist offensive against the KMT in Manchuria leaves the Communists holding Harbin and northern territories

25 June Truman signs an order allowing interned Japanese Americans to return to their homes; many have lost everything and face continuing prejudice

1946

30 JUNE

20 April The Anglo-American Committee of Inquiry recommends moving 100,000 Jews from Europe to Palestine and extending the British Mandate; the recommendation is not adopted

30 June Poland holds a referendum to decide if its people support or oppose communism; the pro-communist result is later discovered to have been fraudulent

◁ **A Greek communist** partisan practising shooting, 1946

△ **Hideki Tojo** on trial in Tokyo, 1946

3 May 1946

WAR CRIMES TRIALS IN TOKYO

At the International Military Tribunal for the Far East, 28 senior Japanese political and military leaders were charged with committing war crimes in Asia between 1931 and 1945. In November 1948, all were found guilty. Seven, including General Hideki Tojo, were condemned to death, and 16 were imprisoned for life. Members of the imperial family were, controversially, exempt from trial.

30 March 1946

CIVIL WAR IN GREECE

After an interlude in the conflict between communist and royalist factions in Greece (see p.218), the civil war reignited. The communists refused to take part in the first elections since 1936, and began guerilla operations. When the British withdrew their support from the royalists, the USA stepped in with military and economic aid.

16–20 August 1946
THE GREAT CALCUTTA KILLINGS

On 15 March, Britain had announced that India would become independent. The Indian National Congress wished for a united India at independence, but the Muslim League favoured partition into majority Hindu and Muslim states. Feeling that Muslim voices were not being heard, Muhammad Ali Jinnah, the League's leader, organized a peaceful "Direct Action Day" on 16 August. A huge crowd of Muslims gathered in Calcutta (now Kolkata), and fighting erupted between Hindus and Muslims. Around 10,000 people died in sectarian violence that foreshadowed the atrocities that went with partition in 1947.

▷ Rioters armed with lathis (bamboo sticks) on the streets of Calcutta, August 1946

1946

1 August President Truman creates the US Atomic Energy Commission to control the development and production of nuclear weapons and nuclear energy

19 January 1947 Poland becomes a communist republic and signs the UN Charter

1 JULY

4 July 1946 The US gives up sovereignty over the Philippines and recognizes the country's independence

▽ The back of a Gulag prisoner's jacket, showing their identification number

19 December 1946
THE FIRST INDOCHINA WAR BEGINS

On 23 November, after a year of low-level conflict, the French bombarded Haiphong, in the Viet-Minh-held northeast of Vietnam. In reponse, the Viet Minh soldiers detonated explosives in Hanoi's European districts on 19 December. The ensuing Battle of Hanoi started the First Indochina War, setting Ho Chi Minh, backed by China, in the north against the French in the south.

▷ A French anti-communist poster from Indochina

14 August 1946
FORCED REPATRIATION TO THE USSR

The British, Americans, and Italians began forcibly repatriating around half of the 6 million Soviet citizens left in Central and Western Europe at the end of World War II. These included prisoners of war and refugees from Eastern Europe. Among them were non-citizens and opponents of Stalin, such as Cossacks, White Russians, Slovenes, Croats, and Serbs. The USSR treated many of the returnees as traitors, sending hundreds of thousands of them to its network of labour camps, known as the Gulag.

10 February 1947

THE PARIS PEACE TREATIES

At the 1946 International Paris Peace Conference, representatives of 21 nations met to draft peace treaties with Germany's former allies – Bulgaria, Finland, Hungary, Italy, and Romania. No peace treaties were signed with Germany and Austria, as they no longer existed as states. The treaties, signed on 10 February 1947, confirmed the territorial losses of the defeated countries. The new territorial boundaries led to the forced migration and displacement of millions of people.

△ Soldiers marking the new border between Italy and Yugoslavia in a cemetery in Gorizia,, Italy

1876–1948
MUHAMMAD ALI JINNAH
Born in Karachi, Jinnah was an Indian Muslim lawyer and politician. He focused on safeguarding Muslim rights in India's independence struggle and fought for a Muslim homeland. Following India's partition (*see p.298*), he served as Pakistan's first governor-general.

12 February Aung San and some minority groups in Burma reach an agreement to unify the country

28 February The KMT government in charge of Taiwan kills thousands in Taipei in a crackdown on protests; martial law lasts until 1987

1947

12 MARCH

27 January Burmese nationalist leader Aung San and the British government agree that Burma will be independent within one year

14 February The UN takes responsibility for Palestine after the UK and USA fail to find a mutually acceptable solution to resettling Jews in the region

▽ **President Harry S. Truman** authorizing the provision of US aid to Greece and Turkey

12 March 1947

THE TRUMAN DOCTRINE

The Truman Doctrine was a policy designed to protect US interests and world peace by providing military and economic aid to "free peoples" struggling against "totalitarian regimes". The doctrine was primarily directed at stopping the spread of communism and underpinned US foreign policy during the Cold War. It was first tested in the Greek civil war (*see p.295*), where US aid helped in the government's fight against communist revolutionaries.

> "Totalitarian regimes imposed on free peoples, by direct or indirect aggression, undermine the foundations of international peace and hence the security of the United States."

PRESIDENT TRUMAN, IN A SPEECH TO THE US CONGRESS, 12 MARCH 1947

14–15 August 1947
THE PARTITION OF INDIA

Three hundred years of British involvement in India ended, and the subcontinent was partitioned (divided) into two new countries – India and Pakistan. Partition triggered one of the largest mass migrations in history, as 15 million people rushed to reach the right side of the border in Punjab. Muslims in India made their way to Pakistan, while Hindus and Sikhs in Pakistan headed for India. Partition broke up communities in which people of different religions had lived in harmony for generations and unleashed violence that claimed up to 1 million lives.

◁ **A distraught boy** sitting on the walls of a refugee camp in Delhi during the Partition of India, 1947

1947

13 MARCH

21 July 1947 The Dutch attack areas held by republicans in Indonesia, dashing hopes of peaceful independence

4 October The USSR creates the Cominform to promote communism and counter capitalist, "imperialist" US expansion

4 January 1948 The British colony of Burma becomes an independent republic known as the Union of Burma

1889–1964
JAWAHARLAL NEHRU

A lawyer and leading figure in the Indian independence movement, Nehru was the first prime minister of India. He was head of a powerful political dynasty that continues to influence Indian politics.

Partition drove 5.5 million Muslims into West Punjab and 4.5 million Hindus and Sikhs into East Punjab

29 November 1947
CONFLICT IN PALESTINE

The UK was caught between encouraging the Palestinian Arab population towards independence and its commitment to creating a Jewish homeland. Unable to find a solution, the UK had turned the problem over to the UN. On 29 November, the UN called for Palestine to be partitioned into an Arab state and a Jewish state, with Jerusalem as a neutral zone under international control. The plan sparked civil war. Violence broke out as both sides tried to secure the lands they inhabited.

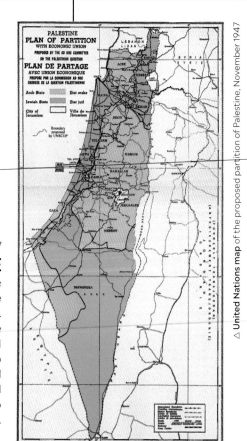

△ **United Nations map** of the proposed partition of Palestine, November 1947

16 June 1948

THE BRITISH MALAYAN EMERGENCY

In 1948, the Malayan Communist Party (MCP), led by Chin Peng, began organizing strikes and attacks against the British in its fight for Malaya's independence. When communists killed three European managers of rubber plantations in Perak state on 16 June, the British declared a national state of emergency. MCP-led insurgents waged a guerilla war on Commonwealth and British forces until 1960. By then, communist influence had waned, and the Federation of Malaya had been independent since 1957.

△ Federation of Malaya
postage stamp

▽ Prime Minister Daniel Malan (*centre*) and his government, 1948

26 May 1948

APARTHEID IN SOUTH AFRICA

Daniel Malan's National Party was elected and put racial segregation, or apartheid, at the heart of South Africa's government. Interracial marriage was banned, white-only areas were strictly enforced, and Black South Africans were dispossessed of their lands. Apartheid lasted 50 years.

3 April The Marshall Plan (*see p. 303*) offers aid to help in the postwar reconstruction of 16 European countries

1948

16 JUNE

4 February Ceylon gains independence after the Ceylonese political elite cooperate with the British; it becomes the Republic of Sri Lanka in 1972

5 June The Halong Bay Agreement unifies Tonkin (north Vietnam) and Annam (central Vietnam) under the Provisional Central Government of Vietnam, but the Indochina War continues

"Every generation shapes its dreams... My generation dreamed of doing away with British colonialism in Malaya."

CHIN PENG, IN HIS AUTOBIOGRAPHY, MY SIDE OF HISTORY, 2003

1948-49
THE FIRST ARAB-ISRAELI WAR

Israel remembers the war of 1948–49 as a war of independence. The Arab world sees it as the Nakba (the "Catastrophe").

14 May 1948 Jewish leaders proclaim the State of Israel as Britain's mandate in Palestine comes to an end.

15 May 1948 Arab states including Egypt and Lebanon launch operations against Israel in response to its declaration of independence.

Early 1949 The Israelis occupy Palestine and expel about two-thirds of the Arab population (c. 750,000 people) from their homes.

24 February–20 July 1949 Armistice agreements end the war. A temporary frontier is fixed between Israel and its neighbours.

5 July 1948
BRITAIN'S NATIONAL HEALTH SERVICE (NHS) IS BORN

The British Emergency Hospital Service, founded in 1939 to care for wartime casualties, paved the way for a government-directed National Health Service (NHS). Widespread injuries, illnesses, and poverty in postwar Britain made its establishment urgent. Launched by Aneurin Bevan, the Labour government's minister of health, the NHS provided free medical treatment for everyone based on need, not on ability to pay.

▷ **Student nurses from Sierra Leone and Nigeria** attend a midwifery course at the National Training School for Midwives in London, 1948

1948

17 JUNE

24 June 1948 The Berlin Blockade begins when Stalin cuts off land access to Berlin; the Western Allies supply Berlin by air

28 June Stalin expels Tito's Yugoslavia from the Cominform for deviating from Soviet Communism

25 June The Displaced Persons Act of 1948 authorizes the immigration of more than 400,000 Europeans, mostly from Eastern Europe, to the USA over a four-year period

26 July Truman issues an order to desegregate the US military after a 1947 presidential report condemns discrimination in the armed forces

1945-48
DEALING WITH COLLABORATORS

Many people collaborated with occupying forces during World War II, some for personal gain, others for survival. After the conflict, some collaborators in Nazi-occupied territories were legally prosecuted, while others were punished by angry mobs. Women were frequently targets for public humiliation. In France, women who had been in intimate relationships with German soldiers had their heads shaved and were shamed in public as punishment for what was called "horizontal collaboration".

▷ **A French woman** having her head shaved as punishment for collaborating with Germans

1887-1975
CHIANG KAI-SHEK

Head of state of the Chinese Nationalist government in 1928–49, Chiang Kai-shek was Allied commander in China during World War II. After the Chinese Civil War, he retreated to Taiwan in 1949, remaining its president until his death in 1975.

"We must make it clear that armed attack will be met by collective defence, prompt and effective. That is the meaning of the North Atlantic Pact."

DEAN ACHESON, US SECRETARY OF STATE, 18 MARCH 1949

25–30 March 1949
DEPORTATIONS FROM THE BALTIC STATES

To consolidate Soviet rule and quash independence movements, the USSR conducted mass deportations and forced collectivization of rural land. In Operation Priboi some 95,500 people from Latvia, Lithuania, and Estonia, including many thousands of children, were deported to work in Siberia for life. Most were given only a few hours' notice of the deportation.

◁ **Prisoners in the Vorkuta Gulag (Vorkutlag),** one of Soviet Russia's major labour camps, 1945

27 August In Norway, the last of 37 people condemned to death for colllaboration is executed; 28,750 had been arrested for war-related crimes after Germany's surrender

5 May The Council of Europe is established; it comprises 10 countries committed to promoting democracy and protecting human rights and the rule of law

1949

23 MAY

22 January 1949 Beijing falls to the Communists after Nationalist leader Chiang Kai-shek resigns the presidency; the Communists take Nanjing in April and Shanghai in May

▽ **The pen used by Dutch statesman** Dirk Stikker to sign the NATO treaty

4 April 1949
THE NORTH ATLANTIC TREATY ORGANIZATION

NATO was created as a security alliance between the USA, Canada, and 10 Western European countries. By 2020, it had 30 members, including 21 EU countries. In May 1955, the Warsaw Pact between the USSR and seven other Eastern Bloc socialist republics aimed to balance the power of NATO and the Western Bloc. Both treaties led to the expansion of military forces that were integrated into the respective blocs.

▽ **Poster map** of the Federal and Democratic Republics of Germany

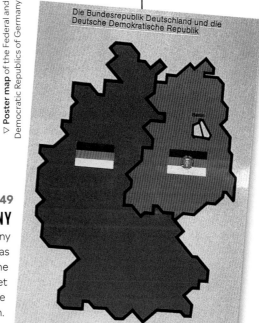

Die Bundesrepublik Deutschland und die Deutsche Demokratische Republik

23 May 1949
WEST AND EAST GERMANY

The USA, the UK, and France consolidated the zones that they occupied in Germany to create the Federal Republic of Germany. The West German Constitution was approved in May and the first government elected in August. On 7 October, the USSR established the communist German Democratic Republic (GDR) in the Soviet occupation zone in eastern Germany. By 1955, both West and East Germany were fully sovereign states, although NATO and Soviet troops remained in Berlin. The GDR and Berlin became a focal point of Cold War tensions.

This map, produced in 1945, shows the four Allied occupation zones of Germany, as well as the territory ceded to Poland and the USSR. In addition, Berlin was split between the four Allied powers. The Allied occupation would last until 1949.

1947-55
THE IRON CURTAIN

When World War II ended, old enmities between allies resurfaced and, with Europe shattered, two superpowers emerged – the capitalist USA and the communist USSR. Stalin's wish to create a buffer of communist states in Eastern and Central Europe led him to renege on promises to allow democratic elections there. On 15 March 1946, Winston Churchill delivered a speech in Fulton, Missouri, attended by President Truman, in which he stated that an "iron curtain" had fallen across Europe, separating the west from the Soviet east.

The rift between former allies continued when Truman offered US support to anti-communist forces in the Greek Civil War. The Truman Doctrine, which pledged US support for democracies threatened by authoritarianism, was put into action in 1948 with the Marshall Plan, a programme to boost Western European economies. Stalin responded in 1949 by establishing Comecon, an organization to coordinate communist economies.

The first major confrontation between the USA and the USSR occurred in Germany, where Stalin blockaded Allied-controlled West Berlin in 1948–49. In response, the USA formed NATO, and the USSR eventually countered with its own military alliance – the Warsaw Pact – as the Cold War between the superpowers continued.

KEY MOMENTS

1947-48 The Marshall Plan
In 1947, US Secretary of State George Marshall proposed to offer economic assistance to rebuild Europe. His plan began in 1948, eventually transferring more than US$13.3 billion in capital and materials. The USSR refused the offer to participate.

1948 The Berlin Blockade
In June 1948, Stalin blockaded West Berlin, hoping to gain sole control of the German capital. The Western Allies refused to back down, and delivered food, fuel, and vital supplies via a series of airlifts (*right*) that lasted until May 1949.

1949-55 The blocs solidify
The North Atlantic Treaty Organization (NATO) was formed in 1949 as a military alliance of 12 nations against further communist expansion into Europe. When West Germany joined NATO on 6 May 1955, the USSR responded eight days later with the signature of their own alliance, the Warsaw Pact (*right*).

(map, left page)

INSTERBURG
KOENIGSBERG
GOLDAP
MEMEL
OST-
BRAUNSBERG
ELBING
IENBURG
ALLENSTEIN
PREUSSEN

WARSCHAU

CZENSTOCHAU

BENZIN
KÖNIGSHÜTTE
KATTOWITZ

LEGEND·ERKLÄRUNG

BOUNDARIES·GRENZEN:

GERMANY
DEUTSCHLAND   1937

OCCUPATION AREAS
BESATZUNGSZONEN 1945

PROVINCES · PROVINZEN

ZONES·ZONEN:

AMERICAN ZONE · AMERIKANISCHE ZONE

BRITISH ZONE · BRITISCHE ZONE

FRENCH ZONE · FRANZÖSISCHE ZONE

RUSSIAN ZONE · RUSSISCHE ZONE

POLISH TERRITORY · POLNISCHES GEBIET

Alle Rechte vorbehalten

Einzelpreis: RM 0.50

1 October 1949
THE PEOPLE'S REPUBLIC OF CHINA

With Chiang Kai-shek's Nationalist cause defeated on the mainland, Mao Zedong established the People's Republic of China (PRC). He proclaimed that Western "bourgeois" civilization and democracy were bankrupt, and "a people's republic led by the working class" was the solution. Within days, the USSR and the European communist bloc recognized the Chinese Communist Party (CCP) as China's legitimate government.

△ Illustration showing Mao Zedong **proclaiming** the establishment of the People's Republic of China

17 October Chinese troops stop at Hong Kong's northern border; the British garrison had been strengthened in case of a Communist invasion

1949

24 MAY

12 August The Second Geneva Convention outlines provisions for the treatment of wounded, sick, and shipwrecked members of armed forces at sea

29 August The USSR successfully tests its first nuclear device, RDS-1 or "First Lightning", in Kazakhstan, ending the US monopoly on nuclear weapons

△ **Emperor Bao Dai,** head of state of Vietnam, 1949

2 July 1949
THE STATE OF VIETNAM

The French formally merged Cochin China with the rest of Vietnam, proclaiming the Associated State of Vietnam. They appointed the former emperor, Bao Dai, as head of state. Most Vietnamese nationalists denounced this, and the struggle for independence continued. At the end of the Indochina War, in 1954, Vietnam was formally divided into North Vietnam and South Vietnam.

1893–1976
MAO ZEDONG

A soldier, Marxist, and founder of the People's Republic of China, Mao restored China's independence and sovereignty. He led China's Communist revolution, including the Great Leap Forward and the Cultural Revolution.

Around 5 million civilians died as a result of combat, famine, and disease during the Chinese Civil War

March 1950–November 1951

THE BRIGGS PLAN IN MALAYA

Two years into the Malayan Emergency (*see p.299*), the British forced 10 per cent of Malaya's population into 400 internment camps called "new villages". The aim was to cut the communist insurgents off from their rural support base. Such practices were prohibited by the Geneva Conventions and customary international law, but the British stopped the mass resettlement programme only when they realized it was ineffective.

△ **A Malay home guard and a policeman** checking a civilian passing through a new village

◁ Chiang Kai-shek posing in front of the flag of the Republic of China

8 December 1949

CHINA'S NATIONALISTS MOVE TO TAIWAN

After two decades of fighting, the Communists defeated the Nationalist KMT and won control over mainland China. Chiang Kai-shek and the remaining KMT left for Taipei, Taiwan, where they installed the rival Republic of China (ROC) as a government-in-exile. Both Mao and Chiang claimed to be the sole legitimate government of China. Taiwan became the last Nationalist stronghold.

27 December The Dutch formally transfer sovereignty to Indonesia's national government after facing international pressure

1950

31 MARCH

22 November The Petersberg Agreement allows West Germany to join the international stage (including bodies such as the Council of Europe)

14 February 1950 Mao and Stalin sign a Sino-Soviet Treaty of Friendship after two months of arduous negotiations

▽ **Senator Joseph McCarthy** presents to a Senate committee, 1950s

9 February 1950

THE "RED SCARE"

US senator Joseph McCarthy delivered his "enemies within" speech, accusing the US government and media of being infiltrated by communists. In the early 1950s, American leaders repeatedly told the public to fear subversive communist influence – the "Red Scare" – in their lives. McCarthy led a series of brutal investigations and hearings, including 36 days of televised hearings in 1954. Most of the accused were innocent. Eventually, lawyer Joseph Welch's rebuke in court and Edward R. Murrow's skilful journalism helped discredit McCarthy and undermine his influence.

25 June 1950–27 July 1953

THE KOREAN WAR

When World War II ended, Korea was split along the 38th parallel into US and Soviet occupation zones. Tensions between the former allies led to the UN assuming responsibility. In August 1948, with US support, an independent South Korea was created. In June 1950, supplied and advised by the USSR, rival nationalists in North Korea invaded the South to unify the country. While China supported North Korea, the UN aided South Korea. The Korean War was one of the first Cold War battlegrounds. At least 2.5 million people died and more than a million were injured before an armistice ended the fighting in July 1953. Korea remained divided in two.

◁ **United Nations forces** crossing the 38th parallel as they withdraw from Pyongyang, 1950

15–19 September 1950 US Marines land at Incheon on the west coast of South Korea; in late September the Americans recapture Seoul, helping turn the tide of the Korean War

11 December Chinese attacks at Chosin, in the north of the Korean peninsula, force a wholescale UN retreat back to South Korea

1950

1 APRIL

19 September The Western Allies agree to end the legal state of war with Germany, a technicality unresolved since 1945, hoping to strengthen West Germany's position as an ally in the Cold War

25 June 1950

THE START OF THE KOREAN WAR

Parties in the communist north and capitalist south of Korea both claimed to be the true government of the country. On 25 June, 75,000 soldiers of the North's Korean People's Army (KPA) crossed into South Korea. The invasion aimed to reunify the Korean peninsula under communist control. The KPA captured the South's capital, Seoul, on 28 June.

▷ **People's Liberation Army soldiers**

19 October 1950

CHINA INTERVENES IN KOREA

After US–UN forces crossed the 38th parallel into North Korea, around 260,000 Chinese soldiers entered the peninsula to support the North Koreans. Having secretly crossed the river Yalu, the Chinese army caught the UN forces by surprise and drove them back to South Korea. Mao Zedong felt China had to intervene in order to protect communist interests.

▽ **South Korean Army officers** observing activities at the 38th parallel, June 1950

18 April 1951
EUROPEAN COOPERATION

On 9 May 1950, French foreign minister Robert Schuman set out his plan to increase European cooperation by integrating the French and German coal and steel industries. On 18 April 1951, the Treaty of Paris established the European Coal and Steel Community (ECSC). France, West Germany, Italy, the Netherlands, Belgium, and Luxembourg agreed to pool their coal and steel production. The ECSC was the first of a series of multinational European institutions that paved the way for the European Union.

◁ **Poster celebrating** the "Day of Free Europe", Berlin, 1952

"There is no future for the people of Europe other than in union."

JEAN MONNET, "THE FATHER OF EUROPE", WHO INSPIRED ROBERT SCHUMAN, 1950

4 January 1951 Chinese troops capture Seoul after UN forces abandon it; UN and South Korean forces retake Seoul in March

28 July The United Nations 1951 Refugee Convention establishes the legal protection, rights, and assistance due to all refugees

1951

8 SEPTEMBER

22 April Holding a vital part of the UN line in Korea, at the river Imjin, the British Army experiences its bloodiest battle since World War II

1 September Australia, New Zealand, and the USA sign the ANZUS Treaty to ensure peace and security in the Pacific

8 September 1951
THE ALLIED OCCUPATION OF JAPAN ENDS

Forty-eight nations signed the Treaty of Peace with Japan (ratified on 28 April 1952), which formally ended the Allied occupation of Japan. Under its terms, Japan recognized Korea's independence and renounced all rights to Taiwan and other territories. US military bases in Japan were allowed to remain. Japan's reparations agreements with its Asia-Pacific war victims were not covered by the treaty and needed to be negotiated separately.

▷ **Hiroshima Peace Memorial** (Genbaku Dome), Japan

INDEX

Page numbers in **bold** refer to main entries.

ACKNOWLEDGMENTS

The publisher would like to thank Cyrus McGoldrick for authenticity reading, Kirsty Seymour-Ure for proofreading, Vanessa Bird for indexing, and Usman Ansari and Pankaj Sharma for high-resolution image support.

The publisher would like to thank the following for their kind permission to reproduce their photographs:

(Key: a-above; b-below/bottom; c-centre; f-far; l-left; r-right; t-top)

1 Dorling Kindersley: Gary Ombler / M. J. Phelps / War and Peace Show (c). 2 Alamy Stock Photo: De Luan (c). 4-5 Alamy Stock Photo: Chronicle (t). 6 Alamy Stock Photo: American Photo Archive (cr). Getty Images: Roger Viollet (cl); HUM Images (r). 7 Alamy Stock Photo: INTERFOTO (r). Getty Images: Hulton Deutsch (l); Smith Collection/Gado (cl); The Print Collector (cr). 16 akg-images: Alain Gesgon / CIRIP (t). Alamy Stock Photo: Science History Images (bl). Dreamstime.com: Caglar Gungor (br). 17 Alamy Stock Photo: PA Images (tl). 18 Alamy Stock Photo: mccool (tl); blickwinkel (bl); Pictorial Press Ltd (br). 19 Alamy Stock Photo: Sueddeutsche Zeitung Photo (tc); Jimlop collection (tr); Shawshots (br). 20-21 Getty Images: Roger Viollet (r). 20 Getty Images: Fototeca Storica Nazionale (cl); Hulton Deutsch (clb); Universal History Archive (bl). 22 akg-images: Andrea Jemolo (tl). Alamy Stock Photo: INTERFOTO (tc); mccool (br). 23 Alamy Stock Photo: Photo 12 (tl); Everett Collection Historical (tr); CBW (b1); Everett Collection Inc (b2); Shawshots (b3); CPA Media Pte Ltd (b4). 24 Alamy Stock Photo: Glasshouse Images (tr); INTERFOTO (c); Trinity Mirror / Mirrorpix (br). 25 Alamy Stock Photo: Sueddeutsche Zeitung Photo (tl); INTERFOTO (tr); Shawshots (b). 26 Alamy Stock Photo: Sueddeutsche Zeitung Photo (t); Science History Images (br). 27 akg-images: ullstein bild (br). Alamy Stock Photo: Chronicle (tl); Dinodia Photos (tr). 28 Alamy Stock Photo: PRISMA ARCHIVO (tr); De Luan (b). Getty Images: brandstaetter images (tl). 29 Alamy Stock Photo: CPA Media Pte Ltd (tl); CPA Media Pte Ltd (br). Getty Images: Rykoff Collection (bc). 30 akg-images: (br). Alamy Stock Photo: Sueddeutsche Zeitung Photo (tl). Getty Images: ullstein bild Dtl. (tr). 31 Getty Images: ullstein bild Dtl. (tl); Universal History Archive (bl). 32 akg-images: Bildarchiv Pisarek (b4). Alamy Stock Photo: Sueddeutsche Zeitung Photo (tl); Sueddeutsche Zeitung Photo (b2); Bildagentur-online/Joko (b3). 32 Bridgeman Images: Prismatic Pictures (t). Getty Images: Universal History Archive (b1). 33 Alamy Stock Photo: INTERFOTO (tl). Getty Images: Roger Viollet (br). 34 Alamy Stock Photo: Everett Collection Historical (tr); Chronicle (bl); Album (br). 35 Alamy Stock Photo: Everett Collection Historical (tl); INTERFOTO (tr). Getty Images: brandstaetter images (br). 36 Alamy Stock Photo: CBW (tl). Getty Images: DE AGOSTINI PICTURE LIBRARY (tr); Pictures from History (br). 37 Alamy Stock Photo: Shawshots (tl); Sueddeutsche Zeitung Photo (tr); Heritage Image Partnership Ltd (bc); Sueddeutsche Zeitung Photo (br). 38 Alamy Stock Photo: CBW (tr); Shawshots (bl); Everett Collection Inc (br). 39 Alamy Stock Photo: Album (bl). TopFoto: (tl). 40-41 Alamy Stock Photo: MPVHistory (l). 41 Alamy Stock Photo: Lordprice Collection (crb); Pictorial Press Ltd (br). Getty Images: Science & Society Picture Library (cr). 42 Alamy Stock Photo: Everett Collection Historical (bc); Heritage Image Partnership Ltd (br). Getty Images: Bettmann (tl). 43 Alamy Stock Photo: The Print Collector (tr); Photo 12 (cl); Album (b1); World History Archive (b2); World History Archive (b3); Sueddeutsche Zeitung Photo (b4). 44 Alamy Stock Photo: Sueddeutsche Zeitung Photo (tr); Shawshots (c); CBW (bl). 45 Alamy Stock Photo: CPA Media Pte Ltd (b). Getty Images: Pictures from History (t). 46 Alamy Stock Photo: Avpics (t). Getty Images: Michael Nicholson (br). 47 akg-images: brandstaetter images / Austrian Archives (tl); akg-images (br). Getty Images: Bettmann (bl). 48 Alamy Stock Photo: dpa picture alliance (tr); Shawshots (bl). 49 Alamy Stock Photo: Album (tr). Getty Images: Bettmann (bl); brandstaetter images (br). 50 Alamy Stock Photo: Shawshots (tl); Pictorial Press Ltd (bl). Getty Images: Keystone-France (tr). 51 Alamy Stock Photo: Pictorial Press Ltd (bl). Getty Images: Chris Jackson / Staff (tl); Pictures from History (tr). 52 Alamy Stock Photo: dpa picture alliance (tl); Sueddeutsche Zeitung Photo (bl); Chronicle (br). 53 Alamy Stock Photo: CPA Media Pte Ltd (tl); Sueddeutsche Zeitung Photo (tr); Shawshots (br). 56 Alamy Stock Photo: Shawshots (tl); John Frost Newspapers (tr); Niday Picture Library (b1); Sueddeutsche Zeitung Photo (b2); Everett Collection Inc (b3); Max Right (b4). 57 Alamy Stock Photo: World History Archive (tr); Shawshots (br). Getty Images: ullstein bild Dtl. (tl). 58 Alamy Stock Photo: INTERFOTO (cr); GL Archive (br). Getty Images: J. Kirchner / Stringer (tl). 59 Alamy Stock Photo: John Frost Newspapers (tr); Shawshots (bc); Photo 12 (br). 60 Alamy Stock Photo: D and S Photography Archives (bl). Dorling Kindersley: Gary Ombler / Royal Airforce Museum, London (t). 61 Alamy Stock Photo: PJF Military Collection (bl); Barbara Ash (br). Getty Images: ullstein bild Dtl. (tl). 62 akg-images: picture-alliance (br). Getty Images: Fox Photos / Stringer (tl). 63 Alamy Stock Photo: Hilary Morgan (tr); TT News Agency (bl); Classic Picture Library (bc). Getty Images: Popperfoto (tl); Hulton Deutsch (br).

64-65 Alamy Stock Photo: Sueddeutsche Zeitung Photo (r). 64 Alamy Stock Photo: INTERFOTO (clb); Vital Archive (bl). Getty Images: ullstein bild Dtl (cl). 66 Alamy Stock Photo: INTERFOTO (tr); Hum Historical (bl). Getty Images: PhotoQuest (tc); David Savill / Stringer (br). 67 Getty Images: Bettmann (tl); Popperfoto (bl). 68 akg-images: Ullstein (bl). Alamy Stock Photo: INTERFOTO (tc). Getty Images: Universal History Archive (tl). 69 Getty Images: Keystone-France (tl); ullstein bild Dtl. (bl). 70 Getty Images: H. F. Davis / Stringer (tr). TopFoto: ullsteinbild (tl). 71 Alamy Stock Photo: Sueddeutsche Zeitung Photo (tr). Getty Images: ullstein bild Dtl. (bl); Bletchley Park Trust (br). 72 Alamy Stock Photo: akg-images (br). 73 Alamy Stock Photo: Historic Collection (tr); Sueddeutsche Zeitung Photo (br). TopFoto: INTERFOTO (tl). 74 Alamy Stock Photo: Chronicle (cr). Getty Images: Hulton Archive / Stringer (tr); Roger Viollet (bl). 75 Getty Images: IWM (tl); Sovfoto (tr); adoc-photos (br). 76 Alamy Stock Photo: Photo 12 (br). Getty Images: ullstein bild Dtl. (tc); Keystone-France (tr). 77 Alamy Stock Photo: Chris Howes/Wild Places Photography (tr); Sueddeutsche Zeitung Photo (bl). 78 Alamy Stock Photo: De Luan (tl). Getty Images: Mirrorpix (tr); MPI / Stringer (br). 79 Alamy Stock Photo: Chronicle of World History (tl). Getty Images: Keystone / Stringer (bl); Bettmann (br). 80 Alamy Stock Photo: Operation 2021 (tr); Sergey Nezhinkiy (bl). Getty Images: adoc-photos (cr). 81 Alamy Stock Photo: Sueddeutsche Zeitung Photo (tl); Sueddeutsche Zeitung Photo (cr); Lordprice Collection (b1); CBW (b2); World History Archive (b4). 81 Getty Images: Hulton Deutsch (b3). 82 Alamy Stock Photo: Shawshots (tl). Dorling Kindersley: Peter Cook / Planes of Fame Air Museum, Chino, California (bl). Getty Images: SeM (c). 83 Alamy Stock Photo: Shawshots (t); carlo maggio (bl). 84-85 Alamy Stock Photo: Stocktrek Images, Inc. (r). 84 Alamy Stock Photo: Everett Collection Inc (bl). Getty Images: Science & Society Picture Library (cl); Bettmann (clb). 86 Alamy Stock Photo: John Frost Newspapers (tl); CPA Media Pte Ltd (br). 87 Alamy Stock Photo: CBW (tl); INTERFOTO (bl); CBW (br). 88 Alamy Stock Photo: De Luan (tl). Getty Images: Bettmann (tr). 89 Alamy Stock Photo: Nigel J Clarke (tl); Photo 12 (bl); CPA Media Pte Ltd (br). 90 Alamy Stock Photo: Shawshots (tc); Archive PL (tr); Sueddeutsche Zeitung Photo (bl). 91 Alamy Stock Photo: colaimages (br). Getty Images: Michael Ochs Archives / Stringer (tl). 92 Alamy Stock Photo: Niday Picture Library (br). Getty Images: SeM (tl). TopFoto: (tl). 93 Alamy Stock Photo: American Photo Archive (tl); Sunpixels (cr); Sueddeutsche Zeitung Photo (br). 94 Alamy Stock Photo: Trinity Mirror / Mirrorpix (tl); Everett Collection Inc (br). 95 Alamy Stock Photo: Historic Collection (tr); Associated Press (b1); Trinity Mirror / Mirrorpix (b2); Associated Press (b4). Getty Images: Bettmann (b3). TopFoto: (tl). 96-97 Alamy Stock Photo: ClassicStock (r). 96 Alamy Stock Photo: incamerastock (cl); CPA Media Pte Ltd (bl). 98 Alamy Stock Photo: Everett Collection Inc (cr); Lordprice Collection (bl). Getty Images: Keystone / Stringer (br). 99 akg-images: Interfoto (bl). Alamy Stock Photo: Gary Eason / Flight Artworks (tl). Getty Images: ullstein bild Dtl. (br). 100 akg-images: picture alliance / WZ-Bilddienst (bl). Getty Images: ullstein bild Dtl. (tc); Popperfoto (tr). 101 Alamy Stock Photo: Chronicle (tl); Pictorial Press Ltd (bl); Pictorial Press Ltd (br). 102 Getty Images: Mondadori Portfolio (tl); Keystone / Stringer (br). 103 akg-images: (tr). Alamy Stock Photo: World History Archive (bl); Sueddeutsche Zeitung Photo (br). 104 akg-images: Fotoarchiv für Zeitgeschichte (tr); ullstein bild (bl). 105 Alamy Stock Photo: Sueddeutsche Zeitung Photo (bl). Getty Images: Hulton Archive / Stringer (tr); Keystone / Stringer (br). 106 Alamy Stock Photo: Associated Press (bl). Getty Images: IWM (tr); ullstein bild Dtl. (br). 107 Alamy Stock Photo: Sueddeutsche Zeitung Photo (b2); SuperStock (b3); Sueddeutsche Zeitung Photo (b4). Dorling Kindersley: Gary Ombler / Fleet Air Arm Museum (c). Getty Images: Keystone / Stringer (tl); ullstein bild Dtl. (b1). 108 Getty Images: Afro Newspaper/Gado (tr); Keystone / Stringer (br). 109 Getty Images: ullstein bild (tl); Photo 12 (tr); IWM (bl). 112 akg-images: (tl). 113 Alamy Stock Photo: War Archive (tr). Getty Images: Mondadori Portfolio (bl); ullstein bild Dtl. (br). 114 Alamy Stock Photo: Penrodas Collection (tr); INTERFOTO (c); The Print Collector (bl). 115 Alamy Stock Photo: Chronicle (tr); Sueddeutsche Zeitung Photo (bl); CBW (br). 116 Getty Images: Sovfoto (tl); Print Collector (br). 117 Alamy Stock Photo: CPA Media Pte Ltd (bl). Getty Images: IWM (tr); Imperial War Museums (br). 118 Alamy Stock Photo: Everett Collection Historical (tr); Everett Collection Historical (bl); Alan Morris (br). 119 Alamy Stock Photo: Sueddeutsche Zeitung Photo (tl); Chronicle (tr); From Original Negative (bl). Dorling Kindersley: Gary Ombler / Wardrobe Museum, Salisbury (br). 120-121 Alamy Stock Photo: Everett Collection Historical (l). 121 Alamy Stock Photo: CPA Media Pte Ltd (cr); piemags (crb). Getty Images: Keystone / Stringer (br). 122 Alamy Stock Photo: Shawshots (tl); Sueddeutsche Zeitung Photo (bl). Dorling Kindersley: Gary Ombler / RAF Museum, Cosford (tr). 123 Alamy Stock Photo: Shawshots (tr); Vlad Breazu (bl). 124 Alamy Stock Photo: World History Archive (tr). Getty Images: Print Collector (tc); ullstein bild Dtl (bl). 125 Getty Images: FPG / Staff (tr); Mirrorpix (bl). 126 Getty Images: HUM Images (tl). 127 Alamy Stock Photo: D and S Photography Archives (tl). Getty Images: Pictures from History (bl); Sovfoto (br). 128 Getty Images: Universal History

Archive (tl); ullstein bild Dtl (br). **129 Getty Images:** Imperial War Museums (tl); Pictures from History (bl); Bettmann (br). **130 Alamy Stock Photo:** Shawshots (bc); history_docu_photo (br). **Getty Images:** Mondadori Portfolio (tl). **131 Getty Images:** ullstein bild Dtl (tl); The Washington Post (tr); NurPhoto (br). **132-133 Alamy Stock Photo:** Hi-Story (l). **133 Alamy Stock Photo:** Everett Collection Inc (cr); Everett Collection Inc (br). **Getty Images:** Mirrorpix (crb). **134 Alamy Stock Photo:** World of Triss (tl); CPA Media Pte Ltd (bl). **135 Alamy Stock Photo:** Everett Collection Historical (bl); Zuri Swimmer (br). **Getty Images:** Fox Photos / Stringer (tl). **136 Alamy Stock Photo:** Sueddeutsche Zeitung Photo (bl). **Getty Images:** ullstein bild Dtl (tl); ullstein bild Dtl (br). **137 Alamy Stock Photo:** Richard Cummins (br). **Getty Images:** ullstein bild Dtl (tl); Buyenlarge (tr). **138 Alamy Stock Photo:** Everett Collection Inc (tl). **Getty Images:** The Asahi Shimbun (br). **139 Alamy Stock Photo:** Chronicle (tl). **Getty Images:** Historical (tr); Hulton Deutsch (bl); Bettmann (br). **140 Alamy Stock Photo:** INTERFOTO (tl); CBW (b). **141 Alamy Stock Photo:** Science History Images (tr); PjrStudio (bl); CPA Media Pte Ltd (br). **Getty Images:** Keystone / Staff (tl). **142 Alamy Stock Photo:** Sueddeutsche Zeitung Photo (tl); Chronicle (br). **143 Getty Images:** API (tl); Keystone / Stringer (tr); Bettmann (bl); Bettmann (br). **144 Alamy Stock Photo:** dpa picture alliance (tr). **Getty Images:** ullstein bild Dtl. (bl). **145 Alamy Stock Photo:** Kabataan (bl). **Getty Images:** Galerie Bilderwelt (tl); Bettmann (br). **146-147 Alamy Stock Photo:** World History Archive (r). **146 Alamy Stock Photo:** SBS Eclectic Images (cl); Everett Collection Inc (clb). **Getty Images:** Historical (bl). **148 Alamy Stock Photo:** Shawshots (tr); The Picture Art Collection (bl). **Getty Images:** ullstein bild Dtl (br). **149 Alamy Stock Photo:** Shawshots (tl). **Getty Images:** The Asahi Shimbun (tr). **150 Alamy Stock Photo:** HelloWorld Images (t); dpa picture alliance (br). **151 Alamy Stock Photo:** John Frost Newspapers (tl); INTERFOTO (tr). **Getty Images:** ullstein bild Dtl. (br). **152 Alamy Stock Photo:** piemags (tl); History and Art Collection (bl); Photo 12 (br). **153 Alamy Stock Photo:** Shawshots (tl); INTERFOTO (tr); INTERFOTO (bl). **154 Alamy Stock Photo:** Niday Picture Library (tr); Shawshots (br). **155 Alamy Stock Photo:** Lebrecht Music & Arts (tr). **Getty Images:** ullstein bild Dtl (tl); ullstein bild Dtl (bl). **156 Alamy Stock Photo:** Photo 12 (bl); Zuri Swimmer (br). **Getty Images:** Bettmann (tr). **157 Alamy Stock Photo:** Matt Jones (tl); Hi-Story (br). **Getty Images:** ullstein bild Dtl. (tr). **158 Alamy Stock Photo:** Pictorial Press Ltd (tl). **Getty Images:** Central Press / Stringer (tr). **159 Alamy Stock Photo:** History and Art Collection (tl); AB Forces News Collection (bl). **Getty Images:** Historical (br). **160 Alamy Stock Photo:** 508 collection (tr); akg-images (br). **Dorling Kindersley:** Gary Ombler / RAF Museum, Cosford (tl). **161 Alamy Stock Photo:** Niday Picture Library (tr). **Dorling Kindersley:** Andy Crawford / Imperial War Museum, London (b). **164 Alamy Stock Photo:** CBW (tl); CPA Media Pte Ltd (tr). **Getty Images:** Hulton Deutsch (bl). **165 Alamy Stock Photo:** INTERFOTO (br). **Getty Images:** Imperial War Museums (tl). **166 Alamy Stock Photo:** Hansrad Collection (tl); Shawshots (tr); Sueddeutsche Zeitung Photo (bl); Chronicle (bc); INTERFOTO (br). **167 Alamy Stock Photo:** piemags (bl); IanDagnall Computing (br). **Getty Images:** ullstein bild (tr). **168 Alamy Stock Photo:** incamerastock (tr); Shawshots (br). **Bridgeman Images:** National Museum of the Royal Navy (tl). **169 Alamy Stock Photo:** Atomic (tl). **Getty Images:** Bettmann (br). **170 Dorling Kindersley:** Gary Ombler / B17 Preservation (bc). **Getty Images:** ullstein bild Dtl. (tl); Imperial War Museums (c). **171 Alamy Stock Photo:** Chronicle (tc); Sueddeutsche Zeitung Photo (tr). **Dorling Kindersley:** Gary Ombler / Wardrobe Museum, Salisbury (br). **172 Getty Images:** Bettmann (tr); Popperfoto (bl); Popperfoto (br). **173 Alamy Stock Photo:** Militarist (tl); Sueddeutsche Zeitung Photo (tr); The Print Collector (bc). **174-175 Getty Images:** Hulton Deutsch (l). **175 Alamy Stock Photo:** Everett Collection Historical (cr); CBW (crb); Shawshots (br). **176 Alamy Stock Photo:** GRANGER - Historical Picture Archive (br). **Getty Images:** ullstein bild Dtl. (tl); ullstein bild Dtl. (bl). **177 Alamy Stock Photo:** Tim Scrivener (tl); Everett Collection Historical (bl). **178 akg-images:** INTERFOTO / HERMANN HISTORICA GmbH (br). **Alamy Stock Photo:** D and S Photography Archives (tl). **179 Alamy Stock Photo:** Sueddeutsche Zeitung Photo (tl); SuperStock (tr); John Zada (br). **180 Alamy Stock Photo:** John Dambik (tl); Pictorial Press Ltd (br). **181 Alamy Stock Photo:** Magite Historic (tr); De Luan (bl); Archive PL (br). **182 Alamy Stock Photo:** Chronicle (tl); Pictorial Press Ltd (tr). **Getty Images:** Universal History Archive (bl). **183 Alamy Stock Photo:** PA Images (tl); piemags/NBP (bl); American Photo Archive (br). **184 Alamy Stock Photo:** Zip Lexing (bl); dpa picture alliance archive (br). **Getty Images:** Bettmann (tl). **185 Alamy Stock Photo:** Science History Images (tr). **Getty Images:** Imperial War Museums (tl); DEA / G.P.CAVALLERO (bl). **186-187 Getty Images:** Imperial War Museums (r). **186 Alamy Stock Photo:** M. Palmer (cl). **Getty Images:** Imperial War Museums (clb); IWM (bl). **188 Alamy Stock Photo:** GRANGER - Historical Picture Archive (tl); Niday Picture Library (tr); Everett Collection Historical (bl). **189 Alamy Stock Photo:** Everett Collection Inc (bl); IanDagnall Computing (br). **Getty Images:** Historical (tr). **190 Alamy Stock Photo:** Pictorial Press Ltd (tr); Peter Vrabel (b). **191 Alamy Stock Photo:** RGB Ventures / SuperStock (bl); Borislav Marinic (br). **Getty Images:** Keystone / Stringer (tl); adoc-photos (cr). **192 Alamy Stock Photo:** Niday Picture Library (tl). **Getty Images:** Frederic Lewis / Staff (br). **193 Alamy Stock Photo:** Niday Picture Library (tl); CBW (br). **Getty Images:** Bettmann (bl). **194 Alamy Stock Photo:** Blakeley (tl); Antiqua Print Gallery (tr); Hum Images (b4). **194 Getty Images:** Roger Viollet (b1); IWM (b2); PhotoQuest (b3). **195 Alamy Stock Photo:** Stocktrek Images, Inc. (tr). **Getty Images:** Bettmann (bl). **198 Alamy Stock Photo:** Everett Collection Inc (tl). **Getty Images:** ullstein bild Dtl (bl); ullstein bild Dtl (br). **199 Alamy Stock Photo:** INTERFOTO (tr). **Getty Images:** Popperfoto (bl). **200 Alamy Stock Photo:** SuperStock (tr). **Getty Images:** Fairfax Media Archives (tl); Bettmann (bl). **201 Alamy Stock Photo:** Pictorial Press Ltd (tl); CBW (tr). **Getty Images:** Galerie Bilderwelt (bl). **202 Alamy Stock Photo:** INTERFOTO (tl); dpa picture alliance (tr); Newscom (bl). **Getty Images:** Mondadori Portfolio (br). **203 Alamy Stock Photo:** Niday Picture Library (tl); PJF Military Collection (b). **204 Alamy Stock Photo:** VTR (tl); Alexander Mitrofanov (tr). **Getty Images:** HUM Images (bl). **205 Alamy Stock Photo:** The Picture Art Collection (br). **Getty Images:** Keystone / Stringer (tl). **206-207 Getty Images:** Popperfoto (l). **207 Getty Images:** Keystone-France (cr); Popperfoto (crb); Afro Newspaper/Gado (br). **208 Alamy Stock Photo:** Glasshouse Images (tl); Photo 12 (bl); IanDagnall Computing (br). **209 Alamy Stock Photo:** Pictorial Press Ltd (tl); Archive PL (tr); Walker Art Library (br). **210 Alamy Stock Photo:** GRANGER - Historical Picture Archive (tl); INTERFOTO (br). **Getty Images:** FPG / Staff (bl). **211 Alamy Stock Photo:** World History Archive (tr); Everett Collection Inc (bl). **Getty Images:** ullstein bild Dtl (tl). **212 Getty Images:** Keystone-France (tl); Bettmann (tr); Sovfoto (b). **213 Alamy Stock Photo:** CPA Media Pte Ltd (tr); StampCollection (cl). **Getty Images:** Museum of Science and Industry, Chicago (br). **214 akg-images:** (tr). **Alamy Stock Photo:** Sueddeutsche Zeitung Photo (bl); Sueddeutsche Zeitung Photo (br). **215 Alamy Stock Photo:** Sueddeutsche Zeitung Photo (tr); PjrStudio (bc). **Getty Images:** Gordon Anthony / Stringer (br). **216 Alamy Stock Photo:** Kevin Griffin (tl); World History Archive (tr); CPA Media Pte Ltd (br). **217 Getty Images:** PhotoQuest (tl); IWM (bl). **Getty Images / iStock:** AlexanderZam (br). **218 Alamy Stock Photo:** Pictorial Press Ltd (br). **Getty Images:** DE AGOSTINI PICTURE LIBRARY (tl). **219 Alamy Stock Photo:** michael cremin (tl); Sueddeutsche Zeitung Photo (bl). **Getty Images:** PhotoQuest (br). **220 akg-images:** ullstein bild (tl). **Alamy Stock Photo:** De Luan (br). **Getty Images:** Umberto Cicconi (bl). **221 Alamy Stock Photo:** Tibbut Archive (tl); GL Archive (bl); dpa picture alliance archive (br). **Getty Images:** Sovfoto (tr); Fairfax Media Archives (bc). **222 Bridgeman Images:** Picture Alliance/DPA (tr). **Getty Images:** Bentley Archive/Popperfoto (bl). **223 Alamy Stock Photo:** SuperStock (tl); World of Triss (c). **Getty Images:** Keystone-France (br). **224-225 Getty Images:** Galerie Bilderwelt (l). **225 Alamy Stock Photo:** D. Trozzo (crb); shoults (br). **Getty Images:** Historical (cr). **226 Getty Images:** Galerie Bilderwelt (tr); Popperfoto (bl); Michael Nicholson (br). **227 Getty Images:** Paul Popper/Popperfoto (tl); Historical (tr); Galerie Bilderwelt (br). **228 Alamy Stock Photo:** piemags (tr). **Getty Images:** Roger Viollet (tl); Smith Collection/Gado (br). **229 Alamy Stock Photo:** Glasshouse Images (br). **Getty Images:** Photo 12 (bl). **230 Alamy Stock Photo:** Shaun Wilkinson (tl); piemags (bl); PJF Military Collection (br). **Getty Images:** PhotoQuest (tr). **231 Alamy Stock Photo:** Stocktrek Images, Inc. (tl); Niday Picture Library (br). **232 Alamy Stock Photo:** philipimage (tl). **Getty Images:** Bettmann (tr); Reg Speller / Stringer (br). **233 Alamy Stock Photo:** FMUA (bl); PA Images (br). **Getty Images:** Education Images (tl). **234 Alamy Stock Photo:** World History Archive (tl); piemags (bl). **Getty Images:** ullstein bild (br). **235 akg-images:** (tr). **Alamy Stock Photo:** American Photo Archive (bl). **236-237 Getty Images:** Mirrorpix (r). **236 Getty Images:** PhotoQuest (cl); Popperfoto (clb); WHA / World History Archive (bl). **238 Alamy Stock Photo:** CBW (tr); Chronicle (br). **Getty Images:** ullstein bild Dtl. (bl). **239 Alamy Stock Photo:** GRANGER - Historical Picture Archive (tl); Chroma Collection (br). **Getty Images:** ullstein bild Dtl. (tr). **240 Alamy Stock Photo:** GRANGER - Historical Picture Archive (tl); Sourced Collection (tr); Shawshots (br). **241 Getty Images:** Hulton Deutsch (br). **242 Alamy Stock Photo:** Alexander Mitrofanov (tl); World History Archive (b2); Associated Press (b3); Sueddeutsche Zeitung Photo (b4). **Getty Images:** Keystone / Stringer (tr); IWM (b1). **243 Alamy Stock Photo:** Trinity Mirror / Mirrorpix (bl). **Getty Images:** Hulton Archive / Stringer (tr); Galerie Bilderwelt (br). **244 Getty Images:** Historical (tl); Historical (br). **245 Alamy Stock Photo:** Chronicle (tl); Eric Nathan (bc); World History Archive (br). **246 Alamy Stock Photo:** Sueddeutsche Zeitung Photo (tl); Matthias Naumann (br). **247 Alamy Stock Photo:** Sueddeutsche Zeitung Photo (tc); The Print Collector (bl). **Getty Images:** IWM (br). **248 Alamy Stock Photo:** Kirk Fisher (bl); The Print Collector (br). **Getty Images:** Keystone / Stringer (tr). **249 akg-images:** (br). **Alamy Stock Photo:** GRANGER - Historical Picture Archive (tl); Nelly George (tc). **250 Getty Images:** Found Image Holdings Inc (tl); Bettmann (br). **251 Bridgeman Images:** Don Troiani. All Rights Reserved 2023 (tc). **Getty Images:** Mirrorpix (tl); Bettmann (bc); Universal History Archive (br). **252 Alamy Stock Photo:** John Frost Newspapers (bl). **Dorling Kindersley:** Gary Ombler / Gatwick Aviation Museum (t). **Getty Images:** Photo 12 (br). **253 Getty Images:** Staff (tl); Sovfoto (b). **254 Alamy Stock Photo:** Chronicle (tl). **255 Alamy Stock Photo:** Glasshouse Images (tr); Glasshouse Images (bl); SuperStock (br). **256-257 Alamy Stock Photo:** CARL DICKINSON (l). **257 Alamy Stock Photo:** World History Archive (cr); CBW (crb); CBW (br); CBW (tl). **260 Alamy Stock Photo:** Sergey Nezhinkiy (tl). Shawshots (tr). PJF Military Collection (bl). **261 Alamy Stock Photo:** World History Archive (bl). **262 Alamy Stock Photo:** ARCHIVIO GBB (tl). **Getty Images:** Bettmann (bl); ullstein bild (br). **263 Alamy Stock Photo:** Niday Picture Library (tl); M. Palmer (tc); Shawshots (br). **264 Alamy Stock Photo:** Tango Images (bl). **Bridgeman Images:** Museum of Fine Arts, Houston / gift of Will Michels in honor of Jim and Erika Liu (tr). **265 Alamy Stock Photo:** Pictorial Press Ltd (tl); Everett Collection Historical (br). **Getty Images:** Keystone-France (bl). **266 Alamy Stock Photo:** agefotostock (tr); PJF Military Collection (bl).

Getty Images: Fox Photos / Stringer (tl); Popperfoto (br). **267 Alamy Stock Photo:** GRANGER - Historical Picture Archive (tl); The Print Collector (bl). **268 Alamy Stock Photo:** Pictorial Press Ltd (tl). **Getty Images:** PhotoQuest (br). **269 akg-images:** (tl). **Alamy Stock Photo:** Sueddeutsche Zeitung Photo (bc). **Getty Images:** Slava Katamidze Collection (br). **270 Alamy Stock Photo:** Vintage_Space (tr); World History Archive (bl); Album (br). **271 Alamy Stock Photo:** Everett Collection Inc (tr). **272 Alamy Stock Photo:** Photo 12 (tl); dpa picture alliance (tr); **Getty Images:** PhotoQuest (br). **273 Alamy Stock Photo:** Shawshots (tr); Chronicle (bl). **274 Alamy Stock Photo:** Chronicle (br). **Getty Images:** Hulton Deutsch (bl). **275 Alamy Stock Photo:** De Luan (tl); Azoor Photo (tr); Shawshots (bl). **276 Alamy Stock Photo:** Shawshots (tr). **Getty Images:** Sovfoto (tl); PhotoQuest (bl). **277 Alamy Stock Photo:** CPA Media Pte Ltd (tr); Photo 12 (br). **Getty Images:** Culture Club (tl). **278 Getty Images:** Bettmann (tr); HUM Images (br). **279 akg-images:** Interfoto / HERMANN HISTORICA GmbH (tl). **Alamy Stock Photo:** World Archive (tr). **Getty Images:** Imperial War Museums (bl). **280-281 Alamy Stock Photo:** Stocktrek Images, Inc. (l). **281 Alamy Stock Photo:** Sueddeutsche Zeitung Photo (br). **Dorling Kindersley:** Francesca Yorke / Bradbury Science Museum, Los Alamos (crb). **Getty Images:** Eric BRISSAUD (cr). **282 Alamy Stock Photo:** SuperStock (tl); Everett Collection Historical (tr); Max Right (br). **Getty Images:** Historical (bl). **283 Alamy Stock Photo:** DOD Photo (tr). **Getty Images:** Pictures from History (bl). **284 Alamy Stock Photo:** Niday Picture Library (t); Pictorial Press Ltd (br). **285 Alamy Stock Photo:** World History Archive (tl); Prisma by Dukas Presseagentur GmbH (bl); Alpha Stock (br). **286 Alamy Stock Photo:** Hilda Weges (tl); MeijiShowa (br). **287 Alamy Stock Photo:** Pictorial Press Ltd (tl); MeijiShowa (bl). **Getty Images:** Pictures from History (br). **288-289 Getty Images:** Sovfoto (l). **289 Dorling Kindersley:**

Gary Ombler / Brooklands Museum (br). **Getty Images:** Universal History Archive (cr); Sovfoto (crb). **292 Alamy Stock Photo:** Associated Press (bl); World of Triss (br). **Getty Images:** Historical (tr). **293 Alamy Stock Photo:** Steve Allen Travel Photography (tc); James Talalay (tr); Associated Press (br). **294 Alamy Stock Photo:** Signal Photos (br). **Getty Images:** Galerie Bilderwelt (tl); Keystone / Staff (bl). **295 Alamy Stock Photo:** Chris Hellier (tr). **Getty Images:** Keystone-France (bl); Photo 12 (br). **296 Alamy Stock Photo:** Lanmas (bl). **Getty Images:** Hulton Deutsch (tr); Pictures from History (br). **297 Alamy Stock Photo:** SuperStock (tl); Georgios Kollidas (tr). **Getty Images:** MPI / Stringer (br). **298 Alamy Stock Photo:** World History Archive (tl); Dinodia Photos (bl); World History Archive (br). **299 Alamy Stock Photo:** World History Archive (tl); Richard Brown (tr); imageBROKER.com GmbH & Co. KG (b1). **Getty Images:** Historical (b2); PhotoQuest (b3); Bettmann (b4). **300 Alamy Stock Photo:** Trinity Mirror / Mirrorpix (tr); CBW (bl); colaimages (br). **301 Alamy Stock Photo:** Penta Springs Limited (bl); Album (br). **Getty Images:** Laski Diffusion (tl). **302-303 Alamy Stock Photo:** INTERFOTO (l). **303 Alamy Stock Photo:** Jimlop collection (cr); Sueddeutsche Zeitung Photo (br). **Getty Images:** Bettmann / Contributor (crb). **304 Alamy Stock Photo:** World History Archive (t); INTERFOTO (bl); CPA Media Pte Ltd (br). **305 Alamy Stock Photo:** SuperStock (tr); Everett Collection Historical (br). **Getty Images:** Rolls Press/Popperfoto (tl). **306 Alamy Stock Photo:** Everett Collection Historical (bl). **Getty Images:** Interim Archives (tl); Bettmann (br). **307 Alamy Stock Photo:** INTERFOTO (tl); Travelman (br).

All other images © Dorling Kindersley
For further information see: www.dkimages.com